OOH AAH
PAUL McGRATH

Ooh Aah Paul McGrath

The Black Pearl of Inchicore

Paul McGrath
with Cathal Dervan

MAINSTREAM PUBLISHING

EDINBURGH AND LONDON

Photographs supplied by *The Star*, Dublin, and Paul McGrath. Thanks to Noel Gavin, Jim Walpole and all their photographic colleagues

To Robert Reid – thanks for the facts and figures

The moral right of the authors has been asserted
First published in Great Britain in 1994 by
MAINSTREAM PUBLISHING COMPANY (EDINBURGH) LTD
7 Albany Street
Edinburgh EH1 3UG

ISBN 1 85158 647 4

A catalogue record for this book is available from the British Library

Typeset in Sabon by Litho Link Ltd, Welshpool, Powys, Wales
Printed in Great Britain by Butler & Tanner Ltd, Frome, Somerset

To Christopher, Mitchell, Jordan and Cillian

Paul

A silken boy of skills sublime
whose graceful stance with speed combined
to give us joy that will ensure
his wonderous deeds through life endure.

A talent o so rare and true
enhanced the lives of all who knew,
his courage through the darkness shone,
his spirit made him carry on.

Through heated cauldrons near and far
his was indeed a shining star.
No bigotry or hate but love,
his gentleness shone way above.

Throughout a world enshrined with strife,
his gallant team enriched our life.
In glorious summers now gone past
our love for them will ever last.

Frank Mullen

Contents

FOREWORD

by Bryan Robson

PAUL McGRATH for me has always been a world-class footballer – he should have been the greatest defender of his generation.

I will argue with any man just how good a player he has been and still is for Manchester United, for Aston Villa and for Ireland. I will also wonder aloud just how much injury has denied Paul McGrath in terms of the ultimate rewards as a player for his club and for his country. He is without a shadow of a doubt a great player – he could have been the greatest defender of them all.

I am proud to have known Paul as a person and to have played alongside him and against him as a professional footballer. I have never quite been able to shake him off either on or off the pitch. On it, we have played against each other several times. Off it, his name always crops up as a class act whenever I discuss the game of football with fans, players or managers.

And we have known each other quite some time. Little could I have known the morning he first arrived at The Cliff from Ireland as a shy 22-year-old just what a talent had landed on our doorstep. I don't remember too much about Big Paul when he came over on trial because he was so quiet. He's always been a quiet lad – it's only in the last three or four years that I think he's come out of himself a little bit and he's opened up when he's talking to you.

From that first day you could see that he had the skill, the presence and the ability to make it as a great player. He always had the ability. It was just a case of getting it out of him mentally and making him believe in himself. He was a class act from the day he joined United. It took him a few years to settle in at the club but once he came into the team and kept a regular place he was in a different league. By 1985 and the successful FA Cup final against Everton he had arrived. He was confident at last. He was believing in himself. The next year, 1986, he won the Player of the Year award at the club and that made such a difference to him. It was the turning point. He had a fabulous year. I came out then and said he was one of the best defenders in the world. I meant it. Then and now.

We have crossed paths for club and country since then. There was always great rivalry in the United dressing-room between players of different nationalities. This club has always had a lot of Irish lads over the years. They are part and parcel of this great club called Manchester United. And Paul has been one of the best Irish players of all to have worn the United shirt. In 1988 we played against each other at the European Championships and the rivalry was something else. I had the same with Norman Whiteside and with Kevin Moran over the years. But when you're out on the pitch you're playing for your country and that is all that matters. Big Paul has been like that and I've been like that. You get on with playing for your country and friendship goes out the window. Playing for Ireland has always made Paul proud. The international recognition has helped him and vice versa. I'm delighted that he's had that success with his country. He's made two World Cup finals and a European Championships with Ireland. That's some achievement.

It hasn't always been easy. At one time I did worry that his personality might hold him back because he's such a quiet and withdrawn lad. You wonder, is he going to do it? Is he going to make it? Is he going to drive himself to do it? He's proved it over the last seven or eight years now that he always had what it takes to make it to the top.

I respect Paul as a person as well, despite all the misconceptions. Friendship has always been important to me. With Paul it developed gradually as I got to know this Quiet Man from Ireland. After training we'd go for the occasional drink, once a month or so, myself and Norman and Kevin Moran. Paul would come with us. We'd have a drink together and I got to know him even more then. People have said that he's had his problems off the field with his drinking and that kind of thing. I think he's the first to admit it, but at the time when he used to go out with Kevin and I he was never a problem. He'd have a few drinks, he was a good socialiser but he was never a problem. He's greatly misunderstood. When I've been in Paul's company and he's had a drink he's always been quiet. He's never caused problems when I've been out with him. That's the way it was. Myself and Kevin would have been the first ones to calm Paul down if he had needed to be calmed down. But he never did, he never stepped out of line.

I think sometimes he received too much publicity. That went against him because of the type of lad he is. When you play for Manchester United, everything is highlighted. There's only a couple of clubs in England where the same pressure applies. You've got Manchester United and Liverpool, and Arsenal and Tottenham in London. It's the "living in a goldfish bowl" syndrome. Things get highlighted more than any other club if the players do something off the pitch. That affected Paul. If people don't see eye to eye with the players they get reported and it's headline news. If Paul had been at a smaller club it would never have been mentioned or never made headline news. He paid a price for that but I believe he had made himself before he left United for Villa. His matches for Ireland were excellent when he was at this club. Some of the performances he put in at United were out of this world. I think the making of him as a player was the first year he won the club's Player of the Year award in 1986. There were some excellent players here at the time and to win that trophy you've got to play really well and have consistency in your game. He had all of that.

I feel sorry for Paul that he has yet to win a championship medal. I know what he went through at Manchester United when he was here – we had some great teams but never quite overcame that hurdle. When Paul was playing to the top of his form we had quite a team without winning that title. There were some really good players here who never won the title though they deserved to. Paul was one of them. It's a shame that a player of Paul's calibre never won the championship. I was just fortunate I caught it at the back end of my career where we've got an excellent team here.

Paul's chance may come. He is certainly highly regarded within the game. The PFA award in 1993 showed the esteem that fellow players held him in. There's been plenty of times that I've been out talking to other players about football and his name always comes up in the conversation. He always gets a mention as being a class player. His peers reflected that in 1993. It was a nice honour for him because it was chosen by his fellow professionals. The award didn't surprise me. I've played with and against world-class players and he's up there with the best of them. If you take into consideration his problems with his knee as well it's incredible what he's done. It's not the most perfect knee in the history of the game. If he hadn't had the problems with his knee he would have really been the best defender in the world. I still argue that he was close to it. But when you consider the problems he's had with injuries you wonder just how much he has been denied.

I did worry that it could all end in tears for him. I saw it happen to Norman Whiteside, who quit the game at just 24 years of age but who was really struggling to survive when he was 21 going on 22 because of his own knee injuries. It's a great contrast now because Paul is still playing and Norman had to quit. It's also a great pity because Norman would have been up there, close to being a great player like Kenny Dalglish. That's how highly I rated Norman before he had his problems with his knee. You looked at Paul then and you just hoped that it wouldn't happen to him. Now he's 34 and he's still going strong. It's a credit to him. And a credit with the performances that he's putting in on the pitch when you consider that he's not even training every day. That shows how naturally fit the lad is.

I still regard Paul McGrath as a friend. I always did and I always will. He was such a quiet lad and he never had a bad word to say about anyone. That's how I will always remember him. I will always have a great affinity with Paul. I'll be proud to call him a friend long after we have hung up our boots. Somehow I think he's going to be around for some time to come. Long may he continue.

Bryan Robson
Manchester United and England
March 1994

INTRODUCTION

by Cathal Dervan

PAUL McGRATH was born a rebel with a cause. He still is – a man with a fight on his hands from the fourth day of December 1959 when he first drew breath in a North London hospital. His first breath was a rebel yell, long before he ever knew what the cause was or even realised that he had one.

For five innocent years he never knew he was different from the rest, never realised his background was unusual in the Ireland he had entered just six weeks later in 1960. Back then a black baby was something to be found in the wilds of Africa where the natives ate each other and where the good people of Ireland sent their money to feed the starving children of the Third World. Black babies were something the priest spoke about from the altar on a Sunday morning. Something the missionaries collected for with the begging bowls. An object of pity and a subject for help as far as the plain people of Ireland were concerned.

Irish women were white. They married white men, had white babies, lived white lives. Black may have been beautiful as far as a pint of stout was concerned but bring a black baby into Ireland at the start of the swinging '60s and you were bound to be asking for trouble.

Ireland back then was the western outpost of Europe and the last bastion of parochialism and narrow-mindedness. Everything was done by the book. The Holy Book. Catholics lived good Catholic lives. Protestants kept to themselves. The minorities, few

13

as they were, were seen and not heard. Jews and Blacks, Muslims and Hindus were objects of curiosity. Something to be stared at, not something to be encountered.

Ireland of the late 1950s was insular and insecure. Mass was on a Sunday. Mass employment was impossible as the young nation tried to come to terms with independence and a new-found economic freedom away from the centuries-old bond with the British empire.

Times were hard. Young men and women found it difficult to get work. The rural communities lost their young to Dublin and beyond in their thousands. Dublin lost its young to London and New York. The country was experiencing mass emigration on a scale not seen since the great famine of the 19th century.

Ireland was still ten years away from real change – but already the facts of life as a progressive Western democracy was beginning to hit home. And be rejected. Irish people who didn't conform were treated suspiciously, looked upon as radicals, different to the norm and not to be accepted. Step out of line and Ireland of the late '50s would punish you with scorn, contempt, anger and rejection.

Paul McGrath's mother discovered that to her cost. Her crime back in 1959 was to go to London in search of work and find herself pregnant and unmarried. The bigger crime as an Irish girl in her early twenties was to fall in love with a black man, a doctor from Nigeria, and bear his child.

Years later nobody would bat an eyelid if the same set of circumstances descended on their family. Back then it was an outrage in the eyes of a close-knit Irish community, something to be hidden away in a closet of the mind and ignored for as long as possible before the horrible truth became a reality. An Irish girl in McGrath's mother's situation found herself with very few friends in a moment of crisis like that. The bonds of friendship and even family disappeared in the event of an unwanted pregnancy in Ireland of the '50s.

Lonely and upset, worried and unsure, his mother returned to Ireland when she discovered the news about her pregnancy – and realised she was to be left on her own by the man responsible for her predicament. The Dublin she returned to in early 1959 was not one of a thousand welcomes. Comfort was a foreign land. Paul McGrath's mother went back to North London and Ealing a broken woman. But ultimately a stronger woman.

Throughout her ordeal she harboured one burning ambition, an ambition to have her baby. A burning desire to do what was best for her baby, a desire to battle through against all the odds and come out on top. His mother, if nothing else, was a fighter. She knew she faced a battle. She was determined to win and win it on her terms no matter what Ireland circa 1959 thought. His mother fought her battle and won.

Yes, there were tears along the way. Yes, there were years of anxiety and worrying, years of doubt and depression. But throughout her ordeal she maintained that pledge to do what was right for her son. She knew the day he was born in Ealing that Paul McGrath would be brought back to her native Dublin, back to the land she was born in, to be raised like any other Irishman.

Paul McGrath will always be grateful to his mother for her determination to see her son brought up in Ireland – and grateful that she succeeded despite all the barriers thrown across her life by narrow-mindedness and bigotry.

Thus they found themselves, a mother and an infant Paul McGrath, on the mailboat to Ireland, the mailboat to a new life and a new hope for mother and child in the winter of 1959-60.

The tears were natural, the upset uncontrollable the day his mother brought him back to the Ireland that had turned its back on her misfortune and the destiny of her newborn son. He was just six weeks old, oblivious to it all and crying tears that had no meaning next to hers when his mother boarded the nightboat to Dun Laoghaire with her bundle of joy – and the object of her heartache – clutched safely in her arms.

Reality forced his mother to bring her only son home. She couldn't look after him on her own in London, and she couldn't get the support she needed to bring him up without a father in Dublin. Like so many Irish girls before and after her his mother found herself in a hopeless situation. She needed help. All she could do was bring her son home – and then take the steps she had dreaded for nine long and painful months.

Paul McGrath's mother cried her eyes out that morning as the waves lashed against the pier in Dun Laoghaire. He wept too and screamed, oblivious to the future that was about to unfold in front of his newborn eyes. Little did he know then the sheer tragedy of the story unfolding, the heartache and the sense of despondency rushing through her veins as the boat came within sight of her native city. Life was painful.

She had known it would be like this for months, dreaded the impending day for weeks, prayed that the inevitable would not come to pass. They were coming back to Ireland, back to the Dublin that had rejected her but would provide a home for her son in one shape or another for the next 22 years, until the day he would leave for Manchester and life as a professional footballer in the bright lights.

Years later he would depart for England in fairytale circumstances, set off for the land where he was born by chance, but not by choice, full of hype and glory, hope and prosperity, the anxiety and the ambitions that every person takes abroad in the search for employment and happiness. But Dun Laoghaire that wet and windy day was a different story. It was the story of a desperate woman taking desperate action. The story of a woman driven to an action she didn't want to take.

Talk to him now and Paul will maintain that his mother must have feared losing him forever that wet and dreary morning they arrived at Dun Laoghaire. She must have known as she handed him over to a Protestant foster agency that mother and child might never see each other again. She must have feared the end of the bond between womb and child as she handed over her pride and joy with a tear in her eye and a dagger running through her heart.

But Betty McGrath, like so many Irishwomen before and after her had no choice in the course of action she was about to take. She loved her son, wanted what was best for him. She knew the only option was to place Paul McGrath in a foster home and pray that one day mother and child would be reunited in love and harmony.

Betty McGrath did what she did that morning with a feeling of loss and a feeling of love. She knew as he went quietly into the arms of another woman that she would see her son again, knew in her heart and soul that things would eventually work out for the best. For both of them.

She knew many Irish girls of her generation had handed their children over to adoption agencies run by the Catholic Church and surrendered all chance of ever seeing their offspring again. She knew there were other unthinkable options she could take with her child.

Betty McGrath was a loving and caring mother despite all her problems, all the prejudices rife in Ireland of the late '50s. She wanted above all what was best for her son. That's why she handed him over to a Protestant agency, why she allowed her first and only son to spend his childhood years with a foster mother and then in a succession of orphanages.

Betty McGrath knew she would never lose sight of her son. The hours of despair, the months of loneliness as she suffered through her pregnancy on her own in a London that didn't seem to care would not be wasted, would not threaten the bond between mother and child.

This is her story. His story. The Paul McGrath story. It is also the story of a mother's love for her son through thick and thin, through everything the world could throw at her. A story that begins with a bump back in 1959 and ends in a triumphant cry for freedom in the 1990s.

To understand Paul McGrath, the awesome athlete and the private person, it is necessary to delve into his background and risk opening the wounds to the world. To understand his life and his battles against depression and alcohol is to understand the lives and battles of many who have gone before him, many who have battled with him already and many who will battle with him in the future.

If nothing else Paul McGrath is a winner. The fact that he has won the battle can act as an inspiration to kids and parents the world over. It would be easy to feel that life owes Paul McGrath – he has given it far more, both pleasure and pain, than it ever gave him in return. But still he won.

This is his story. His battle. His victory. A cry from the heart. A cry for freedom that refuses to be silenced. Forever.

CHAPTER ONE

If You Ever Go Across the Sea to Ireland

DUN LAOGHAIRE – launchpad for a million dreams, resting place for a million broken hearts as they kissed their Ireland goodbye. A harbour town to the south of Dublin, a borough in its own right. Once named Kingstown after an English monarch who had landed there in the times when Ireland was still a colony, a part of the United Kingdom, and its subjects loyal to the crown. A town honest enough to know that throughout time it owed its prosperity to the steamships, the mailboat and then the car ferries that called it home. The boat to England that has always been and always will be a gateway 'o emigration for millions of my fellow countrymen, women and children.

The last sight of Ireland, the first sight of the new world. There were always boats in Dun Laoghaire, there always will be. The boats that have run for generation after generation of lost souls and lost people from that Dublin inlet to the coast of Wales, to Holyhead and beyond, to any of the ports of call that have welcomed Irish emigrants for centuries now.

The boat to England. Then, now and forever – an escape from the hardships of Irish life, from the hardships of unemployment and hopelessness, poverty and despair. An escape from unattainable dreams, from lives that offered little hope for one reason or another. An escape to a new life, a new world, a new meaning no matter what your religion, your sin, your grievance or your gripe against the land of your Irish fathers.

The last stand for your country comes as that boat pulls out of the harbour and turns a course for Wales. So often in the past it was the last sight of Irish land for countless despairing souls, so often the last resting place for their Ireland and their Irishness.

As it was in the late 1950s for my mother Betty, a Dubliner to the core, a young strip of a girl with the weight of the teenage world on her shoulders and an escape to London as the answer to all her problems. The day she took that mailboat to Holyhead and the heaving mass of humanity that was the mail train to London she was, in her mind at least, escaping to a new life, to a new job, to a new base in the English capital that would change her life forever.

As the steam rose deep in the bowels of that British Rail ship she was free – in her mind if nowhere else. Finally free from the shackles of Irish society, she was off in search of the elusive dream, off to follow her goal to the land where the grass was always greener and the streets paved with gold. Years later the lyrics would come back to haunt her and countless other Irish emigrants. "Oh Mary this London's a Wonderful Place," claims the song, words borne of visions radiant enough and tangible enough to fill the head of any teenage girl anxious to become a dreamer with the cause once landed as a stranger on a stranger shore, into the welcoming arms of womanhood and maturity.

Like countless other Irish girls before and after her, my mother became a statistic on an emigration chart the day she took the boat to England. Like the countless thousands who had gone before her, the thousands who followed her afterwards and the thousands who will do so again in the future she swore she'd be back. London was only a temporary refuge for a young Irish girl with ambition nestling in her heart and a desire to succeed in life burning through her soul.

She'd be back alright – but far sooner than ever she expected. And for reasons she couldn't have envisaged in a thousand years.

Life in London was tough for the Irish in the Fifties. The men, glad to get the chance to work in post-war Britain, rebuilt a country that had been ravaged by the Second World War. The young men of Dublin and beyond built the motorways and the city centres, the flats and the houses and the council schemes, the boulevards of broken dreams that are now hallmarks of the modern British way of life. They were the navvies and the labourers, the chippies and the brickies of a post-war generation in a world picking up the pieces. They stuck together, those Irish abroad. They worked together – the companies they started are still to be found all across the England that was to become their second home. They worked together and they lived together. They prayed together, their religion the magnet that drew them together and reminded them of home.

They kept largely to themselves as they gathered their thoughts and their families in enclaves like Kilburn, Camden, Shepherd's Bush, Cricklewood, Ealing and Kentish Town. There the bars were theirs and the life was theirs, as close to home as they could make it. There they swapped their stories and their yarns, looked out for one another, ignored the prejudice and the suspicion that saw boarding houses with the signs "No Blacks nor Irish need apply" festooned across the windows.

They stuck to one another in work and in play. They waited on the sides of the road at six in the morning for the nod from the gaffer and a hand up on to the back of an open truck for the chance to work in the Murphy Mafia, the Irish building clique that put the mortar back into England and cemented a new look for a crumbling land. They worked hard and drank hard.

They suffered the prejudice of any immigrant race, so often not in silence but in the clenched fist of a people immune to resignation and acceptance. They were hard men at work, rest and play with their women at home raising families or often as not out in the hospitals or the factories, working their way to the promised land, working their way to a return to the old sod, a return to the Ireland they had felt obliged to leave.

North London was full of the immigrant Irish in the Fifties – it still is. The shops sold the Irish papers, the *Meath Chronicle*, the *Roscommon Herald*, the *Connacht Tribune*. The pubs stocked Guinness like at home, the music and the culture, the crack and the religion were like they had never left the corner of Ireland that was still in their hearts.

That was the London my mother entered as a naive and innocent teenage girl when she moved to Ealing with a head full of naked dreams and a heart laden with guilt and remorse. The early days were tough. She found a home and job, life settled down and she began work as a cleaner. She had left Dun Laoghaire full of the dreams of any Irish emigrant. Reality was a lot tougher for her and her generation.

Reality was a lonely existence as well. Solace and comfort were in short supply. When they came knocking you answered the door or risked permanent rejection. Comfort in the arms of my mother was the reward of a Nigerian student doctor, the man she loved however briefly, the father I never knew from the time the world welcomed Paul McGrath on that fateful day in 1959.

I have never known the identity of that man – I have never really wanted to. As far as I am aware he was a medical student from Nigeria who went back to West Africa not long after I drew my first breath. That's as much as I know and as much as I want to know. I have never made an issue of it, nor do I now want to become embroiled in emotional blackmail for him, for me and, most importantly of all, for my mother.

Only twice in my life has the identity of my father bothered me. Once as a 17-year-old with Dalkey United when I was about to go abroad for the first time on a club tour to Germany. The passport application was awkward. I didn't want the rest of the lads to know my business. I avoided the question "father's name" for as long as possible. Eventually the passport was rushed through with the help of the TD, politician and sporting man David Andrews.

The second time came about five years ago, one Saturday afternoon before a First Division match against Coventry at Old Trafford. I was in the dressing-room about an hour before kick-off when the steward came rushing in muttering words I thought I would never hear.

"Paul McGrath – your father's at the gate looking for his tickets," said the gateman, oblivious to my plight. What was he talking about? The heart fluttered, the adrenaline flowed. Could it be him after all these years? Then reality sunk in – the Mr McGrath at the gate was indeed a player's father. His son was called Lloyd McGrath and he played for Coventry. It was a simple mistake by the steward – but it got me going nonetheless.

Fathers and mothers were never a fashion accessory as far as my life and my relationship with my own mother were concerned. My mother was left with no choice but to bring me home from London at six weeks of age and hand me over to someone who could look after me until such time as she would be able to take me back and give me as normal a family life as possible. That hurt her then. It still hurts her now. I understand that and I respect her for what she did. She could have turned her back on me completely, but she didn't. She did what was best at the time – for that I will always be grateful.

What was best for me then was a Protestant foster agency and life with a woman called Mrs Donnelly in the very Whitehall streets that produced Liam Brady and nurtured his footballing skills.

The Protestant foster agency was a tough choice. My mother had been reared as a Catholic in Dublin. But Catholics in authority had little regard for young girls in her position. That was why I was handed over to a Protestant agency that wet morning on the quayside at Dun Laoghaire.

Mrs Donnelly was like the halfway house for the kids handed over to that agency. There was a lot of controversy at the time about the idea of Catholic girls giving their children up to Protestant agencies. Holy Catholic Ireland claimed that the Protestants were trying to steal their children and convert them to their faith.

They probably had a point. I consider myself a Catholic without practising these days and one of my greatest thrills was meeting the Pope at the World Cup finals in Italy. Yet I would struggle to find the paperwork that qualifies me as a member of his flock – I was brought up as a Protestant and confirmed as a Protestant in all my time in institutions. And I can vividly remember a group of our Protestant brethren coming down from the north of Ireland every year to recharge the faith and make sure we were being raised the right way, their way.

I wasn't the first child entrusted into Mrs Donnelly's care and I certainly wasn't the last. She had me from the age of six weeks to about five years. She had what must have seemed like hundreds of other kids as well. They reckon as many as 40 kids passed through her door. As far as I was concerned she was my second mother – and my mother was my first mother when she used to come to visit me in those early days. I was better than the other kids – I had two mothers.

Life was hard for my natural mother. She worked hard to maintain the contact between us. She tried to take me home when I was three but it didn't work and I was back with Mrs Donnelly. She always ensured, though, that I grew up knowing who she was and what she meant to me. She always came to see me with a smile and a present. We had our problems but we never lost our sense of belonging to each other. That made it easier for both of us to accept things years later and to rebuild our lives together.

In the meantime I got on with life like any kid. I cried as a baby, walked into things as a toddler, wet the bed like anyone else.

And it was Mrs Donnelly who introduced me to football. I can vaguely remember kicking a ball out on the same streets as Liam Brady with my big brother Denis. He was my big brother as far as I was concerned. Years later it dawned on me that Denis was white and I was black. He couldn't have been my brother in the real sense of the word but as a three-year-old he was everything I wanted from a big brother. He looked after me, he watched out for me, he was the apple of my eye, was our Denis. He was my brother and Mrs Donnelly was my other mother, her extended family was my family.

Mrs Donnelly never made an issue of my background. Denis, my big brother, never made an issue of it. The kids on the street would from time to time. They'd tease me about my parents, about my colour, laugh at me calling Denis my big brother. Their intolerance just typified Ireland at the time. Years later it has changed for the better, even if attitudes could still do with some fine tuning.

That family with Mrs Donnelly at the helm was all I really knew for the first five years of my existence. Every so often my mother would visit – and one day her visit was to change my life. I was put into my Sunday finest. We were going to see my friend Ernest Dereekie at his big house out in Dun Laoghaire. As far as I was concerned it was just an ordinary day out for a mother and her son.

Wrong. This house was no ordinary house. It was a big grey building cast from a Charles Dickens novel and set in York Street out in Dun Laoghaire. The very same Dun Laoghaire streets that had welcomed me home into the arms of a stranger five years earlier, the same streets that had bid my mother farewell on her way to England. This house was an orphanage called The Bird's Nest, the logical progression from the environment of Mrs Donnelly's for the children entrusted to that Protestant agency. I thought I was going to visit my buddy. When we got there another course was already decided for my life.

My mother was handing me over again for my own sake, for my own good – this time to an institution. I was too old for Mrs Donnelly and too much for my mother in her circumstances. We parted in a big playroom in The Bird's Nest. Life was teaching me a lesson. One minute she was with me, the next minute I turned around and she was gone.

Young as I was I felt a sense of rejection, a feeling that still comes back every time I think of it. I knew what it meant to turn around and find your flesh and blood gone. I reacted badly. I cried for hours on end. I cried in the playroom, in the television room, surrounded by kids who had long since surrendered to life in an institution. I cried and bawled to people without ears in the dormitory with the steel beds that was to become my home for the next five years.

That night I threw another black kid, Klasf Lee, into a bath full of water. He was hardly much bigger than me – my anger suggested this was the way to solve my problem, to make him pay for my suffering. I didn't mean him any harm. I was rebelling against this great big grey institution that had overtaken my life. An institution that was to become home for the next five years until I moved to another one and then on to a third one.

Institution. The word itself is enough to frighten most people off. You soon get used to it. You get used to it because you have to. Because it's the norm. Because it's home.

I'm sure my mother has gone through an awful lot of guilt over what happened but I never blamed her for anything nor had any sort of a grudge to bear over it. What I went through as a child hurt me – it also toughened me up, it made me prepared for life and it was to benefit me for many years to come. It stood me in good stead when I first moved to England, when I had to make the big decisions that crop up in a lifetime.

Life made me a winner, fuelled a desire to be number one, to win a tackle or win a match. I grew up in an environment made for winners. I simply hate defeat in any shape or form. Throughout life I have had to stand up for myself. I had nobody to fall back on. It was me against the world – if I didn't win there was nobody there waiting to prop me up.

I have never denied or resented my background. I have often met people in Dublin who know where I came from, where I grew up. There have been times when people have tried to make an issue of it, when people who knew me as a kid have tried to cash in on my hardships through the media. I'm sure they will do so again. Sticks and stones may break my bones but words will never hurt me. Why should I be embarrassed about my background? Why should I be anything but proud of my mother, of my sister and of myself?

I'd like to think that what I have done could be an example for others. I'd like to think that it will help the kids in orphanages now to realise that they are the same as everyone else. That there are no differences. That they can realise their dreams no matter what the pitfalls.

I would also like to change attitudes to children from institutions. Society needs to change its opinions. People think once you're brought up in that environment you've got a handicap. If anything the stigma is more on the other side – it belongs to the smart alecs, to the people who think I've something to be ashamed of. There are people who talk to me about my days in orphanages because they think I'll be embarrassed and shocked. I love to turn the tables and discuss it openly, to make them feel the embarrassment and realise that they're the ones with the hang up and the chip on their shoulders.

I always say yes, I was in that orphanage or that was the school where I was – and then they get flustered and don't know what to do. It's great on my part to be able to do that. Some people are probably embarrassed about coming from my sort of background but I'm not. I'd like to help some of the kids there now. I've been back a few times, though not as often as I should have. I've been involved with the Irish Foster Parents Association as a patron for some of their fundraising. I want to help these kids, show them that there is a place in this world for winners – no matter on what side of the tracks you were born.

CHAPTER TWO

Release

SOCCER made me as a person. It gave me the identity I had been searching for, the expression of my personality that had been looking for an escape valve for so long.

As as kid I was quiet, shy, reserved even. Once I got used to life at The Bird's Nest I adapted quickly. I stood my ground when I had to. I answered back when I shouldn't have. I made my pitch to be the leader of the gang.

All that time I was searching for empathy, for an identity to make me stand on my own two feet – and stand out from the crowd. I found it in the schoolyard of Monkstown Primary School and in the field of dreams that was home to a little schoolboys' soccer club called Pearse Rovers, the best little club in the world.

It's funny the way people change over the years – and how life changes people. When I was a youngster growing up in Dublin I was very different from the other lads of my own age. It probably had a lot to do with my background and the orphanage environment in which I developed but once I found soccer and soccer found me we were made for each other.

I was never one for the high life as a teenager. Even in my late teens when I was out of the orphanage and trying to scrape a living together doing this job and that job, I had no love for living it up at the weekends or socialising in the bars and clubs of south Dublin like most of my friends. My love was football. It was an all-

26

embracing, passionate affair that's still going strong over 20 years later.

My sporting passions probably had a lot to do with my inkling for the quiet life but I just didn't bother to go out clubbing or anything like that. I had one love in life back then from the first day I was introduced to the Dublin and District Schoolboys League and to Pearse Rovers. It's a passion that has stood by me long after the booze, the women and the bright lights have lost their appeal.

Football was my passion, my reason for life. Football was the main thing for me even then when there were so many other things for a teenager growing up in Dublin to explore.

I went to work, I came home, I went out playing or training with the Dalkey lads and then I came back home again and I went to bed. It was the sort of discipline that the youngsters at clubs in England get, except I wasn't signed to anyone and I didn't ever think I would be. I just loved the game for the game's sake. It was one of the few things I could do well, one of the few things that set me aside from the rest. It was the one thing that gave me an identity and I loved it. My life was the game – the game on the street or the game in the park, the game with the club or the game with my mates at work or at school. It was football, football, football – it always has been and it probably always will be.

It was a passion that had always engulfed me, even as a youngster growing up in an institutionalised environment, away from my family but surrounded by youngsters like myself who lived for the game and the friendship and sense of belonging that a team sport like football can give you. The day the lads introduced me to organised soccer with Pearse Rovers they lit a flame for football that has been burning in my heart ever since.

I remember that longing for football and for sport getting a gang of us up off our backsides in one of the Mrs Smiley orphanages, the Glen Silva Home out in Monkstown. We were all sport mad at the time and the back garden in this orphanage was a perfect stage for our dreams of glory. That was apart from one little problem: it was in bits. It was a lovely site with a huge garden but it was just a mess and a place that served no useful purpose for us other than as a place to hide when the homework or the chores associated with life in those places were on the go and someone was looking for you.

We had the venue for our sporting passions on our doorstep, all we needed was the drive to get the gang of us who were into football in the orphanage up and working in our search for somewhere to play.

Eventually footballing justice was seen to be done one day when we just took it on ourselves to get our own pitch in order. We just decided there and then that the place in a mess out the back was big enough to have a soccer pitch. We didn't ask for permission, we just wanted a pitch of our own so we decided to give it a go no matter who was going to object or try to stop us.

The people running the home out in Monkstown could hardly object to what we were up to but it was hard work, much harder than we had anticipated. We had to go around picking out the stones by hand and then we had to level the ground to build the pitch but eventually we got it sorted out. There were about 20 of us working on it and the end product made all the toil worthwhile. We had a pitch of our own, a pitch to be proud of and a facility we could enjoy at all times. It was there to be used and we did. We went out there to play at all hours of the day. If the people minding us were looking for us that was always the first place they went. We had dug out this pitch with our own hands and we were sure as hell going to use it to the full.

I was only 12 at the time but there were lads from ten up to 19 playing on that pitch, taking turns at being Beckenbauer or Pele, Muller or Neeskens. I always wanted to be Charlie Cooke and my team was always Chelsea on that field of dreams.

Even then soccer was a big thing for me for reasons that I still don't understand. We used to have set times to do our homework when we'd come home from school but I'd want to spend all my time kicking a ball around the place. I had no interest in doing anything else. I'd put on the gear, always the blue jersey of my idols Chelsea, go out the back and we'd just play ball, three of four of us, playing three and in and stuff like that. That went on until we were called in and forced to do the homework, then we'd be out again straight afterwards for another kick around. Football was the only thing for a kid called Paul McGrath in an environment based on conformity.

It was the one thing that I was good at. Other young fellows were clever in school, brainy when it came to the homework, brave when it came to answering questions in the classroom. I wasn't into school or classes, teachers or pupils. I was into sport, my sport – the game of soccer.

I suppose there was something driving me at it the whole time. I still don't know what it was or is but I hated losing at anything.

It wasn't just football – if we had a sports day or anything and I was beaten in any event I'd be sick for days afterwards. There was always a thing where I had to be better than everyone else. It was a great help to me to be good at football. That set me apart, gave me my little flag to run up the pole and wave defiantly in the faces of others who didn't understand me, didn't understand where I was coming from or going to.

I wasn't clever like the rest – or even that interested. I was going to school with the other kids from the home alright but I didn't have a notion about doing sums or anything like that, which used to get me into all sorts of trouble. The teachers would always be on my back and rightly so, because I didn't give a damn about anything other than football. They were convinced I'd never make a living out of being a footballer and rapped my knuckles in an effort to get me to put the head down and study instead of getting the head up to meet the ball in Dodder Park or Griffin Park or the back pitches running into each other in the Phoenix Park where it was as easy to score in a game being played on a pitch next to you.

I was one of only two black fellows in the school where I first went and that was quite awkward. In a close-knit environment like Sallynoggin you're bound to get a bit of stick because you're different from the other kids. I was well used to taking abuse back in those days and I was strong enough to stand up for myself and fight my own corner when necessary. I ignored the stick and abuse because I had my football skills to fall back on and football was a great ice breaker between me and the other kids in school and outside. Soccer developed a bond between me and the other kids that race or colour or religion couldn't separate.

When I first graduated from the primary school in Monkstown, where I was accepted as one of the lads, to the technical college in Sallynoggin I did run into problems. I used to get called nigger and suffer racial abuse, which was a bit of a shock to the system at first because in primary school it wasn't that bad.

I knew what they were saying to me was wrong and hurtful but I never resented the kids who were behind it all, nor did I ever let it worry me. I just accepted it most of the time because I knew it was ignorance that was causing the problem, ignorance of the facts and ignorance of the big world outside the little schoolyard that became the focus of our lives for so many days a year.

But there was the odd time I did lash out, especially if it was someone that I could lash out at without fear of the consequences.

If some little fellow happened to say the wrong thing I'd have a go at him. But a lot of the time I had to bite my lip and just ignore it, hard as it was.

Eventually I decided the best way to react to this minor outbreak of racial unrest in Sallynoggin was to laugh at it, to make a big joke out of the whole thing and even at times to poke fun at myself. The brothers were having their problems out in South Africa and America but I was fighting back with laughter over in good old Ireland. The majority of the kids in the school came to accept me better because I laughed at their efforts to expose the fact that I was different from the rest of them. I even used it to my advantage, playing on the fact with the teachers and getting away with murder every so often when I'd step out of line and break the rules.

The other black kid in school was Klasf Lee, the older guy I had tried to drown the first day my mother left me behind in the orphanage out in Dun Laoghaire. He went to school before I did so he probably got the battering before I arrived but he was well capable of looking after himself and soon he had little trouble fighting off the problem makers. Klasf was a shrewd fellow, a sharp operator who knew how to look after himself and he taught me a lot about life despite my earlier attempts to drown him in one of the Mrs Smiley's baths.

The fact that we were black was initially an issue in secondary school but never the fact that we lived in an orphanage, away from our parents. It just wasn't the done thing to have a go at us about that. Colour wasn't an issue. The other kids probably thought we would be more sensitive about that than we were.

The orphanage was okay once you got used to the idea and accepted it. They were hard in terms of discipline – they had to be. They were also keen on education, not that I was much use to them on that front. I liked history, I did okay at that at school. I had a bit of an interest in English. But sums were out the window – physical education was the subject I really bothered about. It was a subject that stood me in good stead in these days as well.

I was a lot more outgoing then than I am now, mostly because I had to be. Down in The Bird's Nest I was alright because I was in amongst my own, a match for any of them. When I moved to Monkstown it was a different story. A lot of the boys I had tormented had big brothers living in that second place. There were whole families living in the orphanages and when they met up with their big brothers they ensured retribution was dished out to the likes of myself for earlier sins.

That made life difficult for the people in charge. The main man in the second place was called Mr Croxton. He lived in the home with his wife, two daughters and a son. We regarded them as part of us and I'm sure the feeling was reciprocated. He was a bit strict in terms of school work and behaviour. He was against me playing football for a long time but he also encouraged us to stand up for ourselves, a lesson in life everyone needs to heed.

When the violence was blatant, with people beating each other up, he'd step in but a lot of the time he didn't see what was going on. We had a gym out the back and our football field. If we needed a boxing ring they were more than sufficient – and out of the way.

Other kids in school used to come and visit the home every so often – and they'd get quite a shock. They'd be impressed because it was a lovely house in Monkstown and we had a football pitch out the back, a swing swinging from the tree and a volleyball court. There was even a stream running down the back, so we had everything that a kid wanted. Mrs Smiley homes they were called, the ones I was in – she was a little old lady who used to come and visit us. It was a nice family set-up, though with the odd punch-up here and there.

Years later I would move home to my mother after a lengthy illness. It was strange but we adapted. We had never lost sight of each other and that was so important in the reconciliation. I never even thought about my upbringing as being unusual and I never blamed my mother for what happened to me. I never resented the orphanages or the fact that we waited 18 years and two illnesses later to live together. I had my gripes about the homes but I got on with life. And it did have its advantages – when you lived in a home with 20 boys there was always somebody to play in goal! I never looked on it as unusual that I was living away from my mother or that other kids found it strange. It was the done thing as far as I was concerned and I was never unduly worried about it.

CHAPTER THREE

Headless Chickens

CHARLIE COOKE has a lot to answer for.

The former Chelsea wing wizard was the inspiration behind my first real effort at playing football. From the time I first kicked a ball with my assumed big brother Denis out in Whitehall until the day I signed for Manchester United I was a Chelsea fan. And all because of one man – the moustached, long-haired, jersey-flying-in-the-wind figure of Charlie Cooke.

For some strange reason the influx of televised soccer into Dublin via *Match of the Day* on a Saturday night and *The Big Match* at lunchtime on a Sunday indoctrinated me into the ways of the boys in blue. By 1970 and the FA Cup final I was a confirmed Chelsea nut. But love had blossomed long before. In fact one of my earliest memories of my mother is of her coming out to see me with a present of a lifetime. She had bought me the authentic Chelsea strip – why I don't know – as early as the age of eleven and I was away with my footballing dreams. I still find it hard to fathom out why the Stamford Bridge side were the recipients of my earliest affections. Perhaps it was the style of the club, the flair of players like Cooke and Peter Osgood and then, a little later, Alan Hudson.

Denis, my big brother at Mrs Donnelly's, was the first coach in my life. Out on the streets of Whitehall where Liam Brady and Joey Malone first learned how to kick a ball we would don our jerseys and take on the world. When I moved into The Bird's Nest it was the same. I was always on at the masters to let me out the back to kick a football, always trying to watch *Match of the Day* past my bedtime on a Saturday night, waiting for *The Big Match* and Brian Moore at lunchtime on a Sunday.

Primary school in Monkstown was my first public footballing arena. Like every other schoolyard in the country it was populated by boys playing football at break-time, at lunchtime and after school. As long as the sun was in the sky we'd have a ball out in the yard. Every kid in Dublin has done it in his time.

Throw down your schoolbag, one of those old football gear bags with Chelsea scrawled across the front, and you had a goalpost. Get a bunch of your friends and you had a team. Challenge another gang and you had a match – of sorts. Like every other bunch of kids we had no idea of tactics or rules. We just put the ball down and chased after it. Positioning was irrelevant – tactics were those new mints from France you bought in the shop on your way home from school. Or something like that.

We were never ourselves on those concrete yards of dreams. Instead we took on new identities every time the imaginary whistle sounded for the start of another kick-around of World Cup importance. The identities changed as often as the weather in Monkstown. One week I was Charlie George of Arsenal. The next week I was Johnny Giles, because I was small for my age. In 1970 we all wanted to be Brazilians like Pele or Jarzinho or Rivelino. Never a defender. Except for one poor unfortunate who always wanted to be the goalkeeper. In 1970 he was Gordon Banks and I was Pele. He made the save. In 1973 he was Jim Montgomery and we were all Leeds players. He made the saves again. That same year he was a clown from Poland – and he had the last laugh on the English strikers lining up in that schoolyard.

Same names, same games. Only the faces and the venues were changed. To protect the innocent, you understand.

I was an innocent abroad alright in those early days of the '70s. I thought football belonged to the schoolyard and the black and white television screen. I never realised there was a league outside of England where Charlie Cooke was the sole guardian of my dreams and Chelsea my dream team. It was only when I made the switch to secondary school that I discovered the truth and the facts of life that really matter – about the game of Association Football.

I was helped by the fact that my peers were all mad into the game. The kids in the home were always willing to play some football. The kids from outside who congregated in the schoolyard in Sallynoggin Technical College, my one and only second-level school, were more than willing to fill me in on the missing details in this jigsaw of life.

Kieran Forsyth was one of the first friends I made at the Noggin Tech. And he knew a thing or two about soccer. He was from the village of Sallynoggin, just down the road from the Glen Silva home, and we hit it off straight away. We became firm friends, initially through football until our shared interests increased. We mitched together, we'd doss together, we'd play ball together at school. Kieran was with St Joseph's at Sallynoggin at the time and I was to end up with Pearse Rovers but that rivalry never got in the way of our friendship.

In fact when I went to the Tech my soccer career really started to take off. I had been listening in awe to the lads at school talking about belonging to a club and playing for your team on a Saturday and it really appealed to me. Tommy Heffernan was in charge of Pearse at the time and he came down one day to have a look at a five-a-side we were playing in the schoolyard. He had a lot of the lads in my year at school in his side and they were always on at him to come and have a look at me. Without me knowing, of course. I was 13 at this stage and I had never played for any team. I was just happy to play away in school and listen in amazement to this talk of a schoolboys' league which they kept inviting me to join. I used to think it must be great to play in an 11-a-side match with all the gear. Then Tommy came down to have a look and said why don't you come and join us. That's how I started.

The first few games I didn't have a clue, I was running around the pitch like a headless chicken. I had no idea about the positions, I didn't know where I was going or what I was doing and I spent the whole time chasing the ball. If he said to me I was right-back I'd have a guess that that's around here somewhere and then off I'd sprint up the pitch past halfway and well out of position up into the forwards.

I fancied myself as a bit of a ball player and I wanted to get the ball and show them what I could do, the tricks I had mastered in the backyard of the home up against the wall. Of course getting the ball at that age group was almost impossible. I wasn't the only headless chicken. There were about 19 other candidates, all haring around in search of that size four piece of leather.

I didn't know the positions at that stage. There are some would argue I still know little or nothing about positioning. It was just such a great novelty to be part of a team, to feel wanted by people like that. I got a kick out of bringing my jersey home to be washed, out of polishing my boots the night before a game, out of packing my gear and buying my bottle of red lemonade for the journey home. Even things like paying your subs used to be a source of wonder for me. The subs were incredible looking back on it now. They were about 30 pence a week not long after decimalisation but it was worth every penny just to be part of a team and to experience that first thrill of winning matches.

It was also a great excuse to make friends. And that has always been an important facet of football in my life. Pearse Rovers made me many friends. It offered me my first encounter with Johnny Young, a kid who oozed talent on and off the ball, the player to watch out for in our side. He became my closest friend in that team and he was my forthcoming ally right until the day I left Dalkey for St Patrick's Athletic en route to Manchester United.

Kevin Keenan was another schoolmate in Sallynoggin. He was my best friend at school. He wasn't much of a footballer even though he tried his luck as a player with me at Pearse – and we got a great kick out of playing against Kieran Forsyth and St Joseph's Boys, even if we couldn't beat them.

My other passion in life, apart from playing, was watching football. I was a serious Chelsea nut from 1970 when they were in the FA Cup final and beat Leeds in the replay at Old Trafford, of all places. One of the older lads in the orphanage followed them and when the Cup campaign started I thought I might as well do the same. It was a wise decision – my first week supporting Chelsea ended with my team winning the FA Cup. That interest was helped the following Christmas when my mother bought me the Chelsea rig-out, the old all-blue number that made me look and feel like Charlie Cooke. Without the moustache of course.

I started to take an interest in the Irish side when Johnny Giles was manager and he started to get a few decent results. I always wanted Ireland to win when they were on television, and a few times I even got down to Dalymount and the famous roar with tickets from Pearse Rovers. But my abiding passion was Chelsea – there was no other team for me.

I got a great buzz the first time I played at Stamford Bridge for Manchester United. I can't remember if we won or lost. That didn't matter. What mattered was that I had made it to my spiritual home. Every time I go back I pay homage to the legend of Charlie Cooke.

It was always a disappointment that they were never linked with me. It's still not too late though. Take note, Glenn Hoddle!

Charlie Cooke was the player I admired most in the Chelsea side at the time. He had the skills of a Brazilian and a Celtic fire burning in his heart. But there were other great stars at Chelsea in those days – players like Peter Osgood, Peter Houseman, Ian Hutchinson, David Webb and Alan Hudson. It was an era for real players.

Two of the best sides of all at that time belonged to the Germans and the Dutch. Together they made a huge impact on my life and on my understanding of this beautiful game. I vaguely remember the 1970 World Cup coming in at us from Mexico in black and white, and marvelling at the skills of the Brazilians, the Italians and Bobby Moore. He was the ultimate centre-half as far as I was concerned – thankfully I had the pleasure of meeting him many times in England before his untimely death.

By 1974 televised soccer was all the rage, with Jimmy Magee's voice to be heard all over Ireland, and the Dutch and the Germans were the heroes in the Sallynoggin playground and beyond. The West Germans were the side I used to love watching play – they had everything going for them both as a team and as individuals. Franz Beckenbauer and the rest of them used to stroke it around and take their time – they looked so comfortable on the ball. We tried that out with the tennis ball in the playground, but we could never quite match the feeling of the Olympic Stadium many miles away in Munich. Or match the skills of Beckenbauer and Netzer. I still can't figure out why.

CHAPTER FOUR

Dalkey Boys Hooray

PEARSE ROVERS was the beginning and the end of the football domain for a teenage Paul McGrath. In fact I had no football ambitions beyond the little club with the big heart, the club that gave the game to Paul McGrath and was still waiting for that ball back.

I was at home with Pearse Rovers. And home is where the heart is. The grass was no greener than it was at Pearse, the crock of gold at the end of their rainbow more valuable than any other. They liked me and I loved them. Oh, to be young and carefree once more. Just like it was in those far-off, heady days of the Dublin and District Schoolboys' League. Ten of us crammed into a car on the way to a game, lemonade and crisps on the way home to Monkstown, all paid for by the unfortunate driver.

I was no longer the headless chicken. I was a competent defender, a more than adequate midfielder and a useful enough striker when the need arose. Of course there was talk of life after Pearse but who listened to such talk when you were having a ball? And who needed it?

Certainly not me. When I was 17 the talk had already started that there were clubs like Manchester United and Tottenham, where our coach Tommy Heffernan had connections, down looking at John Young or myself with Pearse Rovers. Big deal, I thought. I wasn't interested in going up the road to play football, never mind traipsing across the Irish Sea to a strange city in a strange land in search of that elusive dream. I was my usual happy-go-lucky self, living life as I knew it in Racefield, enjoying my football with Pearse at the weekends and mitching off school whenever the chance arose to kick a ball or rob a few orchards. Or engage in all the other tricks that teenage boys got up to.

I was more than happy playing ball with Rovers, kicking ball in the schoolyard and out the back of the home with the guys I had grown up with, the guys I had kicked my first serious ball with. The coaches and the mentors and the fathers of the other lads were always on at me to step up a grade but I wasn't that interested. I was in a safe haven at Pearse and that was my lot for life as far as I was concerned.

We were doing well in the Dublin Schoolboys' League – even if we could never get the better of our great rivals, St Joseph's Boys, up the road in Sallynoggin. I had settled into the game now. I was small in stature but quite a right-back nonetheless. I was no longer the headless chicken chasing the ball all over the field. I was happy. And that counted for a lot in a life crying out for stability.

Circumstances were beyond my control though. Racefield was the third instalment of the orphanage trilogy that had begun for me years earlier in The Bird's Nest. It was out in Dun Laoghaire, the final link between institutionalism and real life, linked to The Bird's Nest and the Glen Silva Home but a world apart – the final haven for children before adulthood, until their enforced exit to the big bad world of normal life.

It was semi-private, smaller and less well known than The Bird's Nest or the Glen Silva Home purely because it needed to be less conspicuous by its very nature. It had a fantastic reputation for looking after its boys. They were both protective and caring. The future was as important as the present in terms of looking after their family in that home.

There were problems around the corner that last season with Pearse Rovers, most of them not of my own making. At 17, as Janis Ian might say, I was to learn the truth about life. The orphanage could no longer offer me a safe home and a safe environment. They were forced by regulations and their own reality to place me outside their care. They knew that when I turned 17 – and they knew my penchant for football was my only hope of survival in the big bad world away from Racefield.

Pearse Rovers couldn't be part of the equation for my future. They catered mostly for schoolboys' teams. They had one adult side but it wasn't up to much and it certainly wasn't going to help me survive amongst the real men of the real world. The club didn't have the infrastructure to guide me through the choppy waters of adulthood.

Behind the scenes all sorts of manoeuvres were under way, most of them without my knowledge. Mr Johnson, the master at Racefield, was on the look-out for a club that would be more than just a sporting facility for a 17-year-old Paul McGrath about to turn a major corner of the road of life. He wanted an umbrella that would shelter my life – and me from life. He knew about Dalkey United because of their reputation in the greater Dun Laoghaire area for sound values on and off the playing fields of Dublin. The fact that John Young had just moved to Dalkey helped their cause and his search as well. Enormously, as it turned out.

Dalkey officials Tom Cullen, Johnny Dunne and Frank Mullen had been down to see John play with us a fair few times before they persuaded him to step up into the Leinster Senior League. John had talent to burn and was to prove a more than adequate player at that level for many years to come. He's still kicking ball at a good level – and I often wonder why he never joined me across the water until he developed a laziness in training.

It was obvious to all of us that Dalkey were good to John. They made him feel welcome, eased him over the transition from Boy's Own football to the kickers and the hard men of the Leinster Senior League. Pearse, unhappy at losing one of their star boys, were happy that Dalkey had looked after their protégé. When Mr Johnson asked their advice they echoed the sentiments all around South County Dublin – I was on my way to Dalkey.

The first contact was made when Mr Johnson phoned Frank Mullen and told him he had a young lad in his home who played a bit of football and needed an adult club. But there was a catch. He wasn't just looking for a new club for me – he was also looking for a job and somewhere to live as soon as I became too old for the orphanage. Mr Johnson never let on how good I was as a footballer or revealed the potential that the lads at Pearse had told him was running through my veins. He needed to get me looked after – and the response from Dalkey about life off the field for me was just as important as how they were going to treat me on it.

Frank put it to his committee, then and now a small close-knit bunch who run the club like a family and do things their way. My name was known vaguely from their trips to see John Young in action and I think he had been going on about me a bit in training. The reports on my footballing ability were favourable. Now all I needed was a new family and job. Not much to ask for really as signing-on fees go.

Then came the masterstroke. Frank spoke to Frank Hammond, a local slating contractor and builder whose family all played football with Dalkey. He explained that there was a kid on the way to the club who was an exceptional footballing talent but needed a home and job of some sort. Frankie Hammond, God be good to him, needed no second invitation. I was to start work as a trainee slater and move into digs with friends of his family, less than a quarter of a mile from the Dalkey club grounds. The rest, as they say, is history.

John Young had already done a good job selling the club to me. When Tom Cullen came to see at the end of the season with the Pearse Rovers under-17s I needed little persuasion. I was on my way to Dalkey. All he had to do was ask. He did – and that summer I found myself winding my merry way up the coast to that cosy little ground tucked in behind the Gaelic football pitch, a ground that is still home to Dalkey United and always will be.

I was carrying more than my boots that first summer's evening when I went training with United. I was carrying anxieties in that mind of mine.

The welcome at the club was everything it had promised to be. Tom explained that I was not to worry about the football. I had, he said, the natural ability to make the transition from schoolboys' football with Pearse to Leinster Senior League with Dalkey without any trouble.

What he never explained to me was the difference between life in the world of schoolboys' football and life in a dressing-room full of grown men, some of them old enough to be my father. They must have thought it was funny when this teenager walked in with the Afro hairstyle and his boots under the arm. I was certainly different to what they were used to – there were a few shouts of Bob Marley aimed in my direction that evening.

I think the other black player in our grade of football at that time was a lad called Ray "Darky" Keogh, who was, by then, the player-manager of Parkvilla in Navan and quite a midfield schemer in his day.

It was a whole new ball game for me on and off the pitch that first evening. In the dressing-room the banter was adult and grown-up, fellows talking about their wives or their children, their girlfriends or your one up the road that they fancied. They were adults and they expected the kids coming into their ranks to behave like adults. They expected you to stand on your own two feet, to stand up and be counted when it mattered.

My anxieties about my background were ill-founded to say the least. They weren't interested in the fact that I was about to leave an orphanage and move into digs. They weren't interested in the fact that my education finished after I had collected the Group certificate and the Intermediate certificate at Sallynoggin Technical College and had given up on the Leaving Certificate at a very early stage. The only thing that mattered as far as they were concerned was my ability to play football. If I could do that I was okay – if I couldn't I was on my bike. No more and no less.

They played hard and they lived hard. They got up to all the usual pranks. Wallets went missing, lipstick appeared mysteriously on collars during matches before the married lads went home to their wives, smelly Deep Heat appeared in the funniest of places. All designed to inject a bit of humour into life. The football, though, was deadly serious.

My first game was at home in Dalkey against a touring side from Germany called Wattenscheid, now playing in the Bundesliga itself. There was a great debate on the sideline before they decided to play me. Frank, Tom, Johnny Dunne, Paddy Larkin, Mick Hayde, Willie Kane and Willie Fogarthy all threw in their tuppence ha'penny worth. I was in.

This was a case of throwing me in at the deep end on a hot summer's day during an annual festival of soccer organised by the club. They told me not to get overawed by the occasion, to relax and let my football skills do the talking on the pitch. It was good advice. Once the game began I settled into my rhythm at right-back and soon realised I could look the part at this level.

I enjoyed it against that German side. Not for the first time was I to admire continental football. Even now I wonder what might have been if I had ever got the chance to play amongst continental styles on a regular, professional basis.

It was ironic that a German side provided the opposition for my first game. A year later I was to leave Ireland for the first time on a club tour with Dalkey, a tour that was to have serious repercussions on my return.

I have great memories of my times with Dalkey. Like the game against a team of hard cases from Dublin called Fatima Rangers when I got sent off for the first of only two times in my entire footballing career. One of their lads called me a big black bastard. I wasn't having any of that and I kicked him where it hurts. It hurt. He went down like a sack of potatoes. Before the referee even had time to get his book out and send me off I was heading for the dressing-room. Partly because I knew I was going to be dismissed anyway. Partly because I feared what his team-mates were going to do to me. I had done wrong – but there was no need for that sort of remark.

When the referee's report went in he said why I was sent off but refused to reveal what their guy had said in my direction. Dalkey kicked up over the nature of the racist remark and refused to pay my fine of £3. Every season since then the fine has come up in the League's audits – every season Dalkey refuse to cough up. Much to the chagrin of Charlie Cahill, the doyen of the Leinster Senior League for so many years and a good friend of mine.

Fatima were a hard bunch, a typical bunch of Dublin lads out to enjoy their ball. Tough as nails. But a great bunch. They had characters in their team, real characters. And the fans who travelled with them were just as colourful.

Backbone of the Fatima Rangers adult team in those days were a family called the Reids. They lived up near my mother's and before long I was part of their gang for the endless five-a-sides that take place around Dublin all over the summer. Their five-a-side team consisted of all the Reid brothers and Paul McGrath. They'd collect me in the back of a truck and we'd all go off together to the game. The players, the supporters on the back and the father driving the truck. Nine times out of ten we'd win the tournaments.

They could play a bit, those Reids. Ger wasn't a bad player. The best of them was Billy who played with me at St Pat's. Another brother, Victor, was at Shelbourne for a while. And the family used to have a great banner in the stands when he was playing. "Rub it in Vic", read the banner. Typical Dublin wit.

Dalkey United made me as a footballer and as a man. I was thrown in at the deep end when I joined the club, put straight into the first team and left to sink or swim. In footballing terms I was a raw 17-year-old let loose alongside guys who knew every trick in the book and a few more besides. I was playing right-back with the style of Curtis Fleming, the Black Pearl of Inchicore Number

Two who followed on from me at St Pat's and is now with Middlesbrough. With Dalkey I was a mere teenager yet I was expected to play like a man with experience.

The Leinster Senior League toughened me up for what was to come at St Patrick's Athletic, Manchester United and Aston Villa. It taught me tricks that I use to this day. It put me up against crafty old whores who thought they knew everything. The "been there, done that, have the tee-shirt" types who tried to kick the new kids all around the block.

Soccer's like that the world over. I experienced it first hand with Dalkey and I never forgot it. The old dog for the hard road, as they say at home. The old guy with the wise head on his shoulders can often trick the youngster into doing exactly what he wants him to do. It was done to me at Dalkey and I have done it to a few young centre-forwards in my time.

That Dalkey experience toughened me up. It taught me how to play hard and fair. Tom Cullen taught me how to live. He was probably the biggest influence on my football career in Ireland. As soon as I joined Dalkey United he took me under his wing and became more like a father to me than the main man of my football team. The officials at that club were all like that to me. They still are. When I'm in trouble even now I know I can turn to them for help. There wasn't anything that Tom Cullen or Frank Mullen or Johnny Dunne wouldn't do for me off the field. If I asked them tomorrow morning they'd do it all over again.

They looked after me. When I needed work they fixed me up with Mick Fenton and Jim Fitzgerald at CP Security. Jim was buried the day Ireland played Italy in the 1990 World Cup. On the altar the priest said Jim would have been proud of me that day.

The Dalkey people did things for me that had nothing to do with football. They got me jobs, places to live. They drove me here, there and everywhere. If I had a problem it was a problem shared, a problem halved and a problem solved very quickly.

And Dalkey United introduced me to the late, great Billy Behan, vice-president of the club, the Manchester United scout and one of the real gentlemen of football in Ireland. The man I owe as much of my success as a footballer to as anyone. When I joined Dalkey, Billy's son, Terry, was already part and parcel of the first team set-up. That gave any Dalkey youngster worth his salt an immediate head start in terms of notice. After all it wasn't every player in Ireland at the time who played alongside the son of the

Manchester United scout who had discovered the likes of Liam Whelan and Johnny Giles for Matt Busby.

Billy introduced me to Sir Matt, the kindest of men in all my time at Old Trafford. Sir Matt *was* Manchester United. I joined the club long after he had retired from management. Only he never retired really from man management. The players in that club were still his boys right up to his sad death earlier this year.

Every day at the ground he'd meet you with that warmest of smiles and the greatest of handshakes. He always went out of his way to talk to me, from the first day he came to watch me play in Ireland with St Pat's. Matt always had time for me even when the rest of the powerbrokers at Old Trafford were staying out of my way. He always gave me one piece of advice, advice he had administered to so many fallen angels in his glory days: "Always let your football do the talking, son – respond on the pitch," were his immortal words. I thought of those words the day he died this year. He was a gentleman, as was Billy Behan, who's now scouting for Sir Matt in that great fantasy league in the sky. What a dream team they'll produce.

Billy's son Terry was a bit of a character in his own right. His dad had played a bit in his time and passed on the skills. The fact that he was Billy Behan's son never worried Terry. He was always the centre of attention, the joker in the pack. With one major advantage – he could play a bit.

Billy's local links stood him and me well. Dalkey were great ones for keeping the scouts away from their nest of young players. They had always kept their cards close to their chests. A few players had gone over to England for trials and been back home before anyone even realised they were missing. A couple of times they kept Spurs away from me when they knew Billy was selling me to United and Sir Matt at the time. There was even one occasion when the then Tottenham manager Keith Burkinshaw rang Frank Mullen up and said that he was sending his top two scouts over to have a look at me. Frank told him in no uncertain terms that he was wasting his time. There was only one place I was going and that was Old Trafford.

Spurs sent the scouts anyway and they ended up on the sidelines at some match out in the Soldiers and Sailors field in Monkstown. I wasn't aware of their presence but the club were and they were determined to keep them away from me after the match. So when we stopped play at half-time I was told there was a change

44

in the plan for togging in after the game. I was told to get into Frank's car and go with him straight back to Dalkey where my gear would be waiting for me. As soon as that final whistle went I was in the car and off down the road to our own clubhouse. By the time the Spurs scouts got to our dressing-room I had already disappeared into the afternoon and they were none the wiser.

That was typical of the way Dalkey looked after me. The club made me. And taught me. They looked after me through the good times and the bad. It was a marriage made in heaven for me the day I walked up the road in Dalkey and joined the club they call United.

CHAPTER FIVE

In Sickness and in Health

LIFE WAS SWEET that first year at Dalkey United until an end-of-season tour that was to change so many things.

By this stage I was settled into the football side of Dalkey, playing away at right-back, sometimes in the middle of the defence, sometimes upfront when they were looking for a goal to get something out of a game. I was making good progress, listening to the coaches and getting a bit of a name for myself.

Every so often Billy Behan would come out to have another look at us, ostensibly to check on his son Terry but more likely, as I discovered afterwards, to check on this kid called Paul McGrath. He told me years later that he liked the look of me from the first day he saw me – and wanted me for Manchester United. That dream would become a reality when I was 22 but there was a lot of Liffey water to flow under the Matt Talbot Bridge before we got to that stage.

Germany was calling in that summer of '78 and I was as happy as the pig in the proverbials. I had never been outside Ireland before, I had never stayed in an hotel before, I had never flown before. These were all things that were new to me as Dalkey prepared for their regular visit to Wattenscheid and a tournament they have graced frequently.

It was also the first time I needed a passport. That didn't present a problem in itself, though I was embarrassed when they asked who my father was. I was old enough to get the passport without parental consent but I delayed and delayed the application until the very last minute. Only the intervention of politician and football lover David Andrews got the documentation processed in time to get me out of the country.

The first thrill was on the Aer Lingus jet taking us from Dublin to Germany. On the plane, right in front of our very eyes, was the great Pele, on his way from a promotional activity in Dublin for Stewart's Hospital. We were like flies around jam looking for autographs off our hero. Eventually he asked us to back off as he allowed some of the other passengers to take some photographs and when all the fuss had died down Tom Cullen ended up with two autographs. Because myself and John Young were Tom's favourites we got the Pele autographs – and I still have mine at home somewhere. Meeting Pele was an experience in itself. My only regret now is that nobody had a camera to record the moment for history. That is a picture I would love to pass on to my children.

Then we landed in Cologne and got the coach an hour or so to our destination in Wattenscheid. The young lads on the youth team and the club officials were despatched off to the homes of our German hosts – I was in a hotel with John Young and the rest of the first team lads.

Like any other bunch of footballers away from home and the demands of normal life, these Dalkey lads were out to have a good time. The first night we all gathered in one of the bedrooms and everyone was getting ready to go out to a disco. I had never seen the inside of a discotheque before – not a problem nowadays – and I just couldn't imagine what it was like. The lads insisted the younger members of the team like myself and John go along with them – and what an experience that was.

It was a real eye-opener. I liked this disco lark. I liked this drink lark. I had a dance with the lads. I had a dance with a girl. I had a drink. Some sort of schnapps. I had some lager. I had whatever was going and I got out of my tree with the drink. The next day I was wearing dark glasses because that was what you were meant to do after a night on the tear. I had the taste of it. Binge number one of my life was up and running. I lived it up for the ten days with the lads on tour in Germany and I loved every minute of it. I loved the football. We had a half-decent side and we got to the semi-final until the host team put us out.

In that last game something happened that was to trigger a bad spell in my life. I took a kick to the head, a severe kick. At the time it was sore, very sore, but only a temporary problem. I picked myself up, dusted myself down and got on with it. I was happy that the blow was nothing more than one of the scrapes and scratches that are part and parcel of football the world over. My diagnosis was wrong. Weeks later the blow to my head was to cause me all sorts of problems. It was the spark to a bout of depression that spiralled and spiralled. I didn't realise it at the time. I was too caught up with the excitement of Germany and going home. When I got back to reality it made its mark.

When we got home the lads were all saying what an incredible experience it had been, how well I had played for my first time out of the country and how it was only a matter of time before I went away to Manchester United. The pressure was mounting.

Life should have been exciting for me and the rest of those young lads at Dalkey when we returned. I was excited. Excited after Germany, excited about the talk of the prospect of trying my luck with Manchester United. Excited and worried. I had spent my life sheltered from real pressures in an environment that was different. Now I was out in the real world and life was a lot tougher than I had expected. There were people placing great expectations on my shoulders. In the past there was always someone else there to fend off those responsibilities for me. Now I was on my own.

I had what can only be described as a severe bout of depression just days after I returned from Germany in that summer of '79. I can't explain why or how. I still don't understand. But one morning I woke up in my digs and the walls had come crashing down around me. I was in that bedroom but I wasn't. My body was there but I was floating above it looking down and wondering what the hell was going on. The house was not the house I lived in. Everything was a blur. It was a doll's house. The body was mine but not the mind. To this day I still don't know why.

Thankfully somebody found me – I still don't know who. I was in no state to recognise myself never mind anyone else. They got me to St Vincent's in Elm Park, one of the top hospitals on the southside of Dublin. They put out messages for Frank Mullen to try and get him to come to my aid. Eventually Frank was contacted by a Dr Byrne in St Vincent's and told that he needed to get there as quickly as possible, that I had been admitted in a terrible state.

When Frank got there the details were sketchy. All the doctors knew was that I had been found in my digs in a kind of stupor. They couldn't get me to talk, to tell them what was wrong. As the first day wore on I was withdrawing further and further into my own little world.

Frank could get no sense out of me. I saw him there and never acknowledged his presence. All I told him was that I wanted chocolate. Not another word was spoken. I was in a sleepish stupor, unable to communicate or make sense of anything. The hospital took a while to develop any sort of prognosis. They even asked Frank if I was on drugs – I have never even tried that sort of escapism nor have I any intention of doing so.

Frank was at a loss to explain what was wrong with me. He had last seen me on our return from Germany and I was flying. He told them about the blow to the head, went off and got the chocolate and I devoured it without saying a word. From the minute I was admitted to the time he left late the next day I never opened my mouth. All I asked for was that chocolate.

They did the usual tests but made little headway. They kept me in Vincent's for a couple of days but there was little they could do. This was a general hospital. My problems were far from the normal type of affliction associated with casualty wards. All that time Frank and Tom Cullen and Johnny Dunne tried to get some sense out of me but to no avail. I was up there with the gang from *One Flew Over the Cuckoo's Nest*.

Eventually Frank, through his contacts as chairman of the Garda Representative Association, made contact with two men in St John of God's out on the Bray Road who were to solve my problems at least temporarily. Pat Tubridy and Don Lydon were specialists at the John of Gods, a hospital famous for its treatment of alcoholics and those suffering with depression. They took me in as a favour to Frank and did more tests. Eventually they decided I was suffering from severe depression though the cause was far from clear.

Those two doctors sorted me out and they reunited me with my mother. They found her through the records at Racefield. She was working in a restaurant in Dublin and living with her mother and my sister Okone out in Crumlin. The news came as a huge shock. Her reaction was everything it needed to be. She was compassionate and caring. And she was there when I needed her. Her presence at my side out in St John of God's pulled me through. The first day she came out to the hospital we shed some tears. I was overcome at seeing her. She was overcome at the sight of me and the state of me.

We fought the illness together. With the help of Frank Mullen, Tom Cullen and Johnny Dunne I made it past that first hurdle on the road to recovery. Gradually I improved. Physically I had wasted away but mentally I was getting there. I put all my problems out of my mind. I concentrated on going home, home to my mother's on the advice of the doctors. They felt the stability that move would give me was just the tonic I needed to pull through.

I got over that first illness relatively quickly. I had to give up the job in Hammond's when I moved out of the hospital and into my mother's place in Crumlin. But life was good. I went back to playing for Dalkey wth relatively few problems. The illness had happened during the close season, the summer of '79. By the time the new season started there wasn't a problem and the lads hardly realised there was anything wrong. That wasn't important. At the time I didn't want them to know my situation.

Billy Behan knew what was going on but he was happy to let the doctors get on with the treatment and wait for me to recover. He had already decided that he was sending me to Manchester United on his personal recommendation. He was prepared to wait for me – and kept United in the picture. That was an incredible act of faith on his behalf. Most scouts would have washed their hands of me as soon as I went into St John of God's. But Billy was different. He had soul and he had compassion in abundance. He knew football was my life. He knew football was going to be my life no matter what happened in that hospital. He waited. A long wait, far longer than any of us anticipated.

I was alright for a while. For a couple of happy months. Then came the relapse. And that was bad. Very bad. For my mother. For my family.

I recovered from the first illness and had two months of normality. Then came the biggest blow of all. It happened one Monday morning. My mother made me my breakfast before she went out to work. A big fry, tea and toast. She took it up to me as usual.

When she went back to collect the plates I hadn't eaten the breakfast. I was sitting up in bed, oblivious to the world.

This time no casualty unit was equipped to deal with my problems. I was admitted to St Brendan's Hospital in Grange-gorman, a hospital that's hard enough to visit never mind stay in as a patient. I needed their hospitality though. I was sick, seriously sick, seriously depressed.

This time there was no easy cure. I was in there for months.

I had visitors. I hardly noticed them. I refused to talk to anyone. To my mother, my sister, my granny, my Aunt Mary. To Frank or Tom or Johnny Dunne or John Young. To Noel Lowth, my mother's future husband. They'd do their best to engage me in conversation over a cup of tea. I'd ignore them, withdraw into my depressed world. My mother found it hard to handle. My family found it hard. My friends found it hard. I was wasting away in front of them. I was sick. I didn't care. I didn't notice. I didn't want to know.

I know now there are times when those closest to me wondered if I'd ever come out of it. Ever be the same again. They persisted. Thank God they persisted.

No matter how much I ignored them they came back. No matter how badly I behaved in front of them they came back. All the time believing where I had no belief. All the time praying I'd get better. All the time talking football, taking me out to the grass at lunchtime and trying to convince me to play football. I'd kick their ball for something to do. Nothing more and nothing less. Football was the last thing on my confused mind. Football was gone. Dead. A thing of the past in my life.

They told me I was suffering from severe depression. I didn't take any notice. My family and friends did. They still believed in me. I would get better. With their help. It was a long and hard struggle. Against the illness. Against myself. Against my lack of interest. But they got me there. They dragged me there. They got me back to reality. They brought me back to life.

They got me discharged from that hospital and back to my mother's. The first steps on the road to recovery had been taken. It was a long road. A lonely road at times. A cruel road. But I got there. We got there. Together. We fought and we won. We got there in the end.

Those problems are long behind me now. Gone forever. Yet still I wonder why me? Why? Why then? Why ever? Why did my family and my friends stand by me? And how? How did I survive? How did I fight it? How did I win?

There was no obvious cause for my problems. I still don't know how it all happened. Some reckoned the trip to Germany and the questions about my background might have triggered it. There's no doubt the blow to my head was severe enough to trigger the depression. Years later a Dr Liebling at the Westbourne clinic in Edgbaston in England reckoned some of the drink I had in

Germany could have been spiked with LSD. I had all the classic symptoms of an LSD-induced trip.

Personally I reckon it was a combination of the blow to my head and my worries about the future, about the prospect of life on trial as a professional footballer. The pressure of speculation about my future got to me. The transformation from schoolboys' league player to prospective Manchester United star had come too quickly to me. It came at a time when I was just exposed to the real world, real day-to-day living and the real problems concurrent with that. Everywhere I turned they were talking about Spurs or United or somebody else having a look at me. There was a pressure building on me from my peers without them realising it or me realising the effect it was having on my life.

Sometimes I think the symptoms of my problems today caused those illnesses. Back then I didn't like pressure or crowds. It was all thrown upon me and I was thinking there were so many people expecting so much of me. I panicked. I totally freaked out and thought, Jesus, this is such a big move, such a big thing not just for me but for the club as well. I wasn't the sort of person then to handle that type of situation. I'm still not sure how I would react even now.

I'm not a gambler in life, I never was and I never will be. The potential stress of leaving your native city and the environment you know to go in at the deep end with no family and no friends was awesome for me then. It was an intimidating task at 22 when I did go to United never mind at 18 when I was struck with the fear of what might be waiting around the corner.

I still don't remember a lot about my time in hospital. I was in no condition to look after myself. For about six weeks I was in St John of God's in another world altogether. My mum and my sister would come and visit me regularly. Frank and Tom and Johnny Young and Johnny Dunne would come every day and talk football. And all the time I couldn't understand for the life of me what was going on.

They say it's an ill wind that blows no good. That double bout of depression reunited me completely, physically and emotionally, with my mother. We had always been in touch but it brought us back together like never before. We turned a corner during that Annus Horribilus for the pair of us, a corner that we have never looked back on since.

And I discovered just what football really meant to me. All the months of brainwashing from Frank, Tom, Johnny Dunne, John

Young and my mother's future husband, Noel Lowth, paid off. When I was in hospital they would systematically take me out on to the grass at lunchtime and kick a ball in my direction. Even when I wasn't talking to anyone they would bring me out and I'd kick that ball back. I didn't want to but I did it anyway. Without realising it that ball kept me going.

When I went home from hospital the second time the lads would drag me along to watch Dalkey play, to watch the team I had left behind a year earlier. That was against my better wishes. I told them straight the first time they suggested it that I was never going to play football again. I blamed football for my problems. I associated it with the illness. I swore I would never wear a football jersey or a pair of boots again.

But they knew what they were at. They knew football was my route back to normality. They knew that Billy Behan, Sir Matt Busby and Manchester United, aware of all my problems and kept up to date with my recovery, were prepared to stand by me as long as I stood by myself and came through this terrible thing fighting. They knew the first time Johnny Dunne brought me out from my mother's to Dalkey for a match that the bug would catch despite all the protestations from a 20-year-old who had vanished off the face of the footballing earth for a year and had sworn never to return. Between them they had concocted a plan of action to lead me slowly back into the fold at Dalkey United Football Club. It worked.

At first I just watched under duress. Then I looked forward to the Sunday afternoons out when Johnny Dunne would pick me up at my mother's and take me to a game, home or away. Then I began to take an interest in doing a bit of training again. Then I decided to go the whole hog and play.

It was the greatest decision of my life. Their therapy had worked. I was back on a football field. Back doing what I knew best. Two years and two bouts of depression later the one passion in my life was still burning as brightly as ever, as brightly as the day I put on my first Chelsea strip and thought I was Charlie Cooke.

Despite all the knocks from life, all the kicks in the teeth, I could still play ball. Nothing could take that away from me.

To my mother, my late sister, my family and my friends, to Frank Mullen, Tom Cullen, Johnny Dunne, John Young, Kieran Forsyth and everyone else involved in that brainwashing at Dalkey United – a sincere thank you. I can never repay them for what they did for me that year.

CHAPTER SIX

St Paul of Inchicore

ONCE I GOT my love for the game back there was only one way my soccer career was going – up.

Tommy Cullen, Frank Mullen and Johnny Dunne had spent hours at my bedside in Dublin persuading me to kick a ball again, begging me to get involved once more with the lads at Dalkey. When their persuasive powers worked the oracle and I began to play like the player of old for Dalkey under the watchful eye of Willie Kane and Willie Fogarty it was obvious to everyone except me that those talents would begin to turn heads again. They did.

The whispering circles of Dublin soccer are great places for gossip and news. Word that the lad called McGrath was beginning to turn it on again for Dalkey spread like wildfire. My name was appearing in the junior soccer pages of the *Evening Press* and the *Evening Herald*. My star was in the ascent in junior circles – it was only a matter of time before the League of Ireland clubs scattered around the capital came banging on the door with a sledgehammer, followed by the local scouts from the English clubs. They duly did.

As soon as I got my act together after Germany and started to play some decent football again there was all sorts of talk about me moving to a League of Ireland club or even to England. There were always guys coming to watch Dalkey who, rumour had it anyway, were scouting for Arsenal or Chelsea or Spurs or whoever was flavour of the week.

You'd see a guy on the sideline that you hadn't noticed before and all of a sudden the half-time talk in the dressing-room would be about the scout from such and such a big club who's here to watch Paul or John Young or one of the other lads. And then there was Billy Behan who regularly came to watch us, probably because his son Terry was playing for Dalkey at the time. But sure enough every time Billy turned up the story went the rounds in Dalkey that Manchester United were interested in Paul McGrath or John Young.

A lot of the time people were looking at John and myself. Dalkey knew of the interest in us from League of Ireland clubs and to be fair to them they did their best to encourage us and to help us move another step up the ladder. Tom Cullen, always pushing me forward, even got myself and John a trial with a couple of local League of Ireland clubs – but we didn't take advantage of the opportunity presented to us.

One of the first trials he got us was with Home Farm, Ronnie Whelan's club, out in Whitehall, and it was a scream from beginning to end. John and myself had grown up together, we'd been to school together, we'd played football together practically all our lives. That night out in Whitehall we treated the whole thing as a big joke and laughed ourselves silly from the moment we arrived till the moment we left.

We thought it was hilarious but Dave Bacuzzi, the Home Farm manager at the time, didn't see the funny side of it all. He actually told us that if we were only there for a laugh to get the hell out of it straight away. Dave was far from amused and, needless to say, we weren't asked back to Whitehall for a second look.

It was the same story at Bohemians a couple of months later – only worse. Billy Young, a gentleman of Irish soccer, was the manager there at the time and his physio was Mick Byrne, the man who years later would perform miracles for me and my knees in his role with the Irish team. The night we went to Dalymount we weren't bothered by the fact that we were about to train with one of the top clubs in Irish soccer, that we were about to be given the chance to join one of the most famous clubs in the history of the game at home. We were there for a laugh. Myself and John got up to the same tricks from the moment we arrived in the Dalymount dressing-room that I was to grace years later when I made my Irish debut against Italy in 1985.

I made a fatal mistake that night – and one which made me determined never to join Bohemians if they offered me all the money in the world. Bohs at that stage were quite a big club and their first team players fancied themselves a bit. The club had always been known for producing good quality players like Gerry Daly, Mick Martin, Fran O'Brien and Gerry Ryan. They were proud of that tradition and looked on themselves as decent ball players in their own right, which they probably were.

What they didn't take kindly to was starry-eyed kids from the southside of town crossing the Liffey and entering their dressing-room with the idea of taking their place in the Bohs first team. That night I committed a cardinal sin in the eyes of the Bohemians first team squad – I sat at the place allocated to one of their star names.

We had got there a good hour before training began and myself and John had planked our bags in the first place we found. It was almost a suicidal mistake. As soon as the senior pro walked in and saw this young whippersnapper sitting in his seat he blew a fuse, told me to get the f--k out of it and learn some respect. I still don't know if he was taking the water or not but I wasn't taking any chances.

I swore there and then that if I managed to get out of that dressing-room I'd never go back. We did train that night with Bohemians but as soon as I left Dalymount to get the bus home I swore that was it with me as far as that club was concerned.

It was probably nothing as far as the Dalymount dressing-room was concerned. I'm sure their players had seen scenes like it dozens of times before but it upset me – and another chance of moving up the ladder was gone out the window.

Dalkey United really thought Bohs would go for me and John but I wasn't all that bothered that I didn't hear from them again. Dalkey weren't doing that badly at the time, we were winning more matches than we were losing and I was still coming to terms with senior football and adjusting to the changes in my body as I began to grow up and fill out. I was still having problems finding a true position as well. One week I was right-back then I went across to the centre, then back to right-back.

I was as happy as Larry at Dalkey and not at all bothered that I'd blown it with two League of Ireland clubs. I was happy with the lads, settled in my own mind again and just enjoying life in Dublin and enjoying my football. Little did I know at the time that Manchester United were still on my trail. Despite all my problems with my health and that illness they were prepared to wait for me. Frank Mullen and Billy Behan had kept in touch throughout my illness.

Billy, to be fair to him, wanted to see my talent given a chance at Old Trafford no matter what happened to me in the interim. He knew I was sick yet he was prepared to wait and more importantly United, through his regular contact with Sir Matt Busby, were prepared to play the waiting game. They suggested a year with a League of Ireland club would sort me out. It would toughen me up physically and mentally, test the water as far as a move to England was concerned. This was all done behind my back, so to speak. I was quite happy just to be back with Dalkey and back in the real world again.

After Bohs and Home Farm fell by the wayside Dalkey approached Jimmy Shields at Shamrock Rovers, then managed by Johnny Giles. They didn't want to know. Rovers were interested in a silly idea of a professional from the League of Ireland, not a snotty-nosed kid from Dalkey.

There was one League of Ireland manager waiting in the wings for me however. Charlie Walker, a true blue Dub, was noted for spotting young talent on the playing fields of his native city and turning it into League of Ireland material. Back then he was the man in charge at St Patrick's Athletic, the man who had succeeded Eoin Hand as manager and watched the team that Hand had built disappear around him.

Pat's were a sleeping giant of Dublin soccer at that time, caught in a wilderness and overshadowed by the likes of Shamrock Rovers, Bohemians and Shelbourne. Hand had built a team to be proud of. They had got to the final of the FAI Cup and lost to Waterford two years earlier but the support was traditional and loyal and there was always a good buzz about their home pitch, Richmond Park, and the famous slope out in Inchicore.

Two of the best players in that losing FAI Cup final side were Jackie Jameson, a cultured centre-forward with the skills of a Charlie George, and Barry Murphy, a tough no-nonsense defender who would later go on to play for Ireland under Jack Charlton. Jameson and Murphy were the heroes of Inchicore as the side that reached the Cup final gave the area back a soccer pride that would not return until the glory days of Brian Kerr's side and a League of Ireland title triumph in the late 1980s.

Jameson and Murphy were the top Saints but money, however little of it there is in the domestic game, talks in League of Ireland football and the pair were to cross the city and put down their stalls with Bohemians in the summer that I finally arrived on the League of Ireland map. Walker knew he needed new players to keep the fans happy that summer. He badly needed a youngster to replace Murphy. He badly needed anyone with a bit of skill, a bit of flair and a bit of go about him to replace Jameson as the folk hero of the Saints' traditional Inchicore crowd. He got the answer to both prayers in the shape of Paul McGrath but he was hardly to know it the first day he made the trip across the southside to watch Dalkey United in action.

I still find Charlie's newspaper accounts of the events that followed amusing to say the least. "It was St Pat's director Tommy Cummins who first told me to go and have a look at Paul playing for Dalkey," remembered Walker. "He had close contacts with the Leinster Senior League and they were all talking about this young coloured lad playing at the back with Dalkey's first team. That's how I ended up watching Paul out in Dalkey. I watched him three or four times playing at the back and in midfield and from the start he looked something special. We needed an influx of young blood at the club and after watching him a few times I decided it was right to move for the player. Finally I tackled Paul up in his house in Crumlin and with a little bit of help from his grandmother he signed for us."

I can remember the rumours circulating about the dressing-room in Dalkey. The manager of St Patrick's Athletic was out to watch the team and there could only be one player he was interested in – me. When Charlie started to come to watch us in matches all the attention seemed to turn on me for some reason. I got a terrible ribbing from the other lads and they kept telling me that I wouldn't have far to travel any more for my football.

Charlie was one of the characters of Irish soccer. As manager at St Patrick's Athletic, the club just down the road from my mother's house in Crumlin, he was well known in the game and it was hard for him to remain anonymous when he was looking for players in the Dublin leagues. You could see his big frame a mile away with his hair flying in the wind and that big smile on his reddened cheeks. Everyone knew when Charlie was at a game and when he started coming back to watch Dalkey a couple of times the rumour factory hit overtime again.

I didn't know the truth, that Charlie knew United wanted me and that St Pat's was only going to be a stepping-stone to Old Trafford. He's lived for years on the claim that he discovered me. That's not quite true – Dalkey handed me to him on a plate on the understanding that it was only a temporary arrangement until I had shown United what I was worth in the League of Ireland and proven that I was still worth a move to England. That was set up by the late Billy Behan.

My modesty and shyness, though, prevented me from thinking he was back to look at Paul McGrath. I felt he was there to watch John Young or one of the other lads. But sure enough one night he came up to the house and asked me straight out to sign for St Pat's. There were a couple of other League of Ireland clubs in the hunt for my signature but Charlie was the first one to put his money where his mouth was and ask me to play for his club.

The money bit was quite funny really. At the time I was working for a security firm called CP Security run by a lad called Mick Fenton and manning the security huts at Blanchardstown hospital. I was back living with my mother in Crumlin and earning something in the region of £15 a week from the job which involved a lot of night work and a lot of overtime. The hours were long and hard and it kept me away from training a lot. It was the first decent job I'd had and I was happy with the money I was taking home. It didn't interfere too much with my football either and that was important. I was quite happy to work for a living and play soccer for enjoyment. Then all of a sudden, I had this offer to make money out of the very thing that I did for pleasure.

The night Charlie came up to my mother's house he said he'd give me £1,000 upfront. That threw me completely – and made up my mind. All of a sudden I was sitting in my mother's front room with a guy who was prepared to pay me £1,000 and £25 a week plus £8 for a win bonus to play the game that I had played for nothing but the love of it all my life.

A thousand pounds was a lot of money in those days and when that figure was mentioned I nearly jumped out of my skin in an effort to sign on the dotted line. When I saw that sort of money flashing up in front of my eyes I thought, "Oh yes, I'll have a bit of that." It was just the spur I needed to make up my mind and all of a sudden Dalkey went to the back of my queue.

Charlie had persuaded me to change for the third time in my soccer life, to leave the security and stability of Dalkey behind and pitch myself in against the real pros of Irish soccer, the guys who got paid to do what I had been doing every week since I was 12 years of age. The guys who knew the ropes, knew the game backwards and knew exactly how to treat new kids coming into their league.

Charlie had talked me into that sort of a move but I have never regretted the day he came into my mother's house and asked me to join St Patrick's Athletic. I knew the first time I spoke to him that I was going to play football for Charlie Walker. It was a move that was to change my life forever – and for the better.

Walker knew how to get a good player on the cheap – he also knew how to keep it a secret.

The night he signed me for St Patrick's Athletic he told me he'd allow me to see out the season with Dalkey United then start life as a League of Ireland footballer the following summer when the Pat's lads would report to Inchicore for pre-season training. There was method in his madness, good method. I was starting to make people sit up and take notice at Dalkey. Other League of Ireland clubs had been around sniffing after my services. If they thought they had a chance of getting me it would keep them away from other players Walker was trying to line up.

Walker also realised that I was slow to adapt to change in life. He would give me time to settle in with the lads during the summer before the season began. There was more chance of an immediate return from one of the best prospects he had seen for a long, long time.

There was also the matter of my representative football with Dalkey United's parent body, the Leinster Senior League, and their involvement in the Oscar Traynor Trophy, an inter-league competition for all the various representative bodies around the country. The LSL, by the very nature of their own competitive leagues, were one of the strongest sides in the competition and I was one of their stars. My prowess at centre-back had kept attacks scoreless up and down Ireland. I was enjoying this representative football and it was helping my profile – if I'd moved to Pat's in the middle of the season I would have automatically become ineligible for the Oscar Traynor Trophy side. As it was, the Leinster Senior League got to the final and we won easily. I still cherish that medal, still recall the team-mates on that side in 1981, less than two years before I would join Manchester United, less than four years before I would win an FA Cup medal at Wembley with the Red Devils.

Valeview's Dave Mason was captain of the Leinster Senior League side that lifted the Oscar Traynor Trophy that season. Like the rest of my team-mates he was later to acknowledge the contribution I made to that victory. In one of the Dublin papers Mason said: "Playing with Paul gave me a very handy tournament.

He was superb for us at the back all the way to the final and victory. And he was a case in point where a player should go to the League of Ireland before travelling to England. It made all the difference to Paul."

That Oscar Traynor Trophy victory was to be the final chapter in the Paul McGrath story as far as junior football was concerned. That May I could afford to be optimistic as I looked forward to the summer, a summer of expectancy. I was reconciled with my mother again, I was enjoying home life at my grandparents' in Crumlin, I was about to embark on a professional footballing odyssey with St Patrick's Athletic that would eventually lead to all the world's great stadiums. To keep fit that summer I played with the lads at CP Security in an inter-firm league – and they reckoned I stood head and shoulders above the rest.

Football has opened many doors for me in my life – and it certainly did with the lads at the security firm. I was quiet then, not one for socialising, but once the talk of a game of soccer came up and there was a chance to play I jumped at it. The other lads asked me if I was interested in playing and I said I'd love to.

I don't think they realised I played at all or the standard I was playing at then, but once I started to play with their team we all became the best of mates. It was a great bit of fun playing on the odd evening during the summer in parks all over the city and then going out for a few pints – of coke, of course – and a bit of craic with the lads afterwards. Nine times out of ten we'd end up in some nightclub or other – and get up bleary-eyed but happy for work the next day. And we all loved the football – it brought us closer together and probably made us work that bit better as well.

One of my closest friends at CP Security that summer was Aidan Crowley, later to become Fr Crowley and now the parish priest in Mallow, Co. Cork. Years later Alex Ferguson would claim in a book that he once had to call a Catholic priest to help me during those troubled times at Old Trafford – but Aidan Crowley was the only priest who ever got close to me on or off the pitch.

We met at CP when I was playing football and working and he was studying to become a priest at Maynooth University and doing a bit of part-time security work to get a few bob together. Like me, his big love in life, aside from the Church I suppose, was football. We were crazy about it and when Aidan asked me if I fancied a game with the works team I nearly jumped with enthusiasm. He wasn't the best player in the world but he was a great man for organising the games and getting the team together – and we've kept in close contact ever since. He's been over to England a few times for games and I've been to see his rectory – complete with football pitch – down in Cork.

Fr Crowley probably said a prayer for me that summer when I embarked on pre-season training with St Patrick's Athletic and signed that first contract as a professional footballer. The big defender was going to need all the prayers he could get – life in the League of Ireland was nothing like anything I was accustomed to. It was a culture shock of the highest magnitude when I first met up with and worked with the lads from the Saints.

I knew it was going to be different the first night I went to train with the Saints out on their old stamping ground in Inchicore. This *was* different. They were faster than the players in the Leinster Senior League, harder, sharper and flashier. They could do things with the ball that I'd only seen on the telly. They were hard and fast in the tackle, strong on the ball, tough as nails. Above all they were pros, they were getting paid to play the game and when your performance made the difference between the win bonus of £8 and nothing, they made sure you knew just how much you owed it to them to perform.

There were players at Dalkey that I thought were brilliant – but they were nothing next to what some of the lads at Pat's were able to do with the ball. And then there were the characters at Pat's, the livewires in the dressing-room and on the field who really opened my eyes to what playing the game was all about.

My closest friend from those days is Joey Malone whose hair was still its natural colour when I first met him but who's since turned a shade of grey with the trials and tribulations of his time as Galway boss and then his moves to Longford Town, Waterford United and now Monaghan United. Joey was brilliant to me from the first day I met him up in Richmond Park. He was as close a figure to Tom Cullen as I could find in St Pat's. Joey had seen it all in League of Ireland terms by the time I got to Inchicore. His advice would stand me in good stead in the years to come. Little things he'd say would always come back to me and he was the sort of friend you'd turn to straight away if you were in trouble.

The first time I played with Pat's I had a long talk with Joey. He knew all about my footballing background because Sean Ryan had done an article in the *Sunday Independent* about me leaving Dalkey to sign for Pat's. We were playing a pre-season friendly that day against a junior club in Dublin and when I saw the picture in the paper and the bit of an article I thought I had it made. I thought to myself that Paul McGrath had finally arrived as a professional footballer. But Joey had other ideas. He took me to one side and told me to ignore what was said in the papers, to forget about the hype and get on with playing my own game. Joey taught me a lesson that day that I've never forgotten.

It's easy to get carried away with what's said in the papers and start to think that you're a superstar in the making and the best player that God ever put life into. Joey reminded me that the only thing that mattered was what I did on the pitch. It was advice that was to help me years later when I was having my problems on and off the field at Manchester United and the papers were giving me a hard time. I always said then that no matter what they wrote about me they couldn't tarnish what I did on the football pitch, the only place that mattered, as Joey had said so many years earlier. Advice that was later echoed by Sir Matt Busby at Old Trafford.

Joey said that day that if I concentrated on football I'd do alright. And, boy, did I need him on my side as I struggled to get to grips with life in St Pat's and the step up to League of Ireland level. I had a nightmare from the word go – and I hated every minute of it.

Charlie Walker sees things differently when he looks back on the early days of a relationship that eventually made me a hero at Richmond Park on the banks of the Camac. The story goes that myself and Walker once had a bust-up before a big game at Inchicore against Limerick when my future was literally on the line. I can remember Charlie coming up to me before the game and telling me that it was time to stand up and be counted. He pointed out that he'd tried me at right-back, he'd tried me in midfield, he'd tried me up front and all the time I was struggling to come to grips with League of Ireland football. That afternoon he told me he was giving me one last chance. I was going to play at centre-half alongside Joey Malone and it was shit or bust. If I did the business in that position I'd make it. If I didn't I was on my way out of St Pat's and probably out of football. These were strong words from Charlie, words I heeded.

Walker remembers it a different way. The passing of time and the heights I've reached have softened a story that frightened the life out of me, a mere youngster at the time.

"In all my years in football I had never come across such an adaptable player," is the way Walker likes to tell the story. "I started him out as a striker and he was outstanding. Then I moved him into midfield and he was equally effective. Then I moved him to centre-half and he was brilliant. That first season at Pat's I just couldn't make up my mind where to play him. I eventually decided to switch him around a bit in the hope that he would eventually find the right spot. We did and he went on to play centre-half for United, for Ireland and now for Aston Villa. I could even have put him into goal for Pat's and have been confident that he would have done a job for us."

The Pat's fans thought the same way. And they struck up a tag that was to stick with me for years. Long before the OOh AAh Paul McGrath chants were born they dubbed me the Black Pearl of Inchicore, a term of endearment that is still with me to this day.

Even then Walker and the fans could see their Black Pearl of Inchicore going back on his roots and following the exodus of Irish soccer talent across the Irish Sea. Near the end of my first and only season in the League of Ireland there was a queue of domestic clubs waiting with the cheque books and the backhanders to pinch my services from under Walker's nose. But just as he had caught them all napping when he signed McGrath from Dalkey United, Walker knew he would catch them all out when the time came to sell the hottest property in Irish soccer.

"I knew that first season that quite a number of scouts had been down to Richmond Park to have a look at Paul – though none of them had the courage to come out with any sort of offer," added Walker. "If I had been an English league manager then it wouldn't have taken me two seconds to sign him. He was that good – but they all waited and hesitated and eventually lost out when Paul went to Manchester.

"There were even a few League of Ireland clubs interested in signing him then. They had sniffed around, put out the usual feelers and I was well aware of their desire to get Paul McGrath.

"I remember doing a piece with Noel Dunne in the *Irish Independent* when I admitted that I had been told about League of Ireland enquiries. But all I could say at the time was forget it. We were not talking about chicken-feed.

"To be honest I was reluctant to part with Paul at the time. He had done a great job for the club. And even if I had been tempted to sell him to another Irish club they would have had to start talking at five figures and work their way upwards. We were talking the sort of sums that League of Ireland clubs just couldn't afford.

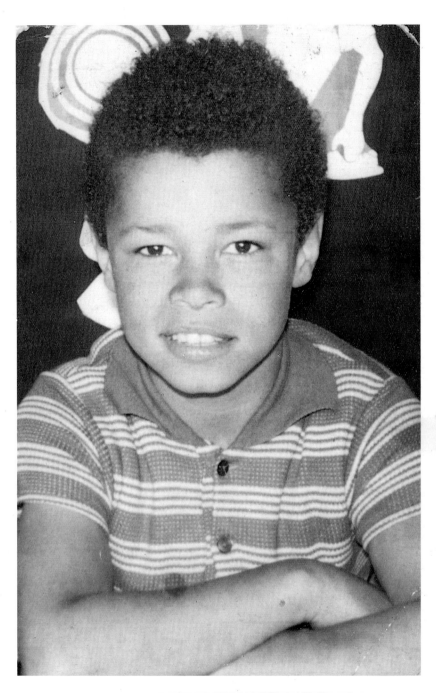

Young, gifted and innocent: Paul McGrath aged 11

The field of dreams: aged 12 on the pitch we dug with our own hands at the Glen Silva home

The boys' own brigade: Paul McGrath aged 12, and Brigade colleagues

A youth amongst men: Dalkey United first team squad, 1979

'We're going to Germany': Dalkey United touring party, 1979–80

It went that way: training at The Cliff, 1986 (Courtesy of Les Williamson)

Knees up: Gary Mabbutt of Spurs meets Paul McGrath of Manchester United, 1986

*In happier times: Paul McGrath, Alex Ferguson and Bryan Robson
(Courtesy of Les Williamson)*

Friend or foe: Paul McGrath v Bryan Robson, European Championships,
Stuttgart, June 1988 (Cyril Byrne/Irish Press)

Waiting for the off: World Cup training camp in Hanover 1988 with Ronnie Whelan and Kevin Moran (Irish Press)

Bosom buddies: Jesper Olsen, Frank Stapleton, Paul McGrath and Kevin Moran

Happiness is ... Paul McGrath and Caroline Lamb, Texaco Awards, Dublin 1994 (Irish Independent)

Like brother, like sister: with Okone, 1991

"We knew the lad had high ambitions, we knew he wanted to try his hand at the professional game. But I don't think anyone realised just how good he was."

Ireland's top sports journalist is Con Houlihan, a columnist with the *Evening Press* in Dublin, an institution of the media and a legend in Irish soccer circles. Houlihan has followed my progress from the very beginnings in Inchicore, a club close to Con's heart, right through to the glories with Ireland and Manchester United and Aston Villa. A piece from one of his earliest writings about me, on the game I made my league debut for Pat's against Shamrock Rovers in the season of 1981-82, sums up the esteem in which big Con holds his fellow Irishman from Dublin.

Houlihan wrote in the *Evening Press*: "In the green spaces between the blocks of flats in Dolphin's Barn they were playing pitch and putt yesterday – a sign that the opening of the soccer season had not been generally recognised.

"But there was a good crowd at Richmond Park where St Patrick's Athletic were billed to play their neighbours Shamrock Rovers. And the east bank of the Camac was like a humble man's St Tropez. Citizens and citizenesses lay in various stages of undress, so drunk with the sun that there was hardly a cheer or a handclap when Synan Braddish led out his men.

"And even the most faithful follower of the Saints would have been stretched to name the eleven in the red shirts and the white shorts. In yesterday's pool St Patrick's had only two of the fine side that made such a great bid for the cup two seasons ago. And inevitably in the pre-match chat there was a note of regret. Barry Murphy would be missed. Of course he would. And Jackie Jameson – indeed.

"But life must go on and indeed so quirky is fate that by half-time the replacements for Barry and Jackie were already being declared freemen of Inchicore.

"The new middle-back is a lad called Paul McGrath whom Charlie Walker plucked out of Dalkey United. He is 'coloured' (aren't we all) – what is more important is that he is a brilliant ball player.

"Indeed his only obvious fault is that he tries to work his way out of trouble – in situations where most would either belt the ball away or push it back to the 'keeper. He is tall, very fast, kicks well with both feet – and is a strong and intelligent player."

Strong words of praise indeed, words that were to be repeated over and over again that season on the terraces at Inchicore and on the back pages of the Irish papers. The fans loved me so much and I felt the same about them. The media loved me so much they linked me with every British club from Land's End to John O'Groats. Eventually, despite all the self-doubt, I would live up to the headlines and move across the Irish Sea – but it took time to settle down in my new home at Richmond Park.

According to the hype I was a natural and the next sure thing to take the plane from Dublin to the lucrative world of cross-channel professional soccer. But that's not how it felt those first few months with St Pat's when I flirted with every position possible from centre-forward to winger to midfielder. I had a nightmare, my timing was all over the place, my first touch was terrible and I found the games racing past me. I'd often come off the pitch at Richmond Park and reckon I'd only touched the ball about five times in all.

As a 21-year-old it was hard to understand why I couldn't do it properly. It was hard to come to terms with what was happening to me on the pitch after having things so easy at Pearse Rovers and Dalkey United.

Charlie had me all over the place in the team in an effort to find my true position but it wasn't working. The fans were growing disenchanted, the team knew I was struggling, the board were starting to question why he had bought me in the first place. The pressure was beginning to mount a couple of months into my first season in League of Ireland football – when Charlie pulled off a wonder stroke that was to get me where I am today.

We were playing against Eoin Hand's Limerick at Richmond one Sunday afternoon and I was seriously worried about my chances of making the bench, never mind getting into the team. When Charlie called me over for a little chat about an hour before kick-off I thought the writing was on the wall for me. "Listen, Paul son," he said. "The directors aren't happy and we've got to do something about it today. I've tried you at centre-forward, I've tried you in the centre of midfield, I've tried you on the wings and it hasn't worked. They're getting impatient so today I'm going to play you at centre-back. If you don't do the business, that's it – you're gone."

His words were harsh but the message was well and truly hammered home. I took it as he had said it. I took it to mean it was time to get the finger out and get things done. If I didn't make it that day as a centre-half against Limerick it was curtains for me in terms of a League of Ireland career.

I knew the importance of the game. I had played there before with Dalkey for a while and and I knew the threat hanging over me made sure I was going to get it right once and for all. It helped that I played alongside Joey Malone and in front of Dave Henderson that afternoon. Joey had seen it all before in the league. He was as cool as a cucumber at the back, which suited me. He liked to play the ball around and so did I and we just clicked straight away. Charlie's threat had worked. We won that match, I had a blinder and from then on Joey Malone and Paul McGrath played like two naturals together at the heart of the Pat's defence.

It was to be the biggest turning point of my career. All of a sudden I found a position in which I would express myself truly for Pat's. I became the regular centre-half alongside Joey and it worked so well that I was to last less than a season with the Saints before the move to Old Trafford. That decision to move me to the centre won me the support of the Richmond Park fans, a very close-knit and loyal group of supporters from Inchicore and beyond who have followed the Pat's through the tough times and the good times.

After that Limerick match I began to find my feet at League of Ireland level and the rewards followed. Every Sunday night I'd go straight from playing to the security job at Blanchardstown hospital and the next morning on my way home from work I'd stop and buy all the papers. I got one or two "man of the match" awards and I'd rush home with the paper to show my mother the good news.

Joey Malone had told me to ignore what was said in print but it was hard not to get a kick and a buzz out of seeing my name in lights like that.

The rewards were getting bigger and bigger as the season with St Pat's wore on. We weren't having the best of times as a team but a few people were starting to sit up and take notice of the Black Pearl. The last month I was with Pat's the Soccer Writers voted me their "Player of the Month". To a guy who had serious doubts about his ability to last at this level that was a great recognition.

The papers were giving me some great publicity, there was talk of clubs from England looking at me and then Turlough O'Connor, Athlone manager at the time, wrote an article in one of the papers that really put my star in the ascendant. Turlough had been a hero of mine when I was a young player with Dalkey. He was the centre-forward with the Bohemians team of the 1970s, an Irish international and a top-class striker. He was also one of the most astute readers of the game in Ireland, a fact proven when he took his native Athlone and then Dundalk to every honour in the Irish game as a manager.

Turlough wrote a long piece in one of the papers about me, saying that if I was anyone else the clubs in England would have snapped me up years ago. Because he was so well respected within the game that story created a buzz in itself but I was hardly ready for what happened a couple of Tuesdays later when I arrived home from work one evening in the middle of March to find Charlie Walker sitting in my mother's front room.

Charlie had been as good to me at Pat's as Tom Cullen was at Dalkey. When I walked in I expected he was there for a cup of tea and a chat about the team and the games and the way I was playing. I never suspected he was there to tell me I was on my way to England.

I can remember the scene vividly. Charlie told me to sit down with a cup of tea and then came out with the words that I've never forgotten. "Right, Paul, I'm here to tell you that Watford, Luton and Man City all want to sign you and Manchester United want you on trial," said Charlie to a room full of disbelieving ears.

"Three of them are all offering cash on the table but United want you over at Old Trafford for a while to have a look at you for themselves. Billy Behan has told them he has no doubts that you'll make it but they want to see you in the flesh before they decide for themselves.

"We can sell you straight away to Luton or Watford or City but my advice is to go to United for a month and see how you get on. If that doesn't work out the others will still be there and still be interested."

I was dumbfounded that night. I'd had trouble enough a year earlier believing that St Pat's wanted me to play in the League of Ireland. Now I was in a situation where three English clubs wanted to pay cash for me and one of the biggest names in European and world football wanted me over on trial for a month.

Charlie reckoned United was the best bet. The fact that he had enough faith in me to let me go away from his team for a month and the fact that we were talking about Manchester United swung the decision. I was to leave Dublin for four weeks with Manchester United.

I had always been a Chelsea fan and I suppose looking back on it now I would have been happier if the Blues had been one of the four English clubs showing definite interest. But United were huge in Ireland. They had a history of great Irish players going through their ranks. Players like Liam Whelan, Johnny Carey, Shay Brennan, Johnny Giles, Tony Dunne, Paddy Roche, Gerry Daly, Mick Martin, Frank Stapleton and Kevin Moran had all flown the tricolour with pride over Old Trafford.

I knew it would be harder to make it with United than any of the other three. I knew United signed dozens of players every year and very few of them ever made it. But Manchester United was special. The name alone symbolised so much for soccer people. There was a magic about the name, a magic about the club, a magic about the fans.

It was a gamble but a gamble I was going to take. After all, I could always go back to Pat's after a month, get back into their team and see what happened from the other clubs if United didn't work out. My mind was made up: I'd try my luck at Manchester United.

The story soon broke in the papers. Everywhere I went there were friends and relations wishing me all the best, saying it was only a formality, that United would be stupid not to sign me once they saw me. The other lads at Pat's were delighted. I'd only been there less than a year but they were all good friends and they were genuinely pleased for me that I was getting the chance of a big break with one of the biggest clubs of all.

The last game I played with Pat's was at Richmond on a wet Sunday in March. It seemed funny that after taking so long to adjust to the standard I was now leaving it all behind after less than a year. I'd never been a great one for change. Now I was uprooting myself again, leaving the cosiness of Inchicore for the bright lights and distractions of Manchester. Would I be able to cope with living in a strange city, amongst strange people, in a strange land? Those questions were hovering away somewhere in the back of my mind. But on the last night with Pat's questions and doubts were forgotten about as we went out together for a celebratory drink and a farewell to old friends.

It was a night that would also change my life. Since the incident in Germany I hadn't really touched a drop of alcohol, certainly not spirits. I'd stayed away from it, frightened by what had happened on that Dalkey tour.

That last night with Pat's I had my first taste of alcohol in a long, long time. Joey Malone was never a great man for the drink due to the fact that he only has one kidney. He was drinking Southern Comfort as his condition means he can't drink pints. He bought me a Southern Comfort and red lemonade to celebrate my big move. I liked the taste of it. I liked it so much I decided I wanted more. In the next couple of years I would have a lot more Southern Comfort. I became hooked, hooked in a way that would have far reaching consequences in the future.

Pat's was a growing-up period in my life. With Pearse or Dalkey I was amongst my own, I was settled and happy. In the year I was at Pat's I was exposed, I was out in the open on my own with my footballing ability as my passport to success or failure.

I made great friends at the club – people like Joey Malone and Harry McCue senior who ran the Swifts at the time. I played with some of the great characters of the Irish game – players like Joey, Fran Gavin and Dave Henderson, the madcap goalkeeper whose father gave me a job putting up fencing to earn a few extra bob. Hendo was one of the best goalkeepers I have ever played with – years later I nearly got into a fight in a Manchester bar because I claimed there were better 'keepers than Gary Bailey back in Ireland, with Hendo top of the list.

Pat's was my club, it still is. It still brings back happy memories, like the Sunday mornings travelling down the country in the back of a coach, sleeping across the back seats because I'd been out working late on the security the night before. That's why to this day I still sit on the back row of the team coach with Ireland and with Villa, despite memories like the lads throwing bottles of water over me on the coach in an effort to wake me up when we'd get to Limerick or Cork or Athlone. I have many other happy memories. Like getting a free pair of boots off John Givens and thinking I was in heaven. Like seeing Charlie Stuart or Con Houlihan or Noel Dunne or Peter Byrne write about me in the papers. They were all things I remember now with fondness, things that made me proud to have been a part of that club.

Some day I may just go back. As a player? As a manager? Maybe even as the owner?

CHAPTER SEVEN

Trial and Error

MANCHESTER UNITED is an intimidating place for any new arrival. A young trialist or a £3.75 million pound signing like Roy Keane will find it daunting. If they don't there's something wrong.

The day I arrived at Old Trafford I realised just what I had let myself in for. I hadn't seen the place before and when I arrived at the ground the history and the tradition of Manchester United suddenly hit home.

The first morning I was brought down to the Cliff along with Barry Kehoe, who was also over from Ireland, and introduced to the rest of the lads in the reserve team squad. The coaches explained that we'd train with the reserves for the first couple of weeks, play a couple of matches in training and generally see how we got on before they made a decision whether to take us any further or not.

I was apprehensive about the whole idea of a trial but I wasn't unduly worried. I knew the full-time training would be a problem but I reckoned once it came down to the football side of things I'd have no problems. As long as I had a ball and a yard of grass I'd be able to stand up for myself.

That at least was the theory. It went out the window the first morning I trained with Manchester United at Old Trafford and they nearly killed me. Maybe they did it deliberately to show the two young lads over from Ireland that this was serious business but they murdered us with running that first day. They just showed me a different level of training that was so physically demanding it was

71

untrue. They ran the legs off us. I just couldn't handle it. I was so far behind the rest of the players in the running that it was actually embarrassing for me. I thought I was reasonably fit until that morning at the Cliff. I just couldn't believe how tough it was but the lads who had been there since the previous summer or before then seemed to find it a doddle.

Throughout my career I had moved up a grade in footballing terms every time I had moved clubs. At Pearse Rovers training, as it was, was all a bit of crack for a bunch of schoolkids growing up together. We trained alright but only to learn the basics of the game and to stop all 22 players in a match chasing the ball like a bunch of lunatics. At Dalkey the training and the football was a lot more serious. Two nights a week we'd meet up at the clubhouse and do a couple of hours running and working with the ball and doing exercises and then playing five-a-sides to finish up. At St Pat's I was introduced to the more theoretical side of the game but the training was still pretty limited. Two nights a week in a concrete yard up in Inchicore, a run-out on a Saturday morning at Richmond Park if you could get off work and a bit of a team talk on the way to the match on a Sunday. That was the sum total of the exertions asked of my body. I was naturally fit and all the training I did at home was to tone up the muscles and get me in shape for the demands of 90 minutes of League of Ireland football every Sunday.

Then I went to United and saw training in a whole new light. This was ultra-professionalism, the human body being pounded and expected to produce performances touching on the superlative. They expected you to go flat out for 90 minutes sometimes twice or three times a week. You were up against athletes in the prime of their health, bodies tuned to perfection. They trained hard and they played hard.

The concrete yard in Inchicore was a million miles away that first month I was put through my paces at Old Trafford. It was like going from a holiday camp to Colditz as far as my body was concerned. That first week I went back to the digs sore and worried. Sore from aching limbs, worried from the anxieties caused by the fact that I was finding it difficult to keep up with players who had been doing this sort of thing most of their lives.

The only thing that kept me going was my own belief in my ability as a footballer. There were lonely nights when I wanted to cry out with the pain of physical exertion. Nights when I lay awake with doubts flying around my head. But the light at the end of the tunnel was always that piece of leather and the couple of acres of grass that held my destiny.

Any idea I had about England being easy was soon put to rest. After the first week Barry and myself were still finding it tough going on the training circuits but once they started to let us play ball a bit we managed to do a lot better. At least now we could hold our heads up high and show these Brits a thing or two.

There were plenty of quality players there at the time to gauge ourselves by. It was a good reserve team squad in those days. There were household names in the making like Mark Hughes, Norman Whiteside, Graeme Hogg and Clayton Blackmore, top-class players just waiting to be discovered. There was a kid knocking around called David Platt who years later would play alongside me with Aston Villa and prove United do make mistakes. The same applied to Alan McLoughlin, who was starting to be talked about at United back then, but he too was shown the door only to embarrass the club with his subsequent performances for Swindon, Portsmouth and the Republic.

There were other young lads over from Ireland, like the goalkeeper Phil Hughes who was to play for the North later on, and a young left-back from Dublin called Pat Kelch who had buckets of talent but was eventually to take my journey in reverse and go home to play for St Pat's and win a league medal with them. There was Billy Garton who looked a fine centre-half until injury robbed him of a worthwhile career at a tragically young age. And then there were Barry Kehoe and Paul McGrath. We were still struggling in the runs but once they got us cleared to play we began to show them a thing or two and convince reserve coach Brian Whitehouse that we weren't just over for a holiday.

I had to miss the first game because of a problem with my clearance from the League of Ireland but then I got my chance in a central league match away to the Newcastle United reserves at St James Park.

Hogg and Garton had been the regular centre-halves on the reserve team and I had watched them closely while I was waiting for my clearance to come through. The big difference between them and the defenders at home was that extra yard of pace. They anticipated things a lot quicker and then when they were surprised by strikers they had that bit of acceleration to get them out of trouble.

I knew what was expected that first night at Newcastle. It was like starting all over again with Pearse or Dalkey or St Pat's, only the magnitude of the occasion was even greater. Typically there were a couple of thousand Geordies in the ground that night cheering on the Magpies, but it went really well for United and for me. We managed to win 1-0 and I supplied the pass for Norman Whiteside to score the winning goal. It wasn't really a pass, more of a clearance, but when the boss said afterwards it was a good pass I wasn't going to argue with him. I had come through my first real test at United with a compliment from the coach and it felt good.

I wasn't worried about proving I could make the first team or anything at that stage. I just wanted to do enough to persuade them to keep me. I'd only been at United for ten days but already I could see enough to tell me that I wanted to stay. It was a different world for a 22-year-old at Old Trafford. Even being part of the reserve team for that ten-day spell brought home the advantages of playing for a club like Manchester United. The facilities were top class, the players were looked after like gods, even the second team's bus for the away matches was superior to anything I had been used to back home.

The fans knew even the reserve players. Hanging around with Norman, it become obvious that even to play in the second team had its fair share of fame around the city of Manchester.

I was enjoying this spell in the limelight and I wanted more of it. I was in digs with Barry, Norman and Phil Hughes and every night we'd wonder amongst ourselves how things were going. Norman and Phil kept assuring us that we were doing as well as could be expected but we were worried. I knew I was struggling in terms of the physical training but as I got more matches under my belt I was growing in confidence about my chances of staying on. The coaches were keeping quiet but Big Ron Atkinson had come down a couple of times to have a look at myself and Barry and the fact that he came back to see us was a good sign.

When the month was coming to an end I was on tenderhooks. I thought I could aspire to the heights of the players already in the reserve team squad but the threat of rejection loomed large on the horizon. How could I go back to Dublin as a failure? Would the clubs who were interested in me before I went to United now forget about me because United had turned me down? Would St Pat's take me back if I couldn't do it at Old Trafford?

When it came to the end of the month, I was due to go home on a Friday for the Soccer Writers' annual presentation dinner in Dublin. I still hadn't heard anything about United's plans for me.

When I went in for training that final morning Brian Whitehouse said to me: "We'll see you on Monday with the lads from your Irish club. The club here want to sort something out with them about signing you. Well done, son."

It was the first I'd heard that United were interested in keeping me and I couldn't believe it. I was over the moon. I was so high I could have flown back to Dublin on my own that night without the aid of an aeroplane.

At the Dublin dinner that night I told everyone I met that I was going to become a professional soccer player with Manchester United. All my mates from Pat's, the players I had played against in that lone season in the League of Ireland and the journalists who had hyped me up all joined in the well wishes. It felt good being back in Dublin knowing I was a wanted man with a bounty on my head from Manchester United Football Club.

While I was home Frank Mullen and Johnny Dunne met the Pat's pair Paddy Becton and Charlie Walker to discuss my deal. The Dalkey lads explained that it was all set up through Billy Behan, there was no cut for Dalkey and I was to get the best deal possible when they returned from a club tour to Germany. All the fears about my future were gone. I knew Pat's would be willing to sell, in fact they were desperate to sell because they had real money troubles at the time. They wouldn't price me out of the market and United, one of the biggest names of all, were sure to offer me a deal I couldn't refuse. Or so I thought.

While Dalkey were still in Germany I was whisked off to United. And, in my opinion, ripped off. Sure enough the Pat's officials that weekend of decision told me I'd be mad to turn United down. They assured me that Ron Atkinson and Charlie Walker would do a deal with my best interests at heart. There was no way I could lose. We were all going to be winners and I was going to be the biggest winner of all.

What they didn't tell me about was their own desperate plight and the financial problems that are still a millstone around the club's neck to this day.

League of Ireland football was a goldmine back in the 1950s and early 1960s when crowds packed grounds like Milltown and Dalymount and Richmond and Whitehall to see the greats of Shamrock Rovers, Bohemians, St Pat's and Drumcondra. There were full houses, great matches and superb entertainment in the era before television and the mass media. But then English soccer began to come in on the television screens of Ireland. Times began to change and those winds of change left Irish domestic soccer trailing in the wake of the GAA as a spectator sport. It was still – and is still – a huge participant sport at junior level but the country just couldn't support the professional clubs trying to pay players decent money.

League of Ireland football has been in a decline for the past 20 years. Nowadays Milltown is, tragically, a housing estate. Richmond has only just reopened and welcomed St Pat's home, Dalymount is a mere shadow of its former self.

The people who run League of Ireland football work long and hard hours, waste their own money and get little or nothing in return. The board at Pat's when I was on my way to Manchester United were in financial ruin. They had debts chasing them all over Dublin. Players' money was late, signing-on fees and wages were a struggle. The club was in danger. Times were so hard they were desperate to sell any player who might make a few bob and get the club out of the quicksand it was slipping further and further into. There was even a story doing the rounds in Dublin at the time about the audit at the bank where Pat's had their account. The auditor was amazed to discover that the account was something like £20,000 in the red but the branch manager had stuck a note to it saying: "Account is okay – they expect to sell Paul McGrath shortly."

They did. Just how desperate Pat's were to sell was to become clearer when I returned to Manchester the following Monday with Charlie Walker and a couple of Pat's officials including Paddy Becton. They went in to see Ron Atkinson to sort out a deal and when I was called into his office it was all done and dusted before I had a chance to really consider what was on offer.

I was put in my place fairly quickly by Big Ron when I entered his office with an earring, a pair of cowboy boots with straps around the ankles and black denims, a poor man's Phil Lynott if ever there was one. Ron's told me since that I looked more like an ageing Jimi Hendrix – and that I had a right band of Electric Gypsies of my own with me that afternoon.

First thing he did was tell me to get the earring out. "I don't sign centre-halves with earrings," he told me in no uncertain way. The earring was quickly removed although recently I have taken to wearing a stud in my ear again – as long as Ron is nowhere to be seen. He'd probably fine me for being fashion-conscious.

It's a good job he didn't fine me there and then for looking cool. I could hardly have afforded to pay the fine for my motorbiker appearance after the deal I signed, not under duress but in ignorance, that afternoon. I was left on my own, told what the offer was – £200 a week before tax, £150 a week after deductions and that was it.

I wasn't happy, I just thought it was ludicrously small and not what I expected a professional footballer to be on at a club with the prestige of Manchester United. I had just left CP Security in Dublin and gone to work with Dave Henderson's father putting up fences. Between the two jobs – football and fencing – I was making as much back at home.

I asked Charlie if I could see him outside the office and I explained that it wasn't enough. I was already making the same money at home between the job and the football. I had played four of the best games in my life during that month on trial and I thought I was worth more than what was on the table.

Charlie listened to what I had to say then went back in to see Big Ron again. Naturally Ron was used to dealing with this sort of thing every day of the week. He knew how far he could push players, he knew how people would react if the chance of a move to Old Trafford was snatched away from them. He was paid to save the club money and when I went back into his office a few minutes later himself and Charlie Walker scared the living daylights out of me.

Ron just said: "Mr Walker tells me you're not too happy with the deal – that's fair enough, so you can head off back to Ireland now."

I was flabbergasted at the ruthlessness of the statement. Being me, I panicked into the bargain. I panicked because I could see the chance of playing for Manchester United being taken away from me. I was caught on the spot and I reacted exactly the way Manchester United wanted me to react. It was that blunt. I stuttered a reply, a reply from a rushed heart instead of a sensible head. "I never said I wasn't happy with the deal. I just talked about it, that's all. I'm happy with it, that's all." Before I knew where I was they had taken advantage of my nervousness and I had signed a piece of paper that made me a Manchester United player at a bargain basement rate.

Looking back on it now I know I sold myself woefully short. I was a fool and I paid the price for it. If I had known then what I know now about transfer deals and the way players are treated properly by the big clubs in England there is no way I would have signed that deal. It wasn't the first time in my career that I was to be betrayed over money by Manchester United.

They pushed me into a corner and I tried desperately to crawl my way out of it. If I had waited a couple of hours I could have listened to the advice of John Givens who was sent over from Dublin by the Irish Professional Footballers Association to help me sort out my deal. They had no money at all but they borrowed the airfare to Manchester by foul means or fair and sent John over to sort me out.

They knew I was going to be taken for a ride by Ron and Charlie and they wanted to protect me. John knew the business. His brother Don had been at United as a kid and went on to play for Ireland. Nowadays John handles the likes of Niall Quinn, Jack Charlton, Roy Keane and the boxer Michael Carruth. Back then he was a part-time official with the PFA – and anxious to see me right.

It was all too late. He made contact with Ron and was told to mind his own business. He contacted the English PFA and was told it was none of their business until I actually became a professional footballer in England. He didn't like the look of the contract but by the time he got to Manchester it was already a fait accompli. I had put pen to paper. Gullible's travels had struck again.

It should have been different had I engaged my brain before signing that piece of paper. I should have listened to the offer and gone away to think about it. I should have waited for John Givens to arrive and talked to Frank Mullen who was back in Germany with Dalkey. When Frank got home and heard the deal I had committed myself to for the next three years of my life he went potty – and rightly so. He was mad with the terms and mad with the fact that the deal had gone through while he was away and without Billy Behan's input. The transfer fee was alright for Pat's but there was no signing-on fee. The wages were terrible. And that was going to be the bread and butter of my life for the next three seasons – by which time I had established myself in their first team.

The transfer fee has always been quoted as £30,000 but in fact St Pat's got a lot more than that. They received another £15,000 when I made my first appearance for Ireland in 1985 and they also got the benefit of a match in Dublin against United which raised quite an amount of money the season after I had signed.

I got the club out of the financial quagmire. They had done well out of the deal for a player who had cost them practically nothing and stayed with them for only a season. Pat's did alright out of the deal but I was far from happy.

I was still annoyed at the fact that my basic wage when I became a professional footballer with Manchester United was only £200 a week. There was no signing-on fee and the wages were pathetic. I was making as much back in Dublin – and they persuaded me to sign a three-year deal which curtailed my potential income further again. Every contract I signed at United after that used the first deal as a base, a poor foundation to begin from.

I was put on the spot that Monday afternoon at Old Trafford. It was made clear by United and Pat's that that was the final offer. I could take it or leave it. I had nothing to gauge what they were offering me against, I had no yardstick to measure it by, no idea just how bad the money was compared to what the other lads at the club were on, and I got caught in a real Catch 22 situation. I desperately wanted to play for Manchester United and make a go of it as a professional player. But I also realised I was selling myself short. I knew the apprentices like Norman weren't on great money but that was part and parcel of the apprenticeship scheme that has always been associated with English football and English clubs. I wasn't signing as an apprentice. I was going to England as a professional but they treated me like a stupid kid barely out of school and they got away with it. I didn't like the deal at all but I still signed because I was naive and afraid of rejection. I felt it didn't reflect the glory or the merits of signing for a club of that stature, for a club that was idolised in Ireland and all over the world.

But there I was signed as a pro and barely making the same money that I was bringing home as a fencer and part-time footballer in Ireland. I know now that I should have gambled against Ron Atkinson that day and called his bluff. I should have stood up to Manchester United and said, "Fine, I'm back off home to Dublin now – I'll wait and see what happens and who else comes in for me."

I should have treated United the way they treated me but I didn't – and they preyed on Paul McGrath, professional footballer, for years to come. I had set my stall out early and they knew they were dealing with a pussycat when it came to talking money and conditions. I had proven myself as a player but let myself down as a man of principle that month at Old Trafford. They played on that fact for the rest of my time there.

I had played out of my skin in four reserve matches. I tried really hard to make every single thing that I did come off. I put the effort in and everyone at the club acknowledged the fact that I had done well during the trial. I wanted to play for that club and I did – but on their terms, not mine. That still hurts to this day. I've seen players hardly worthy of the name command colossal signing-on fees from United and other clubs in England. I've seen guys who would struggle in a decent side make a lot of money out of the game and it still hurts. I know money isn't everything but they should have treated me fairly.

United have changed their ways now. They have the best players in England and they pay them money to match their ability. They can keep the likes of Roy Keane and Ryan Giggs happy and away from the lure of the lira in Italy. But it was so difficult in my day. The past was a different country indeed.

It's easy for me now to look back on those early days at Manchester United and be bitter. I have good reason to be bitter about the money I was signed for compared to the wages the rest of the players were on when I broke into the first team. But soccer repaid me for that early hiccup later on in my career. I've made good money with Villa. I can support my family and set my three young boys up for the rest of their lives thanks to the game. Soccer has been good to me at the end of the day. And whenever I feel low or depressed about the game all I have to do is think back to my fellow trialist at Old Trafford that month, compare my end result with that of Barry Kehoe and be grateful.

Barry Kehoe was one of the best players Ireland produced – and one of the unluckiest. When we went to Manchester that month I knew all about Barry from my time with St Pat's. He played in the midfield for Dundalk and he was probably the most gifted player in League of Ireland football at the time. Barry had been close to big moves a number of times before. Back then he was 20 years of age and over at United with me to take his big break. I honestly expected that they would keep Barry and send me home because he looked so good that month. Everything he did on the training ground oozed class. He was creative and commanding in the middle of the pitch. He took control of games, told lads who were at the club years what to do and they did it because they respected his skills as a player. There was even one night when he played alongside Bryan Robson *and* Ray Wilkins in the middle of the field in a testimonial game and played them both off the park. Barry was that good. He should have played for Ireland in the World Cup and the European Championships. He should have won every honour in the game with United or Liverpool or Celtic or any one of the other clubs who chased his signature for so long.

But life had decided on other avenues for Barry Kehoe. I was devastated for him at the end of that month when United said they weren't going to keep him. I was devastated a couple of years later when I heard the news that Barry had developed cancer. Thankfully he's battled through that illness with the same determination that he showed on the football pitch at Oriel Park for so many years. Not only has he beaten the illness twice but he's also gone back to play for his native Dundalk again and, now, Drogheda under his old boss Jim McLaughlin in the Premier Division of the League of Ireland.

Courage like that makes me realise how lucky I am to have made my living with two of the greatest clubs in the world. Courage like that makes me realise how lucky I am to be in full health with only a couple of dodgy knees to worry about.

When Ireland came home from the World Cup in Italy we played a testimonial match for Barry Kehoe at Oriel Park in Dundalk. Nobody deserved it more. Football owed Barry Kehoe far more than it ever owed me.

CHAPTER EIGHT

Goodbye Ron, Hello Fergie

CANADA never meant much to me until I went to Manchester United – now I will always associate it with dodgy knees.

Being a Dubliner I had heard the story about the great Brendan Behan who, according to Liffeyside legend, went across the Atlantic, saw the sign "Drink Canada Dry" and duly did. But that was as much as I knew of the land on top of America. Until Ron Atkinson put me straight.

It was the end of that first period at Old Trafford, the end of the season I signed myself to Manchester United and committed myself to Ron Atkinson. After the transfer from Pat's I stayed in the reserve team and worked hard under Brian Whitehouse. I was still in awe of the place and the stars in the first team dressing-room, still hero-worshipping those training beside me at The Cliff – stars like Bryan Robson who went out of their way to make me feel welcome. Later he was to become one of my best friends in football.

There I was in awe of them all. The first Saturday I attended a first team fixture at Old Trafford I went into the Grill Room before the game for a bite of lunch. There at the table next to me was John Gidman, a full-back with United and England. Next to him was Ray Wilkins, the most skilful player in all my time at the club – a lovely player, a lovely passer of the ball and a lovely man to boot. Ray was just the business as far as I was concerned. There I was, sitting next to him, having my steak and chips and swallowing my pride with every forkful. One of these stars said hello to me. I nearly choked on the t-bone. They were real. They recognised themselves as human beings.

That has always been the forte of most great Manchester United players. They are human and they realise it. They realise they are lucky to be footballers at the greatest club in the world. I never forgot that sense of humility and belonging that was the hallmark of all the top players at the club – players like Bryan, Arnold Muhren, Kevin Moran and Ray Wilkins – when I joined.

I adjusted slowly to the company I was keeping but quickly to the expectations on the field with the reserve side. I stayed in the side till the end of the season and made an impression on both the coaches and the first team manager. Ron called me into his office about a week before the end of the domestic English season and told me I was going to Canada with the first team squad. I couldn't believe my luck.

Then tragedy struck, a tragedy that haunts me to this day. Our last reserve team game of the season was at Sheffield United. I was demob happy as I made my way to Bramall Lane. I was off to Canada with the first team squad and then home to Dublin to see my family and friends for a well-earned summer break. Life was wonderful. Until a rather ageing striker from Sheffield made his mark on this young upstart defender from Dublin. Literally. He came across me with studs raised, vengeance and venom firing in his heart. I saw the tackle but it was too late. Knee injury number one was up and running before the midwife had time to slap the baby.

Tragedy. The pain shot through my knee and my heart. I was out of the Canadian trip. My return to Dublin was a distressing one. I had never encountered anything more than a pair of broken laces in Ireland. Now I was facing my first cartilage operation. Familiarity has since bred contempt between me and the operating theatre. Ten visits later I feel as if I've been there more often than the average man has been to the thespian theatrical variety. Anyway, I had twisted the knee and had the operation as soon as I got back from my Dublin holiday. I missed the early part of my first pre-season training session then worked rapidly on regaining lost ground. Within a month of the operation I was training fully. A week later I was playing with the reserves. Then came my big chance.

My Manchester United first team debut was brought about courtesy of the Falklands War. Strange but true. The first team played a South Atlantic fund match at Aldershot at the start of the 1982-83 season and I got a game less than six months after I had joined the club. We won quite easily with a sprinkling of first team regulars and a handful of reserves like myself, Norman Whiteside and Mark Hughes. Bryan Robson passed the ball to me that night. I wasn't going to clean my boots ever again after that. Only joking, Bryan.

The Milk Cup was my next port of call with the first team, a game at Bradford the next vehicle for my ambitions. It was a wet and windy night in Bradford. Aren't they all? I was as nervous as a kitten. The television cameras were in and I knew the family back at home would see me in action for United on the small screen for the first time. I got through that one then I made my league debut at home to Spurs in the November because Kevin Moran or Gordon McQueen was injured.

That was my role that first season, understudy to Kevin and Gordon. It gained me 15 first team appearances and three goals that season in all, but as soon as they were fit I was out. I accepted that. I had missed my apprenticeship in England, missed out on cleaning boots and washing floors, and I still felt I needed to learn from the professionals who had the schooling in the game. I watched and learnt from Kevin and Gordon, anxious to study their every move. Kevin taught me what good defending is all about. Thankfully he's still teaching me with Ireland.

I soon learned the first lesson of life at Manchester United as well. Everything at United is measured against the championship. Sir Matt Busby rebuilt the club after the war, set standards as high as the sky for a side weaned on tradition and success. The Busby Babes of '58 and '67 were the yardstick for every United side that followed. No United manager counted for anything until he won the championship. Alex Ferguson knows that though now he has finally ended the long wait; even he was under pressure when the famine continued for season after season. Fergie won the FA Cup, the League Cup and the European Cup Winners Cup – they are mere coins though compared to the currency of championships. And that is the only currency that matters at Old Trafford.

Ron Atkinson knew as much the day he took over from Dave Sexton, long before my time at the club. The players knew we would never really be accepted as United legends until we had taken that championship back to its spiritual home at Old Trafford. We never did in my time there. And that failure came at a price for the manager.

Ron did taste the champagne of success wih United. He won the FA Cup twice but that was only a sideshow as far as the real thing was concerned. I was actually involved in the first successful Cup squad under Ron in 1983 when Brighton took United to a replay but I was only a bit player. I had only been in England a year at that stage and had already recovered from my first cartilage operation. It was a bit far-fetched to expect a Wembley place so soon but I had played in some of the early matches and I was with the party measured up for the Cup final suits and taken down to London three days before the game.

Kevin Moran and Gordon McQueen were the established centre-halves in the side at that time. Any time I got a game was because one or other of them was injured and that was fair enough. I thought though that I'd have a chance of getting the one place on the bench but Ashley Grimes got the nod and I could have no complaints really.

Just to be part of that squad was an honour in itself. I enjoyed every bit of the day for the 2-2 drawn match, the trip up Wembley Way, the walk on the pitch before the game, the atmosphere and the incredible tension as the match swung one way and then the other. The replay was much more one-sided. We won 4-0 and there was a hell of a party that night back at the team hotel and then the following night when the cup was paraded at Old Trafford and through the streets of Manchester.

That summer I signed a new contract at United, another bad deal. I did a lot better than the £200 a week I was on when I first came over – somewhere around £500 a week now – but it still wasn't too hot. I never bothered asking the likes of Kevin for advice as I should have done. Instead I used the same agent as Norman Whiteside and we were both left short of the money our talents deserved. Or so we felt. People will rightly point out that I signed the piece of paper that was my contract of my own free will – but I was naive. To cap it all I signed for six or seven years. I might as well have signed my life away.

Two years after my 1983 Wembley experience we won the Cup again. Gordon McQueen was on his way out of favour and this time I was a fully paid-up United hero alongside Kevin at the heart of Ron's defence.

By then I had made my Irish debut under Eoin Hand – and St Pat's benefited to the tune of another £15,000 for my first cap. That was awkward for Eoin because of his links with the club. And

I always felt I should have been capped earlier. But I went on as substitute in February 1985 for Mark Lawrenson against the Italians when there were about a million people at a packed Dalymount Park. It was a great feeling, even if we lost 2-1.

The following month I started in midfield against England at Wembley. Another friendly and another 2-1 defeat when I was substituted at half-time. I didn't mind too much by then – at least I had played for my country, an honour I had dreamed about from the first day I kicked a ball.

Wembley beckoned again for the 1985 Cup final. We beat Everton and Kevin Sheedy 1-0 in the decider thanks to a Norman Whiteside goal. But everyone remembers that game for just one reason – Kevin Moran's red card. He became the first player to be sent off in a Wembley final. The referee's name is a great quiz question now. I couldn't remember it – until Joey Lovejoy of *The Independent* newspaper reminded me it was Peter Willis. A history maker.

I still feel guilty about that red card. It was my poor backpass to Kevin that let Peter Reid in to pick up the ball and sweep towards goal. I had given Kevin no choice but to go for Reidy after that hospital pass. The referee decided it was a sending-off offence. It was a harsh decision to say the least – and it caused uproar within football.

There was consternation when Kevin was refused his medal after the match because he had been sent off. In fact somebody found it in the Royal Box afterwards and he did eventually receive it. Had they refused to give it to him point blank then I would have given him my medal – after all I was responsible for his dismissal.

Those cups were a great time for United and for the United players. We lived it up to the full, celebrating in both '83 and '85. I can still remember the open-top bus rides around the city, the scenes at Old Trafford, the first league match of the following seasons when hope was at its highest.

That hope was always measured on the barometer of the championship. It was the same for every Manchester United player from 1967 until the night Bryan Robson and Steve Bruce shared the honour of lifting the first Premiership trophy before the game against Blackburn in May '92-'93.

Expectancy was at its highest the season after we won the Cup in 1985 with a superb side including Gary Bailey, Norman, Kevin, Bryan, Gordon Strachan, Mark Hughes, Jesper Olsen and Frank

Stapleton. We won the first ten games, went 15 unbeaten at one stage, yet we still blew it. Liverpool won the league, Everton were second, West Ham were third and we finished in a position that doesn't even merit mention. Failures again.

A sign of things to come. At the start of the following season we couldn't win a game to save our lives. And sure enough the day came when Ron Atkinson paid the price for his failures as a Manchester United manager, and the man who had signed me from St Patrick's Athletic was on his way out of Old Trafford.

He called us into the gym at The Cliff one morning in October of 1986 and we knew it was the end before he even opened his mouth. You could see it written all over his face as he prepared to tell us the news that he had been sacked less than 18 months after winning the FA Cup. Our bad start to the league was the reason for his dismissal.

It was a time of regret for the players, a time for guilt and sorrow. Realism soon dawned that we had let the big man down. He had built a team that he felt could lead United back to the glory days of a First Division title. He had welded a side together to take on the best in the land and we had let him down with a bang. Oh yes, we had flattered to deceive when we won the FA Cup final against Everton in 1985 – then we had gone ten games unbeaten at the start of the following season. But eventually we faltered.

We failed to produce the goods on the field and it was Big Ron who paid the price of our failure.

It was a very hard time for me personally. Ron was the man who had taken me away from part-time football in Ireland. He had offered me the chance to become a professional footballer, a chance that I had only dared to dream about back in my native Dublin.

I still feel bitter for Ron about the way he was let go by the club. United reneged on Big Ron the day they let him go. They never gave him a proper chance that season. Just because we got off to a bad start they sacked him.

Managers are always the ones made to pay for failure. Players can get on with it, welcome the new man in and carry on with their life and their well-paid lifestyle. The manager often loses his control over the players once they cross that white line and enter the playing area. Their mistakes are his mistakes, their fatal errors are the measurement of his worth as a manager. We let Ron down but we were still at United and he was on his bike. I felt so bad for him the day he called us together and told us it was the end of the road. You could sense the disappointment in his voice, feel the emotional trauma.

I felt like crying for Ron that afternoon. I had got on very well with him. He was very easy to relate to and he was a great fellow to work for. He had his moments like the rest of football managers but by and large he was a funny man who got on well with his players. He got a lot of respect from the lads. We knew he had his days when he could rip you to shreds but by and large he treated you like an adult not a child at a boarding school, like some I could mention. He was just the sort of manager who'd see you in a club having a few pints and wouldn't bark at you. He'd more than likely come over and have a drink then tell you to take it easy.

I did have dressing-downs from Atkinson a couple of times. He had a go a few times after games where I had played badly and he still does that occasionally when he feels I've let Villa down. Of course he would vent his anger on players at times but I was never involved in a long-running feud with the manager when he was at Old Trafford. In fact, if he was still the boss at United, I'm sure I'd still be there.

I was no street angel and house devil in his time. I had my ups and downs, my share of the spills that mark any relationship between player and manager. A couple of times he'd bring me into his office and tell me that I had been spotted drinking in this pub or nightclubbing in this discotheque and he'd just say: "Take it easy, don't give people something to sell to the papers. Watch what you're doing." He'd never just say he was going to fine me for this, that or the other. He'd just say calm it down and talk straight to me about it, tell me to get my act together.

He was the sort of person people associate with Manchester United, he had the image and the style to go with a big club like that. But he didn't fit the bill at the end and it was a sad day for United when they let him go. The fans liked Ron – they still do – but at a club like United you have to get the results in the league or pay the price.

The players knew we had let Ron down – for some reason we couldn't get it right at the start of that last season. No matter what we did we just couldn't get a sequence of wins going or find anything like the form we were capable of producing. Mark Hughes had gone to Barcelona and he was a huge loss. Perhaps the club should never have let him go, although it was hard to turn the money down and harder still to deny him his chance on the continent. He's since proved his worth to United again when Fergie brought him back from Bayern Munich.

We should have managed without Mark that season. Even in games where we'd play well we'd lose 1-0 and nobody could explain what was going wrong. It was a nightmare time for Ron and the players. The first couple of bad results were put down simply to a poor start. Once it became a sequence of bad results the pressure came with it. Every time we'd lose we'd get slaughtered in the press. People would claim we were letting down the name of Manchester United and all the time the pressure was growing on Ron's job.

Once things go wrong at a club like United it doesn't take long for people to start calling for someone's head. That year it was Ron's turn to become the target for the terrace taunts and eventually those chants began to find their way into the boardroom. Before we knew where we were Ron was on his way out of Old Trafford.

Ron had blooded me, he had shown me what First Division football was all about and I will always be grateful to him for that. But now I was at a crossroads. I didn't know what the future held for me or the club. Like the rest of the players I was caught in limbo, wondering who would arrive next as Manchester United manager.

There was all sort of speculation in the papers. People were talking about Brian Clough. They were talking about Bryan Robson becoming a player-manager. Bryan will one day make a great manager for United but back then he was just that little bit too young for the most pressurised job in English football. If the job became vacant tomorrow morning I'd have no doubts now about his chances of making a go of it.

When I discovered that Fergie was the man for the job my alarm for my future grew. I wondered if he was big enough to manage a club like United. Over the seven years since then he has proved his pedigree. And he's won every honour. But anyone will agree it takes time to settle in at that club – either as a player or as a manager.

United is a one-off club. It's the biggest club in England, one of the biggest worldwide. It has such a name. It's a fabulous place, a daunting place for anybody coming into the club from outside. Most players want to go there but it can be frightening – if the crowd take to you then you're okay. But they can be a funny sort of crowd if a player doesn't perform to the high standards expected. I was lucky they took to me. Sometimes there were things that I did that I should have been slaughtered for but the crowd turned a blind eye. Not everyone was treated like that though. There were players there like Alan Brazil who I thought was a magnificent footballer but the crowd never gave him a chance. Every time he touched the ball there'd be boos from his own United fans never mind anyone else.

That was a bit sad. From my point of view I loved the crowd there. They developed the "Ooh Aah Paul McGrath" chant. I should have claimed copyright on that – I'd make a fortune out of Eric Cantona these days. Kevin Gallacher at Blackburn also has a version of it. Even the *Daily Star* have used it for an advertising campaign at football grounds all across England. Imagine the money I could have made if I had taken out the copyright.

I was only booed once by United fans. That was near the end of my time at the club when there was speculation that I was going to sign for Terry Venables and Spurs, and they booed me in a match against Luton at Old Trafford. It was upsetting and annoying. It summed up how low my relationship with Fergie had become when the crowd were turning against me.

I always got on with that crowd. Even in the hard times they used to stand by me when the papers were slaughtering me with stories of drinking here, there and everywhere. The crowd used to ignore it. As long as I was seen to be doing it on the pitch on a Saturday afternoon I was alright in their eyes.

Fergie refused to see it like that when he arrived as boss. He just saw my drinking for what it was, a breach of club discipline and the standards expected of United players. He was more concerned about what I was doing off the pitch than on it.

Obviously the club does have a big reputation and I was just trying to keep it up. In fact it had a reputation then within football as a home for heavy drinkers and I was just jokingly trying to uphold that. For the pride of the club of course. Memo to Fergie – that's a joke!

Fergie did seem to ignore my playing side. My attitude was that I was playing football to the best of my ability and the crowd appreciated that but he didn't.

Before he arrived we discussed as a team his appointment. Gordon Strachan told us one or two things about what he was like from his days at Aberdeen and with Scotland. He warned us that

Fergie would lose his temper here and there but Gordon's attitude was that he was a good manager because he'd won things with him at Aberdeen. All we could do was just wait and see what happened. What will be, will be.

He seemed fairly straight the first day he was introduced to us but his first game in charge soon changed my opinion. We were away to Oxford and I was picked to play in central midfield because Bryan Robson was injured. I was taken off at half-time. When that happened I thought, "Oh, Jesus, we're not going to be suited." As soon as I was brought off that day I just knew it was never going to be the same for me at Manchester United.

I just came off and accepted it. I didn't go on the attack or anything like that. At that time I was tied to United for six years. I was just thinking that I didn't want to stay under this fellow for the next six or seven years. I just knew that wasn't going to happen and that was the way it turned out.

There were a few things that happened. I was fined for doing certain things, having a drink and stuff like that. I was fined for being late for training a few times, which is fair enough, but then my grudge came when I asked for a transfer in his first season and he said no. I asked if I could go to the papers and he refused permission.

At that time he was coming out in the papers with all sorts of stuff about me and I had no comeback because I wasn't allowed to talk to them. I found that strange. He was coming out saying Paul's after doing this or that, that Paul wants this transfer, that he can go, there's no way we want him in our club if that's his attitude. But I had no right of reply.

I had to live in Manchester in the middle of all that flak. I had to face the fans. Even now, years later, I'm still explaining to people in Manchester what happened between me and Fergie. I was desperate to tell them my side of the story then but I had no comeback because he had told me not to speak to the press.

On the transfer front I still feel I was kept in the dark. I definitely know people came in for me and were put off by someone at the club. Somebody at the club was saying that I was not to be trusted, that I had a drink problem. Graham Taylor later told me he came in for me for Villa when I first went on the list and was told that I was a million pounds and that I wasn't a very reliable professional and all that sort of stuff. I still don't know who said it but it was a right bit of nastiness.

I'm glad I didn't find that out at the time because the rows behind the scenes might have got a little bit worse, even physical. Not only with the manager but with whoever was giving this information out to other clubs.

CHAPTER NINE

Z-Europa

GERMANY in 1988 was the magical moment when Irish soccer finally stood up to be counted.

We had spent years living in the shadows of the other home nations, years suffering the old jokes about Irish soccer, years in the European doldrums. There had been hard luck stories, no luck stories, bad luck stories. But they all ended in that merry month of June 1988 when Ireland took its rightful place amongst the soccer nations of this earth.

It was the first time an Irish side had ever reached any major finals. The 20 players who went to Germany with Jack Charlton that glorious summer were history makers – and we never even realised it in the weeks leading up to the championships. We were too wrapped up in the hype and the hope that surrounded that trip to the Euro finals, a trip made more in expectation that realisation.

I never even thought I'd make the final squad of 20 when I lay on a hospital bed in Manchester after yet another knee operation the previous November. I was having more problems with my left knee and the club had put me in for another orthoscope and another op in the week Ireland were due to play Israel in a Dalymount Park friendly.

We'd already wrapped up our European qualifying campaign with a 2-0 victory against the Bulgarians in Dublin, a game when I scored one of my few goals for Ireland and Liam Brady was unjustly sent off. Liam had had a running battle with one of their players all afternoon and there were a few scores to be settled after our defeat in Sofia when we rightly felt we had been robbed. We settled the scores alright. They knew they were in a match that afternoon. The little black books were out – we played as Big Jack might have done in his day as a player. We got our men just like in the best Westerns – and overturned that Sofia result. The Bulgarians had come to Dublin and discovered that they weren't as big as they thought they were.

I can still remember the buzz in the coach on the way to the ground that wet October day. Most people had written us off in those European qualifiers but we knew a win against Bulgaria would keep the back door to Germany open – and answer a few questions lying at the back of our minds since Sofia.

Retribution was duly administered at Lansdowne with the only cost a red card for Liam when he delivered his own personal justice on their hardman under the referee's nose. But if that red card was unjust the punishment meted out afterwards when Liam subsequently received a four-match competitive ban, later cut down to two games at the finals, was way out of line with the offence. By the time we got to Germany he had picked up a cruciate ligament injury playing for West Ham and would never get the same chance with Ireland again. That was cruel for him and hard on his country.

But still that day in Dublin was a bit special. Even if the Bulgarians were hot favourites now to beat Scotland in Sofia that November and qualify for the German finals we could live on in hope. That result gave us a chance for the Euro finals, if only a glimmer of hope. We reckoned we'd blown our luck in the drawn games at home to Belgium and Scotland, games when we had failed to make the impressive displays in Glasgow and Brussels count for anything. The victory against Bulgaria – revenge for that dreadful night in Sofia – did give us a shout in the final shake-up.

But qualifying for Germany was the last thing on my mind when I lay stretched out on a bed in a Manchester hospital that fateful November. Ireland duly played Israel on the Tuesday, won 5-0 and David Kelly hit a hat-trick on his first international appearance. It made him an instant folk hero with the fans. And the long blond hair – since cropped – made him an instant hit with the Dublin girls.

I heard that result on the radio and I was glad for the lads and glad for Jack that the winning run had continued. I wondered how

David was settling in with the squad and I drifted off to sleep, never thinking what lay in store for Irish soccer just 24 hours later. I'd even forgotten that Scotland were playing in Bulgaria the next night in the final group game. I just assumed that the Bulgarians had already done enough to qualify.

The next afternoon I didn't pay too much attention to the fixtures as I watched England hammer Yugoslavia out in Belgrade on the box. England had gone to Yugoslavia with the problems of the world lying on their shoulders. The English press were slaughtering Bobby Robson as they have since slaughtered my old boss Graham Taylor, calling for his head, getting ready to fry him if England lost to the Yugoslavs. Robson was getting the sort of treatment from his media that would never be handed out or tolerated in Dublin. The knives were constantly out, the scavengers looking for any meat on the bones of an England team just one game away from European Championship elimination.

But England that afternoon were a different class. Peter Beardsley and Gary Lineker did the business. Bobby Robson's boys were through to the European finals for the first time in his reign and my old mate Bryan Robson, magnificent on the day in Belgrade, was about to captain his country in another major finals.

I felt good for Bryan that evening as I settled down for a snooze after dinner in my hospital bedroom, a room more at home in a hotel than a hospital ward. I hardly even remembered that Scotland were playing in Sofia that same day, didn't even take any notice of the fact that the last remaining act in Ireland's European Championship group was about to unfold.

I think I was even asleep when a nurse came rushing into the room to tell me that Gary Mackay had scored in the dying minutes for the Scots and that Ireland were through to the European finals for the first time ever. I had no idea who Gary Mackay was or what he looked like – but had I got hold of him that night in Manchester I'd have bought him all the Guinness in the world and thrown my arms around him.

I couldn't come to terms with the fact that we had finally qualified for a major finals after all the years of trying, the tears and the torment for the Irish fans and the players.

That night it suddenly felt good to be Irish, even better to be an Irish soccer player. We were now on a world stage. We were now up there alongside the English and the Germans, the Dutch and the Russians, the Danes and the Italians and the Spaniards.

I felt like getting up and walking like Lazarus from that hospital bed, out to join the celebrations that I knew would be going on already in Hale as the Manchester United Irish celebrated the impossible dream, celebrations that were only echoing what was going on back home in Dublin. Scenes of elation that were to become the norm for a nation starved of soccer success for generations.

It had all started two years previously when Eoin Hand finally accepted that international management was not to be his forte. I felt sorry for Eoin because he was a nice man – too nice for that level of job. As ever his resignation was followed by rumour and speculation. Johnny Giles was favourite to get the job back, though there were dark horses in the shape of Bob Paisley, Brian Clough and one Jack Charlton.

I felt convinced that the FAI would stick with tradition and give the job to an Irishman. I was wrong – for the first time the job went to an outsider. And even that came after a typical FAI change of heart. The new manager was decided on a vote. After the first vote Bob Paisley was the man in charge of the Republic. But protocol demanded a second casting of the votes. Somebody switched their vote and Jack Charlton became the manager of Ireland. The rest, history as they say, began when he took charge of the Irish side for the first time in February 1986 for a get-together at Lilleshall.

Jack came down that day with Newcastle United defender John Anderson, a loyal servant to Ireland who never really got the caps he deserved. John drove Jack from Newcastle – and had us in stitches when he arrived. Jack had got into the car in Newcastle, stuck a tape about fishing into the cassette player and never said a word to John for the rest of the journey. He had started as he meant to go on.

My first meeting with him was impressive. He laid it on the line. He was going to do things his way. Nobody was bigger than the team. The senior pros who had influenced Eoin towards the end of his reign were put back in their place. Things like going home to your parents in Dublin on the Monday night before a game were over and done with. This was serious business and it was time to be serious. The squad were in it together. We were to eat together, drink together, sleep together, mix together, move together. We were to give our all in an Irish shirt. If we didn't like it we could kiss international football goodbye.

Jack of course had one huge advantage over any Irish candidate or any Irish player. He had won a World Cup medal back in 1966. He knew what he was talking about and we soon knew what he meant.

That first day he told me he admired me greatly as a centre-half, his own position, then added that my days at the back were over for the time being. I was to be a central midfield player in his plan of action. He was doing this because I was too good a player to waste at the back. That remark won him a special place in my heart.

The first time we really took the whole thing seriously was when Jack brought us to Iceland for a three-nation tournament with the home side and Czechoslovakia that first summer. It was quite a squad. The Oxford pair John Aldridge and Ray Houghton had joined the fold and they were probably the most significant signings Jack made in all his career as a football boss.

He proved himself to be the only boss that summer as well. And boy was I glad I hadn't yet discovered the art of going missing. David O'Leary was sensationally left out of the original squad when Jack felt he had a glut of centre-halves. David went ahead and booked his annual family holiday in Sardinia. Injuries forced a re-think on Jack's behalf. He called David up. David had already paid for the holiday and went to Italy instead of Iceland. Almost three years later he was still paying the price when only an injury crisis got him back for a World Cup qualifier in Seville against the Spanish.

And so we went to Iceland without David – but with some real characters like Mick Kennedy, a tough midfielder with Portsmouth at the time. He came to the fore against the Czechs – he made a tackle so hard that he ended up with a couple of Czech teeth embedded into his elbow. He's still looking for the owner.

More importantly, we won that tournament. It was a nothing competition but it was the first time Ireland had won anything, anywhere. The celebrations in the hotel had to be seen to be believed. Iceland isn't the easiest place in the world to get a drink, we had no trouble finding it. And when the FAI president Pat O'Brien, a lovely man from Cork who died tragically just a year later, said it was only the beginning of great things to come he was more than a touch prophetic. None of us could imagine what was to follow.

The following September we served notice of our intentions with a draw in Brussels against a great Belgian side. We went to

Glasgow and beat Scotland at Hampden Park on a night that probably ranks as the best team ever to play for Jack. There was Packie in goals, me at right-back, Kevin Moran and Mick McCarthy in the middle, Ronnie Whelan at left-back. Midfield consisted of Ray Houghton, Liam Brady, Mark Lawrenson and Tony Galvin. Upfront Frank Stapleton and John Aldridge. What a side – then and now if you could call on those great players. Mark got the goal that night, though by the time we got to Germany he had been forced to retire injured, a cruel blow to a player who had embarrassed England every time he played for us. That was the game when the world started to take note of the Jack Charlton revolution that was sweeping through the Irish side. It was only a hint though at the glory to come, at the days and nights of celebration for our soccer-mad country across Europe and America.

That promise first materialised in Germany at those European Championships. That was the first time we took ourselves seriously, thanks to Gary Mackay's goal against Bulgaria. It was the first time the fans travelled abroad in such huge numbers. The first time the Green Army showed the soccer world how real fans could enjoy themselves without fear of riots or recriminations.

When the draw for the finals put us in with England, Holland and Russia we were given no chance. Every day I reported for training at The Cliff or Old Trafford somebody would try and wind me up about the England match, tell me that I was wasting my time going to Germany at all.

If I thought I had problems getting myself fit again in time to go to the Europeans I really had problems with injury once I got there. I know now that I should have been on the first plane back to Manchester after just ten minutes of that famous victory over England – and all because of an injury to my left knee that was to necessitate yet another operation later that summer. I felt the cartilage pull after just a couple of minutes of that match when I had a shot on the England goal before Ray Houghton scored.

We were all worked up and hyped up about the game and when it started I went around like a headless chicken in midfield for a fair few minutes. I was tugging at Robbo, chasing here, harrying there, pushing this player, tackling that player, winning the ball and giving it to Ronnie Whelan to do something with it and get it out of my way.

Then I saw the pitch and the English defence open up in front of me with Peter Shilton in trouble when the ball came back out after an Irish corner and I just knew I had to have a pop at goal. I did. The ball screamed wide and I did my knee in yet again.

As I came down on the left knee I felt something go. I knew straight away that I was in trouble, that the game was going to be a real battle from then on in just for me to survive. I hobbled through the half, inspired by that incredible goal from Ray Houghton and made it to half-time. But I really thought it would be curtains for me any minute.

At the half-time break Mick Byrne, the Irish physio, was brilliant. He told me not to worry about the injury, that God would get me and Ireland through the next 45 minutes as we tried every trick in the book to protect that Ray Houghton goal. Mick has the healing hands as far as the Irish squad are concerned – and he certainly worked a miracle for me that afternoon in the Neckar Stadion. He piled ice on the knee, loosened up the joint and told me not to worry. But I honestly didn't think I'd get out for the second half never mind last until the end of the game.

I knew it was gone straight from then and that the rest of the game was going to be a struggle. Sure enough in the second half I was reduced to hobbling around trying to throw a tackle in here and there, trying to get in the way of Robbo and Glenn Hoddle when he came on late in the match and threatened to pull us back with some brilliant balls and a quality of passing that England had missed before his introduction.

My knee and Ireland managed to survive that frantic second half but I knew the rest of the European Championships was rapidly escaping from my gaze unless something miraculous happened.

There was great slagging beforehand at United. The English lads would slag us and we'd have a go at them. We'd have bets with Robbo and the rest of them, bet them money and champagne that they wouldn't get a kick. I think Robbo still owes me a few bob for that Ray Houghton goal.

Jack said before the game that we had nothing to fear from England but I don't think we even believed him never mind the fans or the press. I know I was really uptight. Liam Brady had been dealt a double blow by suspension and injury and his experience was going to be missed. Mark Lawrenson had retired injured and was already picking up his pension by the time we left our training camp at Finnstown House for Stuttgart. That meant I was in midfield for the European Championship finals, our debut on such a stage and that probably explains my pre-match nerves before the England game.

It was a sweltering hot day in Stuttgart. Some of the English fans had been misbehaving and there was a lot of tension in the air at the Neckar Stadion. This wasn't just a football match as far as the Irish people were concerned. It was a chance to avenge eight hundred years of colonialism, as one of the papers put it afterwards. It was a matter of pride for the Irish race and for Jack, a man who had been ignored by England when they were looking for a manager some years earlier, a man who has arguably since become the most successful English boss at international level since Alf Ramsey.

Defeat was unthinkable as far as the great footballing minds of England were concerned. Familiarity may breed contempt in terms of the teams knowing each other so well but England had, after all, given the game to the world and who were the Paddies to deny them their moment of glory? That was their outlook. Defeat would be unbearable as far as the Irish were concerned.

We got off to a perfect start courtesy of Ray Houghton, moments after I had done my cartilage. I can still see that goal. A Chris Hughton free-kick, a Kenny Sansom miskick, a John Aldridge touch and a Ray Houghton header to prompt the song "Who put the ball in the English net – Rayo, Rayo", still sung to this day. When that ball went in I froze. We had been denied by fate so often in the past. I waited. For flags and whistles and anything to deny us our moment of glory. Incredibly the goal stood.

Now we faced our biggest battle. Once we went ahead I knew England would move heaven and earth to get back at us. They did but we had a god between the sticks called Packie Bonner. That was his best afternoon for Ireland, even better than Genoa when he saved the penalty from Daniel Timofte. Talk about the hands of God, he had a sheet glass window across his goal – that's the only way to explain how he kept a clean sheet and Ireland in it.

I ploughed on for the second-half against England, taking a chance with that knee but battling on for Ireland, for Jack, for myself. It was easy to get inspiration and confidence with the sort of heroic performances all around me. That second half was probably the longest 45 minutes of my life but we hung on in there and got the result that Ireland and the Irish had only dreamed of. We had beaten the country that gave the game to the world. We had beaten the cream of English soccer. We had launched our first major championships appearance with a victory against England, of all people.

Philip Greene, just then recently retired as soccer commentator with RTE Radio, came up to me in the dressing-room afterwards and said that he thought he would never see the day when Ireland would take on England at soccer and win. There were messages coming into the dressing-room from the Taoiseach and the President of Ireland. Jack was taking calls from all over the place, from people desperate to celebrate the impossible dream, desperate to congratulate him on the achievement of a lifetime, victory against his own country. He was ecstatic, his countrymen were in a state of shock. Mick Byrne our physio even ended up on the front page of the *Daily Telegraph*.

It was so hard for England to take the result. If we had been in their position it would hardly have raised an eyebrow across the Irish Sea. People expected us to just make up the numbers and lose out in Germany. Not beat England. They had such a standing in world football then that to get beaten by a bunch of Paddies was just unacceptable.

Talk to Irish fans now and about 50,000 will claim they were in Stuttgart that afternoon. It's a bit like the Easter Rising at the GPO in Dublin in 1916 when there were two million people in there with Padraig Pearse, according to myth, or the time when Bono and U2 started gigging in the Dandelion Market in Dublin and about 5,000 people used to pack their gigs, if you believe where people say they were. In fact there were about 8,000 Irish supporters in the Neckar Stadion – and they had the time of their lives. We heard them throughout that match, shouting us on, giving us the energy to keep going in search of that elusive win. After the match they were ecstatic. They drank into the night. And so did we.

Jack handled it perfectly. Our hotel was not off limits to the fans. They were in for a few hours, they celebrated this dream with us, they drank with their German hosts, they showed the world how football supporters should celebrate. And we showed the world how an Irish team should celebrate a win of that magnitude. We let our hair down with Jack's blessing. In moderation of course.

Jack knew what it meant. He told us to have a few pints and a sing-song. I stuck to the orange juice for once. There were fiddles and guitars all round the place. Even Liam Brady got up on a chair with a guitar he couldn't play and started singing. There were bodies dancing and swaying all over the place. We just couldn't believe that we had beaten England – and we made sure it was going to be a night to remember after an afternoon I will never forget.

Once the curfew arrived at midnight we went off to bed – with a bit of gentle persuasion from Mick Byrne and Charlie O'Leary of course. I awoke the next morning with a hangover, borne not of alcohol but of happiness, a lump the size of a tennis ball on my knee – and a disbelief that we had actually beaten England in the European Championship finals.

But it was true alright. We were getting news of the celebrations back home where it seemed the whole country had gone mad. I would have given anything to go back to Dublin that Sunday night for the craic and then return on the Monday for more treatment.

That was what my European Championships now consisted of – along with a handful of the Irish team. The flight from Stuttgart to Hanover for the second match was agony. I could hardly move with the pain in my leg. I knew there and then there was no chance of me playing against Russia. So did Jack and it was time to put Plan B into action. Plan B consisted of a call-up for Kevin Sheedy, then at Everton, and the proud owner of the best left foot in Ireland since Christy Brown or Liam Brady.

Kevin came into the side against the Russians and was just brilliant. So were the rest of the lads. Sitting in the stand that night I could hardly believe what I was watching – an Irish side playing the Soviet Union off the field.

We got off to another great start. Ronnie Whelan has always been one of my favourite midfield players in England. We had a lot in common: we were both brought up in Dublin, we both played League of Ireland, we both made our way to England from Dublin clubs. He was from the same Home Farm nursery that produced his legendary namesake Liam Whelan, a Busby Babe who tragically died in the Munich Air Disaster with Manchester United. Ronnie's father, also called Ronnie, was a great League of Ireland player himself and had once scored a very famous goal against England at Goodison Park. Sadly he died in 1993. But at least he got to see his son play at the highest level for Ireland and Liverpool. And he could be proud of the way Ronnie junior hit the Russians with one of the Irish goals of the century that night in Hanover. It was a volley that has been shown time and time again on television and will be for many years to come. It was a goal that should have inspired an Irish win. John Aldridge was denied a certain penalty and we fell level to a late goal from the great Protasov. Still, three points from the first two games was more than anyone dared dream about before we had left Dublin. Now we even had the audacity to talk in terms of a semi-final spot.

Not that I was getting too excited about the prospect of getting Ireland there with a win against Holland in Gelsenkirchen the following Saturday. My knee was in agony. But for the healing hands of Mick Byrne, the Irish physio, I would never have made it. Mick had a bit of a job on his hands at the end of the week. Mick McCarthy was walking around with his legs in bandages – he looked a bit like an Egyptian mummy. And Packie Bonner was in agony with his back.

The walking wounded are never a problem as far as Mick is concerned though. As a physio he is in a different class. Mick treats all the lads like they're really special to him, he looks out for us, he pampers us and coaxes us. He's not just the physio, he's the psychiatrist, the psychologist, the agony aunt and the godfather of the Irish team rolled into one.

He gets wound up from time to time. Like the match in Latvia when Tony Cascarino and Andy Townsend had him running around for ages looking for a chess set they didn't really want. Or the time in Moscow when the lads stuck some funny pictures into his passport and got him into all sorts of bother at immigration.

But Mick is irreplaceable as far as the Irish soccer team is concerned. He has been ever since the day Johnny Giles brought him on board. Every time we meet up he's running around after the lads, doing things for them, getting things organised, listening to them whinge about this and that. Mick knows better than most that professional footballers need to be pampered and he does it so well. When he knows you need to hear words of reassurance that's exactly what you get. In the most convincing manner possible. The morning of that Dutch game in Gelsenkirchen Mick told me he would get me through the game and he was true to his word. I did a fitness test along with Packie on a training ground behind the team hotel. Jack had his doubts about me. So had I. Mick said I'd make it. He had the final word and he was right.

I played in that game and I should have scored early on with the sort of header that was bread and butter to the likes of Frank Stapleton or John Aldridge. I missed – and I was to curse it afterwards in a stadium that was a sea of orange with a splattering of green, white and gold away in one corner. How that corner wanted that ball to go in.

Luck was not on our side that day. We had injury problems when Chris Morris was forced off at half-time and I spent the second half at right-back, part of a rearguard action against the rampant Dutch. We survived for 81 minutes – until Wim Kieft scored the goal that sent us home before the semi-finals.

Holland and Russia were through. They would meet in the final itself and we were vindicated when the Dutch won the European Championships. England finished bottom of our group, beaten in all three games. That gave me something to smile about at the start of the following season when I went back to United with my head held high.

In the meantime though there was some serious partying to be done. We had a hooley in the team hotel that night, then we went out on the town till dawn. We drank our way home on an Aer Lingus charter, all the while unaware that Dublin was packed with people out on the streets to welcome us back as the champions of Europe – in spirit if not in reality.

Nothing prepared us for the chaotic celebrations of Dublin Airport that Sunday lunchtime. The airport, the road into Dublin, O'Connell Street itself. All packed with well-wishers, people anxious to get a glimpse of their heroes, to shake a hand, to say thank you. People proud to be Irish and proud of the 20 players and the coaches who had borne their jersey and their flag with pride in Germany. It was the start of the communal celebration that was to cause me so much pain in future years. The start of a success story that has changed the face of Irish soccer irrevocably. The start of the big money for the Irish football authorities, the start of the bandwagon for everyone else.

It's just incredible how one game in Irish soccer history changed the whole face of the sport as we knew it and the perception it has amongst the ordinary people of Ireland. A sport that has played second fiddle to the GAA and their Gaelic football and hurling for so long is now the biggest sport in the country, and close to becoming our national game whether the traditionalists like it or not.

No other sport has given Irishmen, women and children the sense of identity that has developed with the national soccer team since Jack Charlton took charge. No other sport has given Ireland the international recognition and the pride in our country. No other sport has aroused the passions that began in Germany in '88, became a river of emotion in Italy two years later and now engulfed the Atlantic itself on the way to America 1994.

Soccer has achieved so much over the last six years. Now the powers that run soccer in Ireland must stand up to the challenge and make that success count for something.

I speak from a position of strength. I grew up playing the game in Ireland, from schoolboy league all the way through to the international team. I know what it is like for the youngsters changing in their father's car in the Phoenix Park, for the amateurs paying to play in Bushey Park, for the trailblazers down the country in leagues where soccer has never been before, for the League of Ireland players performing in front of hundreds rather than thousands week in and week out. That's the link that is forgotten when the World Cup bandwagon swings into motion again. World Cup success in itself is great but we must ensure there is a knock-on effect for the Irish game.

I know that it can change back to the old ways just as quickly. Sure, we have more people than ever now wanting to see the international team, wanting to meet the players, wanting to travel the world with us and that in itself is a great thing and it is a great honour to be part of it. It won't last forever though. Once the bubble bursts we will all be brought back down to earth with a bang. Yes, Italy '90 and USA '94 will remain forever in the memories of the nation but it is very important that Irish soccer realises that one swallow doesn't make a summer. And accepts that the games around the corner and up the road are just as important to the public perception of our team and our sport after the World Cups.

I have been a League of Ireland player. I have played in the Leinster Senior League. I have played in the Dublin Schoolboys' Leagues and I have played on pitches all across the country. More than most of the players in the Irish squad I know what the reality of the game at home is really all about. I know what the kids playing soccer for the first time in Ballymun and Tallaght and Kilbarrack and Killarney and Wicklow and Donegal are going through, the thrill of that first jersey, that first 11-a-side game that I experienced with Pearse Rovers. I know the conditions that the fans and the players have to put up with at League of Ireland grounds every wet and cold Sunday during the winter months.

The international scene hasn't had a direct link with the League of Ireland or the junior leagues or the schoolboy set-up at home for a long time now and that has got to change in the wake of USA '94.

When I'm home I love to get the chance to go down to see a League of Ireland match, to go and watch Pat's in particular or Rovers at the RDS or my old mate Joey Malone with Billy Bagster and his Monaghan United side. Yes, I would love to see our own stadium in Ireland, a place where people could go and watch the national team in comfort under floodlights without us being at the beck and call of the IRFU or the GAA or any other rival sporting body. But I would rather they plough the money that they have made from Germany and Italy and now America into the domestic game at all levels. That's where the real need for investment is. And where the success of the World Cup can really have a long-term effect on the future of Irish soccer.

I have seen the people at home involved in senior, junior and schoolboys' football and I know the handicaps they are working under week in and week out to keep the game alive and to give the players the chance to play football. There are some great players in the League of Ireland, there is some fantastic talent coming up through the ranks at all stages but in so many cases it is too much of a battle against all the odds for that talent to come to the surface and that is something we have got to change. We have the money now to start spreading it around and to improve the facilities and the standards for Irish soccer.

The money is there so that we shouldn't be relying on a rugby pitch for our international soccer matches – with or without floodlights at Lansdowne Road. I know I speak for the rest of the lads when I say that at some stages of the year we just dread the thought of a match in Lansdowne Road, especially when the rugby season is in full swing. We normally go there on the Tuesday before a match and I have often asked myself how we are supposed to play soccer on a surface like that. The IRFU look after their own needs and you can't blame them for that. We should have had a ground of our own, worthy of the national side, years ago. The money has been wasted in the past and now we're left with a situation where the players arrive at Lansdowne and plead with the boss to get the pitch sorted out so we can play ball on it.

Money is needed in League of Ireland football and the junior game as well. If the coaching was better then far more homegrown players would be coming on stream for Jack Charlton's senior side. I also feel the time has come to channel funds into the coaching side of the game in Ireland. When I travel abroad and I see the facilities that are available in coaching, sometimes in countries a lot more primitive than ours, it makes me very angry. Our youngsters are not getting the coaching they deserve and that has got to change. Work has started under national coach Joe McGrath but it needs more financial support from the FAI. In the long term a proper coaching network and system will benefit the national team as well because the youngsters coming up through the ranks will be better players.

Maybe then we will see more Irish-born players on the national team because they will have the benefit of the same level of coaching as the sons of emigrants in England. A lot of the kids would still go to England but the League of Ireland would benefit and those players who would be good enough would still get up to international standard.

I know I was a late developer in terms of going to England but I would still encourage Irish kids to come to English clubs. The apprenticeship schemes are well worked out, even if the lad has the sort of talent that Norman Whiteside had when he was 16 there is a certain sort of logic in making him clean boots and work his way up the ladder. It teaches the kids a lot about the way they should behave in an adult world and it makes them appreciate the game far more when they do work their way up the ranks and into senior soccer. If I had served an apprenticeship in England my problems might have been halved.

CHAPTER TEN

Alex Ferguson –
Ouch, Ouch, Ouch

ALEX FERGUSON. A name that brings a lump to my throat every time I come across it. Alex Ferguson. Two words that stick in that throat every time I have to mention him. A man. A manager. A nightmare as far as I am concerned.

For me the bitter end with Ferguson came early in 1989 – after the rift that rocked Old Trafford in January of that year there would be no going back for the pair of us.

In effect my real problems began in October of 1988 when I went into a Manchester hospital for a series of operations on my knees, a direct result of that England game at the European Championships the previous June in Germany. I thought I was going in to have the cartilage repaired after more aggravation, but it was surgery that was to uncover some startling problems for the Black Pearl from Inchicore.

Speculation in the English press suggested that this visit to hospital had revealed a serious flaking of the bone on the dodgy right knee, the same condition that had forced Gary Bailey and Steve Coppell to quit Manchester United in previous years. Surgeon Jonathon Noble, the man in charge of nearly all my many knee operations at the BUPA hospital in Walley Range, carried out two orthoscopes on the damaged right knee then performed major surgery in an effort to repair the damage. His report discounted the story about flaking of the bone – but he was concerned about the long-term prospects for Irish football's most famous knees.

It was a time of concern for me personally and for my family, and it was a worry for United who had seen one of their best prospects plagued by injury ever since my arrival from Dublin. But I have always been a fighter. I knew the operation would put an end to plans Ron Atkinson had to reunite the pair of us out in Spain with Atletico Madrid. And the surgeon was blunt with his post-operation analysis of my situation and my future. I was told in no uncertain terms in hospital that October that my career expectancy could be as low as three months. I knew those knees were bad but I was determined to fight on. The operation cleaned out the knees and the rehabilitation began again for a player well used to the inside of the treatment room at Old Trafford and to the healing hands of Jim McGregor.

Progress was slow at first. Life for Paul McGrath was once more measured in hours – hours of pain, hours on the exercise bike, hours spent with weights and exercises designed to strengthen, strengthen, strengthen the muscles and the joints around the knees. Football was only a distant memory. The tools of my trade, the boots with the screw-in studs that had provoked such excitement years earlier, were nowhere to be seen in that sweaty treatment room at the training ground or down at Old Trafford itself.

Saturday is the day footballers live for, the day their body clock tells them it's time to go out on the park and do what they do best, the day when the professional footballer shows the world why he's paid to kick a ball. Saturday is the day that makes all the pain worthwhile, the day that makes all the effort in training mean something, the day that makes the loneliness and the isolation from the real world seem irrelevant. When you're fit and in the first team Saturday afternoon is everything – when you're injured and out of consideration for that starting line-up, a Saturday afternoon is the loneliest time in the world, even in a stadium like Old Trafford when it's jammed with 50,000 people.

Professional football in England knows how to look after its injured players – up to a point. If the injury is picked up in a first team game then the player remains part of the first team squad for as long as he's out injured. That means he keeps picking up the win bonuses like the rest of the players. What it doesn't allow for is the feeling of helplessness and desperation that races through every injured player's mind. When other players are spending Friday nights in their own homes or, quite often, hotels, putting their feet up and getting a good night's sleep before the next big game the injured player is left to his own devices, subject to the distractions not normally available to a fit player less than 24 hours before action. Some players can cope with the new-found freedom caused by injuries, while others flinch at the very responsibility of free time. The dangers for those found wanting are enormous – as I was to find out.

Injury is nothing new to me since that faceless gentleman from Sheffield came across my knee with his studs raised in that long forgotten reserve team game. I've experienced every type of pain and treatment possible yet I am still one of the players who can't cope with long spells on the treatment table. At the height of my injury problems back in 1989 I wondered about the future, wondered about the pain, worried about my ability to earn a living for much longer in the only trade I really knew. Life and fate had contrived to decide that I would serve only one apprenticeship, would know only one way to work and one way to make a living – to play the game I loved. It was more than my profession, it was my life – and the very profession that had made me also threatened to break me.

The pain of injury, the pain of non-involvement was at its worst on a Saturday afternoon. The other lads tried to make me feel involved but they had their own responsibilities to worry about, their own pre-match nerves, their own feelings of inadequacy or ability before the next big game of their careers. All I could do was limp around the ground and watch those contemporaries play their football, my football, against the big names of the First Division. Sure I would pop my head into the dressing-room before the game and wish the lads the best of luck, knowing in my heart and soul that I should be in there with them, part of the family, not the long-lost cousin in to say hello every now and then.

Sure I would chat to anyone who said hello, talk about the injury, talk about the comeback, all the time wishing the cause of the pain would disappear like a bad dream and I could return to normality, to the normality of the playing pitch and my own field of dreams. Fans at Old Trafford, like fans everywhere, were curious almost to the point of intrusion. They would stop me for autographs on the way from the car park to the ground, delve into a very private grief and always ask the same question. The answer, like the question, was always the same. "When will you be back Paul?" "Get back soon, Paul, we need you." "Sure it won't be long now, the knee is healing fine – and sure why would the lads need me anyway? Aren't they doing alright without me?" would come the inevitable response from a man resilient on the outside and hurting badly inside.

And all the time the silent doubts lingered at the back of the mind. Just how bad was the pain? Just how bad was the soreness in the knee? Just how pronounced was the flaking condition? Would life ever be the same? Would the game ever witness Paul McGrath in full flight again?

The doubts were there but so too were the reasons to be cheerful. As a footballer I had a lot to fight for in that winter of my discontent and Fergie's malcontent. United wanted some class badly. Meanwhile, Ireland were in the throes of proving themselves in a World Cup qualifying campaign and Jack Charlton had privately and publicly told the player suffering in silence at Old Trafford that I was central to his plans whatever my injury problems were. Those words of encouragement from an Irish boss who had stood by me through thick and thin helped to fuel the fires of desire burning in my heart.

The promise to Jack and to myself was cast from the same pledge. I would be back. I would return to the United first team in glory and the Irish team in expectation of the World Cup finals. Damn the begrudgers – I would prove them all wrong, I would refuse to follow Gary Bailey and Steve Coppell down that long and dark tunnel towards retirement and a place in the statistics books, another player finished long before my sell-by date, cut down in my prime, butchered by a vicious boot and a surgeon's blade.

Battles were nothing new – I had long before won battles with life itself. This one would be easy. Determination was etched in steel in that sweaty treatment room, it was stencilled in the look of meanness mirrored in my face as I lifted weights, lifted weights and lifted more weights. The hunger went around in circles every time the knees with no future turned the pedal on the exercise bike. The desire went public every time I met a United supporter and told him to put money on Paul McGrath putting that red shirt on again. The effort was bared to the human eye every time a reporter asked the question – comeback?

They were left in no doubt – they knew and I knew the injured party would be back. No wheel was left unturned – I changed the habits of a lifetime, I even cycled from my new home in Hale into the training ground in Salford every day in the company of fellow injury victims Colin Gibson and Norman Whiteside in an effort to speed up the recovery process. There was always a goal – first I said I would be back just two months after the series of operations that had threatened the career itself. A month later I was to make it.

By December of 1989 Alex Ferguson was talking not just in terms of a return by the player, he was talking openly about rebuilding his defence around Paul McGrath once the player got back to fitness. The signs, if nothing else, were encouraging for the manager and the player.

October was a wicked month. November was a little better. December was heaven itself. On 10 December 1989 Ferguson told the local press: "When Paul is fit he will come straight back into the centre of our defence but I will play him as a sweeper behind Steve Bruce and Mal Donaghy. We will play five defenders at the back but I emphasise that it will be an attacking formation. Paul is a lucky lad and is good enough to be able to step back in with very little match practice. He could walk into a role like that because he is so talented."

The intent was there from Ferguson to ignore his personal problems with the other Paul McGrath and utilise the man's footballing ability to the best means possible as far as Manchester United were concerned. That was one of the few positive elements of the relationship between player and manager, a relationship that was to sour so dramatically and so quickly in the course of the next six months.

To understand the problems that were to follow between Fergie and me it is necessary to delve a little into the background of our dissimilar characters. Fergie comes from a staunch Protestant background in working-class Glasgow; I was brought up in working-class Dublin and proud of it. Idealistically our two worlds were far removed. Ferguson supported Rangers as a schoolboy. My contemporaries, Protestant orphanage or no Protestant orphanage, were sided well and truly with Glasgow Celtic. Politically, socially and historically we came from opposite sides of the fence – looking back now I knew we were never going to meet in the middle.

Ferguson, by virtue of his background and upbringing, would never be able to understand the spirit of a Celtic Irish soul that drove me on in the thirst for life and my hunger for a good time. He could never work out where I was going, I could never understand where he was coming from. To the Irish, having a good time is life itself. It's an escape from the realities of life, a release valve from the pressure of living. To some Scottish Protestants it appears having a good time in an hour of need is akin to turning your face away from responsibilities and flying in the face of reality.

The two of us were always going to disagree on the way I reacted to this biggest injury worry to date – the disagreement that followed still rancours in this Celtic soul. There is no love lost between Alex Ferguson of Manchester United and Paul McGrath of Ireland ever since our paths went two irreconcilable ways in January 1990.

The Cliff was never so welcoming as the day I began my comeback from that series of three knee operations at a midweek practice match behind closed doors at the training ground in the days after Christmas. The long and lonely hours of work with Jim McGregor were beginning to pay off. The rehabilitation was almost complete. I could finally see light at the end of the tunnel. That practice match between members of the first team, the reserves and the 'A' team was a chance to test the knee, a chance to kick a ball in a semi-competitive environment again. It was a success. All working parts were in order. I left the field after 90 minutes physically tired and emotionally drained but happy nonetheless. Relief at last. I'd had just six games all season before those three operations – now at last I was on the way back.

The practice match was the beginning. More light crept through the tunnel on New Year's Eve when I captained the 'A' team in a game against Lancashire rivals Liverpool at The Cliff, a game United lost but nobody really cared. The Black Pearl was back. It was a Saturday and Paul McGrath, professional footballer, was finally back doing what he should be doing on a Saturday afternoon – playing football.

That return couldn't have been better planned. I had missed 12 league games in my spell out injured and our season was falling apart. United were due to play Liverpool in one of the earliest televised games at Old Trafford 24 hours later on New Year's Day, a game we dared not lose in front of our own fans. Player and manager had no doubts that I would be ready for a rapid return to first team duty after just those two reserve outings.

After that 'A' team game I was the centre of attention once more as far as the Manchester press mafia were concerned. After such a lengthy lay-off it was a pleasure to be in the news again. I told them: "I feel shattered but all I need now is games and I'm ready for whatever the manager has in mind for me. I've had a good week in training and I've had no problems with the knee today."

Ferguson knew exactly what he had in mind. After that 'A' team outing the United manager told local reporters: "Paul will definitely be on the bench against Liverpool tomorrow. He eased himself through today and I will have no hesitation in calling on him if I need him tomorrow." He was true to his word. Ferguson did indeed name me on the bench for that home clash with Liverpool in front of the nation's cameras.

It was a start. I was happy just to be back in the first team squad – the delight knew no bounds when I was brought on as a replacement for the injured teenager Lee Sharpe, then playing at left-back for United and only beginning to make a name for himself after his move from Torquay United. It was the icing on the cake on an afternoon that was sweet for me and Manchester United. My comeback took place in a 3-1 win against United's fiercest rivals at the time. Ferguson was a king again as far as one half of Manchester was concerned – but the real bonus for the fans was the fact that their Prince called Paul McGrath was back on his throne.

Christmas and the New Year mean one thing for a footballer – games, games and more games. Festivities are out the window. The comeback was complete at Ayresome Park 24 hours later when United finished their festive programme with a 1-0 defeat against Middlesbrough and I began and ended the game at centre-back. Once more I was delighted to be back. Once more I was tired and emotional. Once more I was able to look to the future.

The papers' talk reflected it. "I was more than a bit shattered after the 'Boro game but it was good to be back and now I am looking forward to the FA Cup game against QPR on Saturday," I explained to the local press. That was on the Tuesday, the day after United had lost at Middlesbrough, the day I started only my seventh first team game of the season.

Talk amongst the United fans was already turning to the third round FA Cup clash with Trevor Francis' QPR at Old Trafford the following Saturday, 7 January. United were struggling in the league. All talk of the championship had long since evaporated at a ground that had waited every year since 1968 for a team to finally exorcise the memories of the Busby era and the last United team to lift the title. Ferguson was under pressure. He had guided the club to second place in the league behind Liverpool the previous season but already United were trailing badly in Arsenal's wake as George Graham stormed to the title at Highbury.

The FA Cup campaign that was to begin at home to QPR was United's last chance of glory that season, our last stab at success. Ferguson knew it and the players knew it. He also knew a fit Paul McGrath was vital to his plans for the Rangers game. Form is everything – I had done well enough in the defeat at Ayresome Park to prove to Ferguson that I merited a place in the team.

The comeback was all it was hoped for as far as the club and the player were concerned on the long journey back from the North-East on the Monday night. That night I was happy, I had every right to be. The next day was a day off for the United players, a chance to have a drink with my mates and celebrate the fact that the wheel of fortune was turning once more in my favour. Wrong!

When I woke up that Tuesday morning I felt a tightness and a pain in my right knee – it was, I hoped, no more than was to be expected in the aftermath of three games in three days and a return to the big stage. I was wrong.

The knee was reacting alright, reacting badly to the ardours of playing again. It was stiff and sore, it was objecting to the demands of heavy ground and heavy tackles so soon after surgery. The signs were ominous for a player who knew his knees inside out. It was too much, too soon. I knew in my heart and soul that week that I would not make the team for the FA Cup clash with QPR. I said as much to Jim McGregor when I went in for training and treatment on the Wednesday. I said as much again when I spoke to Alex Ferguson about the game and the team on the Thursday. Deep down I knew that I would not be able to play on the Saturday. I told the manager so that Thursday afternoon.

The conversation remained private. When the Manchester papers speculated on the Saturday morning that Paul McGrath would "keep his place at the heart of the United defence against QPR" they were widely off the mark. Ferguson had, as is his wont, told his players the team to play against QPR at training on the Friday morning. I hadn't trained, opting instead to receive more treatment on my injured knee. I knew I wouldn't be in the team.

I didn't raise even an eyebrow in surprise when Ferguson named the side and the remainder of the squad and my name was nowhere to be seen. I knew I was injured, the other players at The Cliff that morning knew I was injured, Alex Ferguson knew I was injured. To this day I will swear that the entire dressing-room at The Cliff that Friday knew I was out of action for the following afternoon's Cup-tie against QPR.

That belief has long been contradicted by Fergie's description of the events that followed. My insistence that I was relieved of first team duties by Ferguson that Friday is vital to any understanding of the way events would unfold over the next 24 hours. United, like every professional club around the world, have a strict code of discipline for players on first team duty. They must not drink for at least 48 hours before a game, they must not be seen in public the night before a Saturday fixture. They must not do anything that would affect their performance for the team or undermine their ability to perform in a game or bring the club into disrepute. They are not allowed to engage in media interviews or television appearances on the eve of a big match – all things that I did between the time Alex Ferguson named the side to face QPR and the appointed time when the players gathered for the match the following afternoon.

Ignorance was not my excuse, I knew the rules for players actively involved in first team action. They had never been a problem before, I had never broken them before, never had any reason to run into disciplinary problems because of my behaviour in the days and hours leading up to a big game. Yes, I had had my problems with Ferguson but never over preparation for playing games.

If I was involved with the United first team that Saturday I would have gone home to Claire and the kids as usual after training on the Friday, gone to bed for the afternoon, got up for a couple of hours, watched television, had my dinner, eaten the usual Friday night feast of chocolate and gone back to bed for a good night's sleep before the important Cup game.

But that Friday was different. I was not in the United team – I was not even on the bench. I had no first team involvement therefore I did not have to abide by the rules that Friday night. I was injured and free to do what I wanted with my time.

When I left the training ground at lunchtime on the Friday I was off duty, responsible only to myself under club rules. I was on my own time. I had finished work until I reported for treatment on the Saturday before watching the game against QPR. I was a free man, as was my great drinking partner Norman Whiteside, a long-term injury victim and a player with no chance at all of playing for at least another two months. McGrath and Whiteside, bosom buddies, great mates, partners in crime, were free to spend their Friday as they wished.

That meant only one thing. We decided to go for a drink before appearing together on the Granada television Friday night sports show *Kick-Off* with Elton Welsby, a programme that previewed the major sporting events of the weekend in the North-West and focused on the weekend's big FA Cup-ties. Television scares me at the best of times, and my hatred of television cameras is well documented. Faced with those public invasions into my very private lifestyle I seek solace in only one thing – alcohol. I needed a drink that day to calm the nerves before one of my few television appearances.

Together with Norman Whiteside I was quizzed on the programme about the Cup match, about the injury crisis at United that had claimed the two of us as part of its victims. It was a big joke, the whole thing. We spoke openly and honestly, joked about the game, joked about the injuries, enjoyed ourselves on air without fear of any repercussions.

To many watching in the goldfish bowl that surrounds a club like Manchester United we publicly enjoyed ourselves too much. Popular theory in the whispering circles that eventually find their way back to Old Trafford decided that McGrath and Whiteside were drunk. The club, as ever, immediately received phone-calls claiming as much.

Ferguson, a strict disciplinarian at Aberdeen and with Scotland at the 1986 World Cup finals, was alerted to the phone-calls. He was not a happy man. He had seen the programme and his own opinion deemed that McGrath and Whiteside were going to be in trouble when they reported to the ground the following day. We were oblivious – the pair of us did not know anything about the hostile welcome that was to await us on our arrival at the ground. I had no hint at the row that was to unfold when I turned up as expected to watch the game against Rangers and get some treatment on my injured knee.

The problem had compounded for Ferguson earlier that morning when Lee Sharpe was ruled out of the game at the last moment with a bad dose of flu. The youngster had no chance of playing against Rangers – and Ferguson had little cover at the back with the exception of one Paul McGrath, then injured and in no state to play a game of football.

When I reported in I was subjected to a dressing-down for my behaviour on the eve of a big game – a game I knew I wasn't involved in – and then told I was playing in Sharpe's place. Ferguson felt that my presence alone would boost the youngsters around me. His assistant at the time, Archie Knox, said a morale-boosting return would give the team a lift. Privately the United manager wondered if my problems were all in my mind.

His suggestion that I should play met with a groan of disbelief. I wasn't stupid, I knew my preparation was all wrong for such a big game, I knew I was in no fit state physically or mentally to play in one of the biggest FA-Cup ties United had faced since they had won the competition back in 1985. I knew I wasn't ready for the game, wasn't fit to play the game, wasn't even considered for the game 24 hours earlier. The row that ensued in the dressing-room at Old Trafford was a classic of its kind.

I was in enough trouble for my antics the previous day – now I was openly questioning the manager's decision to use me in a Cup match of such importance and insisting that I wasn't able to play. The two of us exchanged words at a pace of knots, eventually almost coming to blows when I said I would play – and that any comeback was on Ferguson's head.

Then the United physio Jim McGregor intervened. He put his head on the block for me that lunchtime in the dressing-room and I will always be grateful. Jim knew my knees as well as I did; he said there was no way he was going to be responsible for what happened if I did play. The danger was so great that my career could end that afternoon, he said. He was not prepared to have that on his conscience. He made sense of the whole thing, pointed out quite rightly that if I did play and ruin myself I would hold it against him in years to come.

I just thought Fergie was being ridiculous. If he had said on the Friday morning that I was on standby, part and parcel of the first team squad for that game, I would have prepared properly for the match. But no – I wasn't in the team on the Friday because I was injured. Then I was expected to make a miraculous recovery and play just because Lee Sharpe had picked up flu. After the mother and father of all rows he finally accepted that I wasn't going to play, ordered me to report to the ground on the Monday morning with Norman Whiteside for a showdown and then got on with the game.

The match itself ended in a draw. Worse was to follow for

Fergie when Bryan Robson swallowed his tongue and only the prompt action of Jim McGregor saved his life. Fergie, still fuming with me, practically refused to address the press conference in the old tunnels at Old Trafford afterwards. He just claimed it was one damn thing after another that season to a local press who began to float the stories that I had pulled out of the game just an hour before kick-off and that I had been seen drinking heavily with Norman the day before the match.

They were right that I had been drinking but wrong about the circumstances. Anyone who sat in the dressing-room at The Cliff that Friday morning knows I was not named in that side to play QPR. I wanted to tell them but I had been warned not to talk to the papers on my way out of Old Trafford that Saturday evening.

I'd been called in by Fergie before. That Monday morning I thought it was just going to be another routine dressing-down, a stiff warning and the customary fine deducted at source from my wage packet the following week. Wrong again. It was far more serious than that.

I suspected something was up when I arrived at reception rather sheepishly that morning and found Gordon Taylor, chief executive of the Professional Footballers Association, waiting for me. Heavy-duty discipline was on the cards.

Gordon has been a good friend to me over the years. I needed only to look at his solemn face that morning to know this was the real thing. I was right. It was like the condemned man meeting the judge and jury before he was found guilty and sent out to hang. The case for the defence of the defender rested with Gordon – my own PFA delegate Colin Gibson had nothing to do with this one.

The lynching mob was headed by Fergie along with chairman Martin Edwards and the club secretary Ken Merrett. They knew what they were up to. I was to leave that meeting convinced that Fergie had decided over the weekend that this was his chance to get rid of Paul McGrath, bane of his life, forever.

They had it all well planned. Before I went in Gordon took me to one of the directors' offices to have a chat and dropped the bombshell. They were thinking of getting rid of me. Fergie had had enough. This was the final straw.

It was, he said, serious this time. They wanted me to take a pay-out and quit the game forever. He had been left in no doubt by Fergie that this was the club's decision, it was his job to tell me. The way he was putting it I was prepared there and then to accept. My mind was all mixed up, my knees were sore and it seemed like the only option available to me at first glance.

The offer, such as it was, was £100,000 plus a testimonial in Ireland, not at Old Trafford. It was a pathetic offer from a club the stature of Manchester United to a player who had been brought over from Ireland at 22 years of age with little or no support off the field, to a player who had given his all to the club, to a player who was insured for a whole lot more. That's the way I see it now. Then it was easy to see the money in front of my eyes, to take the money and run. Or rather limp away from Old Trafford and from life as a professional footballer.

The way Gordon was putting it I was seriously thinking of taking the offer. It seemed a big deal, two years' money and a United side flown to Dublin at their expense for a testimonial that would generate more money.

They must have felt it was like giving sweets to a baby. Until the baby woke up to the reality of what was happening around him and kicked up.

I started thinking – a dangerous habit for me at the best of times, an even more dangerous one as far as this proposition was concerned. Why would I get a testimonial off United in Ireland? The FAI would have looked after me with a game in Dublin anyway. I had after all injured my knee playing for the Republic at the European Championship finals in Germany, a fact United had recognised when they sought an insurance pay-out off the FAI for that injury.

If United were going to give me a testimonial anywhere it would have to be in Manchester. They owed me one, even if I felt that recent events had done me enough damage with the fans to ensure the crowd would ignore that one in the main. I'd probably have got a testimonial from Ireland anyway and I wouldn't have wanted United to play in it if they had written me off and sent me to the knacker's yard. I told Gordon that if there was going to be any testimonial I wanted it in Manchester against City at Old Trafford. I even doubted that it would make money after the bad press I'd received over the previous week.

The way it developed he was saying I'd come out of it with £100,000 from United and a testimonial. There's no way my contract, with five years left on it, was worth just £100,000 before tax.

Gordon Taylor was left in a very awkward position that morning. On the one hand he realised that United were serious about me quitting the game completely, on the other he realised what it meant to a professional footballer to be told the time had come to pack it in. Realising the club's position he had to encourage me to take the deal. He pointed out that I'd made a few bob, that the PFA would get me into a coaching scheme or get me something else. They weren't just going to leave me there, to see me quit and abandon me as United intended to do. That at least was a source of comfort on a morning where there was precious little of that commodity in supply.

Outside it seemed a good idea to pack it in – inside that meeting room the chill of the reception soon brought me to my senses. There were no friendly welcomes. It was straight down to business, straight down to finding the convict guilty and ending it all. Without any warning they started to discuss money and insurance and pay-offs. This was my career they were ending, as coldly and as ruthlessly as breaking a turkey's neck at Christmas.

Martin Edwards was the judge delivering the verdict. He said Alex Ferguson couldn't put up with it anymore, that the wayward son had pushed the boat out too far this time. There was no trace of sorrow or sympathy in his voice. I was in the wrong and I was on the way out, another statistic on a first team balance sheet trading in commodities called professional footballers not human beings. It was just another meeting for him, there was no sympathy for this Red Devil.

Fergie took the witness stand. He said one or two obvious things about my knees and my discipline, quoted from a dossier prepared for the trial. He wouldn't have any more of my indiscretions. I was out and that was the end of it.

They thought they were offering me a great deal, that I would touch my forelock to the Lord of the Manor and say thank you, sir, three bags full, sir, I'll go off to Ireland now like a good little boy and pack up my troubles in my old kit bag.

I just sat there and listened. I left Gordon to do my talking. I was in no state to offer a defence or an opinion. It was time to shut up and put up. I needed the cocoon of my family and my few close friends to talk this one through. I sat tight. When they'd finished their rantings and ravings, threats and offers, I said I'd get back to them. No more and no less. No commitment and no comment.

When I left I was still shocked. A lot of the time I had listened to them all without hearing a word they were saying. I was like an observer high in the gallery, watching and listening without being a part of the whole thing.

We left in silence. I passed Norman on the way and just glanced at him. We needed no words. He knew I was in trouble. I wondered what his punishment was going to be. He was the lucky one, he got away with a fine and a month's community service at Lilleshall, that human garage where they rebuild broken-down footballers.

I left that building as a footballer on the way out. Thoughts were racing round my head like the ball flying in the air at Wimbledon. The end was near if it all went according to Fergie's plans. I was having second thoughts though. This was my life, my livelihood. Life as a security guard and a fencer back in Dublin held no appeal at that stage of my career.

I needed to talk. I did. To Claire, to Robbo, to Norman, to Kevin Moran. To anyone I valued. The more I talked the more I talked sense. Football was more than my livelihood. It was my life. It was all I knew and all I wanted to know. I had five years left on my contract and belief in my knees. The drinking I could curb, the pain I could control, the self-doubt I could erase. All I wanted to do was play football. My mind, for once, was made up. They could stuff their ultimatum to quit, their testimonial and their insurance pay-out. If it meant spending those five years in the reserves I'd play on.

They had planned to announce to the world that my career was over on the Thursday, the day after the Cup replay. By then they had been told that I was playing on and to hell with the begrudgers.

Initially I was told to stay away from the other players at the training ground. When I reported for treatment I was shunned. It was no more than I expected. Eventually I made an appointment to see Fergie and threw the bombshell back in his face – I would not quit. He was visibly devastated. He told me in no uncertain terms that I had made a mistake of the highest order, that there was no guarantee that I would ever play in his first team again. Life in the reserves, that was the prospective price for being a rebel.

I asked for a transfer. That was turned down. They were prepared to let me quit but not to let me move to another club. Bitchy to say the least.

I have no doubts that PFA chief Gordon Taylor was one of the mainstays in keeping me in the game at a time when United wanted me out. In the newspapers at the time, looking back on the crucial talks, he said: "I'm delighted that Paul's career was soon back on the rails. He worked hard to overcome his problems after those meetings. Paul is a quality player that neither the league nor Manchester United could afford to lose at the time. There was some good straight talking done at the meeting and it seems to have worked."

The United players knew through the Old Trafford grapevine what was happening to me. They were left knowing where they stood in no uncertain terms later that week when Ferguson banned us from drinking in public everywhere except post-match celebrations. The manager had suffered enough at the hands of Norman and myself, he was not going to get caught out a second time.

In the meantime I was sent to Coventry as far as the first team was concerned and I trained with the reserves and the kids at The Cliff. I resurfaced a few days after my dressing-down amid press reports that I had turned down Fergie's offer to quit and was determined to make one last effort at rescuing my Old Trafford career.

It was a tough time for Claire and the children. There were constant streams of reporters calling at the house. They even questioned Christopher on his way home from school about his daddy. It was not an easy time for any of us.

Two days after the fateful meeting, as the United first team prepared for a league match with West Ham and another FA Cup draw against QPR, I was banished to the Central League and a reserve team game against West Brom. Fergie was reported as being furious at my "preparation" for the original QPR game but he did begin to speak again about his wayward child. "Paul is approaching full match fitness but there is no chance of him being involved in either of our two big games at the weekend" were his words of wisdom at the time.

Within a week, though, the ball was back in my court. I was back in the first team, making my return to a mixed reaction from a 46,000-strong Old Trafford crowd as a substitute in the FA Cup second replay win over QPR. I replaced the injured Steve Bruce that day and was set to keep my place for the Cup-tie against Oxford United at home the following Saturday. Fergie would only say: "I won't fuel speculation on this business beyond saying that Paul knows exactly what his situation is at this club."

By this stage other clubs were beginning to sniff around Old Trafford in an effort to land me and use United's misfortunes to their gain. My old team-mate Lou Macari, then manager at

Swindon, enquired about the chances of getting me on loan and was told where to go. So was ambitious Blackburn boss Don Mackay who had already tempted Ossie Ardiles and Steve Archibald to Ewood Park in the days long before Jack Walker's millions and Kenny Dalglish. Nowadays any player would jump at the chance to go to Blackburn but back then they were far from fashionable. However, just to be linked with a loan to the flat cap club was such a relief to me at the time.

There were rumours that Kenny Dalglish tried to sign me for Liverpool. Reporters rang my house on a number of occasions and said they could get no joy from Fergie but there was interest from Liverpool. I'd have loved to have talked to Kenny, and told him that I'd have walked to Anfield to sign for Liverpool. Fergie was saying I wasn't available even though I had asked for a move months earlier, before this row to end all rows.

While all this was going on off the field, on it I was doing my best and making progress again. Six weeks after the showdown I was well and truly back in the team as a fixture after four starts and two appearances as substitute. When I was named in the side to play Bournemouth in the FA Cup on 16 February, Ferguson said: "Paul's fitness is returning and he is being treated like any other player at the club. His performances are better because his fitness is returning and his timing is coming back."

Time was running out though for Ferguson the manager and McGrath the player. Throughout all my troubles Jack Charlton kept faith in me and maintained his stance that he was only interested in what I did for Ireland. In March 1989 I played in midfield for the Republic in a scoreless World Cup draw against Hungary in Budapest when I should have scored only for a great save from a goalkeeper called Peter Dzistil.

On my return to Manchester I remained in favour and chalked up my eighth successive appearance for United against my current side, Aston Villa, in Birmingham. Thankfully Graham Taylor took note of my display that day, in a performance that even pleased Fergie. The United boss said: "McGrath is now right back to his best. Without doubt he is now in excellent form. Paul showed me against Villa that he's definitely on the way back. He's a big lad who needed big games to get back to his peak. His stint in midfield for Ireland certainly helped. Paul was in overdrive at times at Villa and I'm very pleased with the way he has rehabilitated himself."

A month later Ferguson and McGrath were back to their old

ways. I was substituted against Forest and Millwall in a run of ten games in the first team and Ferguson made it clear that Bruce and Donaghy, a £650,000 signing from Luton earlier that season, were his two first choice centre-backs. "They play well together and have a good understanding," he said. I was to finish up with 18 First Division starts and two stints as sub in my final season as a Manchester United player. Behind the scenes though I knew I was on the way out.

As our relationship came nearer and nearer to an end Ferguson made it clear that my future lay elsewhere. It was also obvious to other clubs looking for a centre-half.

French side Lyons began the chase as early as 21 April when their move for Celtic and Ireland captain Mick McCarthy looked set to break down. Lyons looked at me as an alternative in a £500,000 deal but eventually got Big Mick and that was one escape route cut-off. I didn't have to wait long for more options, however.

United were desperate to land a top quality centre-back once Ferguson decided that he wanted rid of his biggest headache – me. They had all but sealed a deal for Swedish captain Glynn Hysen from Italian side Fiorentina in the middle of June that summer and had begun talks to sell me to Trevor Francis at QPR or my old boss Ron Atkinson, just back in the English game from Spain at Sheffield Wednesday. Francis was prepared to pay £600,000. Billy McNeill at Celtic was also interested as his move for Pisa's Englishman Paul Elliott looked set to collapse. I spoke to Celtic at the end of the month but nothing more came of it.

The following month United's fiercest rivals, Manchester City, made a cheeky bid to take me across a city divided by football when the then City chairman Peter Swales confirmed that his manager Mel Machin had indeed spoken to Fergie about me. Ferguson hit back at the interest when he claimed that I was not on the transfer list and had four years of my contract to run. He said he had no plans to let anyone leave Old Trafford at that point in time. I groaned when I read that. The World Cup was waiting at the end of the rainbow that season and I needed first team football to get to Italy with Jack's Army.

But Ferguson still had the knives out. That summer he ordered me to report back for pre-season training four days early despite the fact that I had been involved with World Cup matches for Ireland right into the early days of June. While other international players like Bryan Robson, Mark Hughes, Neil Webb and Brian

McClair enjoyed their last four days off I worked on stamina with the YTS kids. It was the final insult. I was going to leave, come hell or high water. I prayed that the interest from City, Aston Villa or Sheffield Wednesday, as reported in the newspapers, was genuine.

Wednesday boss Ron Atkinson knew me and my problems well enough. But he even wanted twice the trouble – he wanted me in a double deal with Norman Whiteside worth £900,000! Ferguson was only prepared to sell us as a pair for £1.2 million – and didn't really want to send us to the same club anyway.

Thankfully the week I reported back for training was the week that Graham Taylor finally showed his hand in public. He wasn't bothered about reputations or problems. He wanted me for what I was – a first-class footballer who could do a job for him. I was at a barbecue one late summer's night in Bryan Robson's back garden when the phone rang. It was Fergie for me, said Bryan. I picked up the receiver. There was no hello, only "I've given Graham Taylor permission to talk to you. This is his number, the deal is done between the clubs. Goodbye." That was the gist of the conversation. No pleasantries. Just straight down to the business the two of us had waited so long to conduct, the end of a relationship that suited us both perfectly. The minute I spoke to Graham Taylor that night I knew my hell was over.

Ferguson has since gone public on our differences. And he's got one thing right in his book *Six Years at United*, written with the legendary David Meek from the Manchester *Evening News*. He claims very early in the book that he was on a collision course with myself and Norman Whiteside as soon as he arrived at the club. He's right about that – I probably knew even before he arrived that we were just not going to get on at all. I had spoken about him with Gordon Strachan who had been his man at Aberdeen and the omens were not good. From what I could make out Alex was a staunch Scotsman from a different perspective altogether to mine. He was also a strict disciplinarian who did not like his players drinking in public. Ouch.

After Ron Atkinson that was the last thing I needed. As soon as he did arrive in person at the club I knew my worst fears were going to be realised. I played in his opening game away to Oxford at the heart of the midfield – and was fairly quickly substituted by Jesper Olsen. I was not happy with the position and not happy with the new manager. But this was a time to shut up and put up, do the job, enjoy the life off the pitch that playing for United affords you in Manchester, and wait and see.

In fact that first season under Fergie I was to play 38 games in all for United, plus one appearance as substitute – not bad considering all the problems I was having with my knee. It was the following season that we fell out, with a vengeance.

Some of the claims in his book are preposterous. One I even thought was libellous and I did issue a legal letter at the time. That particular claim was reprinted in the *Sun*. Only the advice of my solicitor that a legal case would take years and eat up a lot of my money before a judgement was made, in my favour or not, kept me out of court against Fergie, the *Sun* and the *Evening Herald* in Dublin who repeated the allegations.

Fergie, through David Meek, claims that although he had a kind of sympathy for me it was a quite different relationship to the one he enjoyed with Norman Whiteside. He sensed that I was on a self-destruct course.

Funny then, how I've managed to play on for four years since he threw me out of Old Trafford, played in two World Cup finals with Ireland, been Irish Player of the Year for three years, Villa Player of the Year, the PFA's Player of the Year and the *Daily Star*'s Starfacts Player of the Year for two years running.

He asks in print if I lacked the intelligence to understand what was happening or whether I had gone too far down the road to ruin. He's not sure but he made the claims anyway. That was all I needed – a kick-and-tell manager, as James Lawton described it so eloquently in the *Daily Express* when the book came out.

Alex Ferguson claims the club offered me every facility and advice they could think of. Sir Matt Busby is supposed to have spoken to me along with the club doctor Francis McHugh. I don't recall those alleged conversations. "We even got his parish priest to try and help," says Fergie.

What a load of rubbish. Perhaps, Alex, if we ever speak again, would be good enough to name this parish priest whom he alleges spoke to me. And could he explain why he called a parish priest to sort me out? What could a parish priest do for me?

What Fergie forgets, apart from the name of the priest, is the fact that I am not overly religious – and the fact that I wasn't brought up as a Catholic. I was never christened a Catholic, I was brought up in a Protestant orphanage in Dublin. Parish priests were never the norm in my life apart from Fr Aidan Crowley who worked with me as a security guard while he studied before training to be a priest at Maynooth.

Fergie says the car crash (which I talk about more at the end of this book) that left me in hospital and banned me from driving was the turning point in my United career when I survived and asked for a transfer. He's right about the drinking binges myself and Norman would go on. We'd be in this pub or that pub and all the time somebody would ring Fergie at the club and give him a progress report. I can just imagine him now sitting at his desk with a map of the Greater Manchester area plotting our drinking route, putting down pins wherever we'd been spotted. I'm glad he was keeping note of where we were – usually by the end of the night we wouldn't have a clue if we were in Hale or Altrincham – and we'd care even less.

I've had my bad times and I'm not afraid to admit it. But a lot of my problems stemmed from the fact that I was a Manchester United player living in the goldfish bowl that is Old Trafford. Ever since the glory days of George Best and his headline-making antics off the field it has been difficult for Manchester United players who are in any way out of the ordinary. Best put the club and its players under the spotlight of the news reporters and we've never been able to shake them off since. Some will say George's legacy to the club was the great goals and the great performances. I say it was the womanising and the drinking that put him in the spotlight and caused us all problems years later. Best made stories about United players fashionable and profitable.

Every time I had a drink in a Manchester bar there was somebody waiting to ring the papers. Every time I was spotted out with Kevin or Bryan or Norman there was somebody waiting to ring the gaffer or put it into the gossip columns. If I had been a player with Blackpool or Bury or Bolton nobody would have cared if I was out socialising or womanising or drinking more than my share. I would have been the same as any Joe Soap then and left to my own vices. Even if I had played for most other First Division teams I wouldn't have had as many problems with living in the glare of the spotlight as I did.

The media and the fans think they own the players at United and it does create a lot of tension and a lot of pressure when you're there. If a Manchester United player steps out of line every newspaper reader in England wants to know about it. That is always going to cause problems for their players. It adds to the pressures of a footballer's life in a very unfair and unjust way. The media jump on the United players for the slightest little thing and they don't let go until they've milked it to the full. That's why Alex Ferguson has had to protect Ryan Giggs since his sensational introduction to the English scene. It's why United have been so protective of Lee Sharpe since he first came to the fore.

I made mistakes at United. I know I had real problems coping with the pressures of life at the club. I know what I did off the pitch was wrong from time to time but it was my own doing and it should have been left with me and me alone. Sure there were times when I stepped out of line in terms of socialising and drinking but it was my way of releasing the tension. There are people in every walk of life who react to pressure like that but they don't all get crucified by the media.

I'm not great with crowds at all. I'm not great with handling all the publicity that is part and parcel of being a professional footballer with a big club. My escape valve was to turn around and have a few pints. It gave me the confidence to deal with those situations. Sometimes I went over the top and paid the price. If people concentrated on what you do on the pitch it would be alright. I know what I did off the field was wrong at times but it was my release valve, having a few pints and a bit of a laugh and sometimes getting drunk. That was my way of getting away from it.

I was still a professional despite all my problems. When it came down to games I didn't drink for 48 hours before a match. That was the rule and I stuck to it. I take playing as a professional seriously. I always did – with United, Villa and Ireland.

CHAPTER ELEVEN

Taylor Made

THEY SAID I was stupid the day I walked out of Old Trafford for the last time as a Manchester United player. They said I would never find another club as big as Manchester United. They said I would regret the day I left until the end of life itself. They were wrong on all three counts.

The evening I took that phone call from Alex Ferguson at Bryan Robson's barbecue informing me about Graham Taylor's interest in my services was one of the best evenings of my life.

I was going nowhere fast at Old Trafford. I had been reduced to the level of 'A' team captain in one game, snubbed by the manager as we finished second in the table behind Liverpool the year before, told to report early for pre-season training. The previous 12 months had been sheer hell. I had lost all sight of heaven until that phone-call from Graham Taylor. It was the answer to all my prayers. I needed a clean break. From United and from Alex Ferguson. We were wearing each other out.

The argument suggests I lost out by leaving. That's a point of view – it is not my point of view. I left and Fergie won the title. You could argue I lost out there. I left and went on to win every award imaginable for my performances with Aston Villa and Ireland. You could argue he lost out there.

I will argue till the cows come home that I have been the winner ever since the Sunday evening Graham Taylor told me to get my act into gear and to get to Villa Park fast. It felt good to be wanted again.

Here was a manager who knew his trade inside out. A manager who had transformed Watford from nobodies into a First Division force. A man who had rescued Villa from the brink of relegation and built a side that would finish second in the league within two seasons. A manager who knew his own mind and his own plans for Aston Villa. Most importantly of all, a manager who wanted me.

I couldn't help but be impressed when I first sat down to talk serious business with Graham Taylor. There were no agents involved. Just me, my wife, Graham and his chairman, Doug Ellis. They laid it on the line. They wanted me to be part of their new Aston Villa. They wanted to build a team that could challenge for the title. They felt I was cheap at £450,000 from a United only too willing to get rid of me at any price. They were prepared to take a chance on me – if I was prepared to row in with their plans.

Row in? I'd have swum down the Manchester Ship Canal backwards to push that deal through after those talks. Graham told me he would look after me financially. He did. He gave me far more than Spurs had offered, far more than I was on at United, and I couldn't understand that from a supposedly smaller club. He said not to be greedy, that he would look after me. For the first time in my life a club offered me money that I felt mirrored my talents. That felt good. So did the way they handled it all. If he felt I was missing out in certain areas of the contract he would look after my interests. He did. To this day I do not believe there is a crooked bone in Aston Villa. The manager and the chairman then were first class. Doug is still chairman – and it is well known how highly I regard the current manager.

I had no further dealings with Graham Taylor before I first reported for training at Bodymoor Heath a couple of weeks prior to the start of the 1989-90 season, a World Cup season for me and for Ireland. The medicals were all done and dusted by then and my knees had already been introduced to Villa physio Jim Walker, their best friend ever since. Graham had looked at the results of the medical and admitted that he had seen better knees in a butcher's window. But he wasn't worried about them. If I was prepared to sign for Villa he was prepared to put up with my knees.

Together with Jim Walker he devised the training routine for my knees that left me in the gym most of the week and out on the training pitch for the five-a-sides on a Friday. Graham placed great emphasis on man management. He respected my opinion, he treated me as an adult and that won him so much respect from me. By doing that he rebuilt my own confidence in my knees, in their ability to work at my pace. And he certainly lengthened my career by keeping me away from the heavy training grounds and in the relative comforts of the gym with the exercise bike. The benefits are plain to see. I have yet to play less than 36 games in a season for Aston Villa – I hardly managed a full season once in all my time at Manchester United.

The day Graham Taylor signed me was one of the best days of my footballing career at club level. That includes winning the FA Cup with United, winning the PFA's Player of the Year award or signing on at Old Trafford after my move from Ireland.

The reason I say that is simple. Graham Taylor was prepared to take a chance on me. He was prepared to look me in the eye and level with me the day I signed at Villa Park. He knew I was trouble the minute I walked through the door. My reputation had painted Birmingham red before I even turned off the M6 in search of Villa Park. He ignored that though. He sent me for the medical and when I came back he laid it on the line. He had seen worse knees, he had seen better knees. He knew I was a risk in terms of injury – and he made it clear that he knew all about my reputation. Fergie had tried to sell me and Norman Whiteside as a pair but he wanted only me. He needed a centre-half and he was prepared to take the risk with me.

He was as good as gold that first meeting. He said the rules were rigid at the club in terms of discipline. As long as I abided by them he would do whatever I needed to get me through. He looked after me financially, he doubled the money I was on at Old Trafford and I just thought that was incredible for a club that was supposed to be living in the shadow of Manchester United. Together with Doug Ellis, Graham Taylor made me feel wanted again. I will always be grateful to him for that. And I was a sorry man the day he left Villa by mutual consent to take over England.

I always knew he would succeed Bobby Robson as soon as it became apparent that Robson's career as England boss was over. Graham had done it his way at Watford and brought the club into the big time. He had rescued Villa from obscurity and turned the club around. He had made shrewd signings – he was later to call me the biggest gamble of his life. The risk he took was signing a player with dodgy knees and a dodgy reputation the summer after his club had been lucky to avoid relegation. Had I failed, Graham believes he would have paid the price with his job.

As it was he was out of Villa Park inside a year anyway – to answer his country's call. That one season I worked with him I realised just what a good coach – and a nice man – Graham is. Whatever his problems with England he convinced me I could play on. And he convinced me that we will see him back in management soon. He's too good on the training pitch, working with players, not to be.

I would like to think he feels a sense of pride every time he sees me play now. He can bask in the reflected glory of my career because he saved it.

Any worries I had about leaving a club of *Jurassic Park* proportions behind for the quiet life were soon dispelled. Villa Park has always been one of the great stadiums. When the current work is finished it will be one of the really great stadiums in England. That is a testament to Doug Ellis – and a tribute to the supporters who have staggered me with their loyalty and their passion ever since I arrived from Manchester.

When I left United I left some of the best fans in the world behind me. I found their match in Birmingham. The Villa fans have been brilliant both to me and the team since I came here. They have suffered through two near things in the championship and still they come back. They applaud good football no matter who plays it. And they have really looked after me. Even when I've done stupid things off the field they've stood by me. They welcome me back with open arms. They have a laugh with me about the odd drink or two that's reported in the press. And just lately they've started singing my name to the tune of *Kumbalay My Lord*, and adding "we're not worthy", a lift from *Wayne's World*. I feel I am not worthy of them and their support. Nothing would please me more than to give them a title or a cup before I finally pack up my bags and my boots and head back to Ireland.

I'd also love to win something for Ron Atkinson. I was delighted when he took over from Jo Venglos. Czech import Jo was a great coach but his lack of experience in English football went against him. That can never be said of Ron. He loves good football. He loves good players like Mark Bosnich and Shaun Teale, Steve Staunton, Ray Houghton, Earl Barrett, Andy Townsend, Garry Parker, Sid Cowans, now at Derby, Dean Saunders and Dalian Atkinson. He likes the flair of Dwight Yorke and Steve Froggatt, the experience of Nigel Spink, the promise of Bryan Small, Neil Cox and Ugo Eghiogu. In fact he loves us all at Villa. And so do I.

The thing I really like about Ron though is his attitude to the game. If I'm ever going to win a title it's going to be his way. That is the only way to play.

I've been close twice with Villa – in Graham's last season before he rightly got the England job and again in season 1992-93. Close and yet so far. The story of my personal championship crusade.

Failure in the 1992-93 season had a lot to do with belief. I don't think that we fell away at the end – or that United were that much better at that stage than we were. It had a lot to do with belief – you either believe you're going to do something or you don't. If you don't then you're never going to achieve anything. I honestly think that's what happened to us that year, similar to what happened to us in Graham Taylor's last year in charge. There were too many young players who didn't understand what winning was all about. They didn't have the hunger or the experience that comes with winning prizes and they just went when the chips were down.

I've thrown a league winner's medal away three times now. Once with United and twice with Villa. I wonder now if I will ever see one. At United we lost the title to a Liverpool side that was probably the best in Europe. At Villa in my first season we gave it to a Liverpool side that was probably the best in Europe. Then in 1993 we gave it to a United side that was the best in England but which then flopped in Europe.

I didn't understand losing it the first time with United or Villa and that made it a bigger disappointment for me in 1993. I realised just how close I was to the ultimate prize as a club professional. So close and yet so far. I may never get that close again.

It was similar to Villa getting knocked out of the UEFA Cup the following season. I know I don't have too many chances of ever being there again. It's the same with the league, it's the same with the cups. I try to give it my all. I did the Wednesday night we got knocked out by the Spaniards in the UEFA Cup. That was more of a blow to me because I understand that I won't get the chance next year or the year after. If I was 23 I wouldn't be so worried. I'd think if we came second that we'll be back there again. I probably thought that when we played Juventus with United in the Cup Winners' Cup in 1986 but it doesn't happen like that. Sometimes you have to lose first before you can win. United had lost the league the previous season before they won it in 1993. I hope Villa have learned from it.

But I honestly don't think that I'll be around sampling football at the top for too much longer. I keep saying that year after year when we've lost in this, we've lost in that, we've got beaten here or there. Leagues and cups and things like that are running out for me. I'm getting older and older. I'm 34 now and I'm not going to have that many more chances. That's a fact of life. Not fiction.

Soon after I joined Villa I had a right go back at Fergie in the *News of the World* and it landed me in all sorts of trouble. He was getting knocked by all sorts of former players at the time and I was just the latest to hop on the bandwagon. Only I had very good reason to have a go at him.

Martin Leech interviewed me for the article and it was very relaxed. We talked over a couple of bottles of champagne and I got it all off my chest. What came out was the truth. I probably wouldn't have said what I said so strongly if I had been drinking Coke but it was what I felt at the time about him and how I still feel now.

I expected United to have a bit of a whinge but I was amazed at the outcry led by Martin Edwards. He was insulted that anyone should speak about his beloved Fergie like that and on United's insistence I got hauled before the FA, charged with bringing the game into disrepute. Apparently United gave the Lancaster Gate officials an ultimatum. If the authorities didn't take action against me they would sue me for slander against Fergie. Touchy, to say the least.

The thing that really upset them apparently was my suggestion that Fergie should lighten up and relax, have a drink and learn how to enjoy himself. United got their way, the FA threw the book at me. I was fined £8,500 and found guilty of bringing the game into disrepute. It was a record fine at the time – I think my old friend Vinny Jones has surpassed it since for his hard man video.

I was sick. The newspaper ran a poll and the supporters came out in favour of me. I thought I couldn't have said anything that badly about him. If he did like a drink – and I suggested he didn't – I would have gladly given him £200 to go and buy a few good bottles of Scotch. Instead I got rapped across the knuckles by the FA and fined £8,500.

CHAPTER TWELVE

Ciao Italia

QUE SERA SERA – We're going to Italy.

Every Irish man, woman and child will remember that song, a song that echoed from a few brave Irish fans at ticketless Belfast in September 1988, the glorious aftermath of the European Championship campaign, all the way through to the majestic Olympic Stadium in Rome and the end of an odyssey that had seen us fulfil that song's dream.

Euro '88 was only the start as far as the team that Jack built was concerned. It was only the stepping-stone to greater things as we prepared for a World Cup qualifying series that threw us in with Northern Ireland, Spain, Hungary and Malta.

When the Irish squad gathered in Dublin in the September following those Euro finals I was confident about playing in a World Cup finals for the first time. My knees had acted up after Germany and I went under the knife once more but I was back with a vengeance at Old Trafford – and attracting interest from outside Manchester. That interest came from Terry Venables and Spurs, encouraged by my Dublin mate Krish Naidoo, a fanatical Tottenham supporter.

By the time we got back together in September 1988 for the potentially tricky trip to Belfast and the opening qualifier Terry was ready to make his move. We reported as usual on the Sunday night, when I received a phone-call from Terry asking if I was interested in a move to White Hart Lane. He had spoken to Alex Ferguson –

the United boss was delighted at the prospect of getting rid of me and had agreed a deal worth £600,000 with Tel, then rebuilding his Spurs side after his return from Spain and Barcelona.

The move appealed to me. Venables was the best coach in England. Spurs were a huge club. I was having trouble at United with Fergie and trouble at home with Claire. She had left me at that stage. A move seemed a good idea.

It was agreed that I could leave the Irish camp on the Monday and fly to London for the day, for talks and a medical. I crept out the next morning – it took the press about 12 hours to catch up with the fact that I was absent, this time with permission.

Terry was everything I thought he would be. He looked after me financially in the deal, he impressed me with his plans for the club, his ideas on the game. The doctors, however, didn't like the look of my knees. One specialist suggested I had two years left at most. Terry, though, was happy to take that chance. He wanted me and I wanted to play for him.

It seemed everything was in order for me to go back to Dublin to join up with the Irish squad and move to Spurs the day after the game in Belfast. I played at Windsor Park and we drew 0-0. We should have won. Tony Cascarino had one effort taken off the line by their 'keeper Allen Knight that I was convinced was a goal. The linesman and the referee judged otherwise. Still, a point was a good result in Belfast and we were on our way.

I returned to London on the Thursday ready to sign for Terry Venables. Then the deal collapsed. Claire came home and decided she didn't want to move to London. She was ready to give our marriage another chance so long as we stayed in Manchester.

It is one of the great regrets of my life that I didn't sign for Terry Venables that day. I know he wanted to work with me and I really believe my career would have benefited from working with him. I should have followed my instincts and moved to Spurs but I didn't.

Money was a problem as well. Not from the Spurs end, from my own. I had two agents working for me and they wanted a 20 per cent cut of everything I earned on a five-year contract at Spurs. Between them and the taxman it just wasn't worth it. I had to turn Terry down – and give those agents £1,500 cash just to get them off my back. They were ringing me at all hours of the day and night, trying to sell me to Switzerland, to English clubs, anywhere, just to get more money. They wanted £5,000 to end a contract I had never signed. I just gave them that £1,500 to get them off my back; it was expensive but it was worth it.

By the time Ireland played in Spain that November, when Steve Staunton made his debut, I was back on the treatment table and there followed my real problems with Fergie. The one thing that kept me going through all of that was Jack Charlton's loyalty. He never forgot me or worried about what was happening at Old Trafford. He even sent Maurice Setters along to a couple of reserve matches to have a look at me. That meant so much.

In March 1989 I put those worries to the back of my mind for the scoreless draw against Hungary in Budapest. We had a huge travelling support with us. Many fans had gone out early to watch Marcus O'Sullivan hit gold at the world indoor athletic championships on the Sunday. Poor Marcus couldn't understand where all the tricolours had come from at the indoor arena when he picked up the 1500-metre gold medal. We should have won in Budapest as well. I was denied a goal only by a brilliant save from their 'keeper, one of two Dzistil brothers.

That April we humbled the Spanish in Dublin, thanks to a goal credited to their midfielder Michel but given in my mind anyway to Frank Stapleton. We were on our way. A packed house against Malta and Hungary six weeks later for two great wins, and a Paul McGrath goal, convinced the Irish public we were going to Italy.

They were right. The following season I was given a new lease of life by Graham Taylor at Aston Villa and Ireland benefited. We hammered Northern Ireland 3-0 in Dublin then off we went to Malta in November for the game that put us through.

The fans emigrated again. We left on the Monday after I had picked up the inaugural Opel award as Ireland's international "Player of the Year", a great honour which I won the following year as well. We left more in confidence than hope before the fog which descended on Dublin and caused so many fans travel problems. Some even arrived at the ground on the Wednesday at half-time, with their suitcases under their arms. They were happy though.

A win that afternoon in Valetta and we were definitely there. The sun-kissed island in the Mediterranean had never seen anything like it. Malta became Irish. The fans travelled out in their thousands – there were 20,000 people at the game and it seemed as if they were all Irish. They had a ball. When one of the planes came into the gate at Valetta Airport there was a black guy taking

the luggage off. ' Ooh Aah Paul McGra
McGrath," sang the fans.

There were stories about collections for I
English planes who couldn't believe the good
fans. Stories like the one about the captain on
the passengers not to put their eye on the bl
because she was his.

The party atmosphere carried itself on
Ta'Quali stadium. I played right-back, John .... scored two
great goals and we were there – we had qualified for the World Cup
finals, the first Republic team to do so.

The party that night was unbelievable. The lads had a drink
together in the Hilton Hotel to celebrate then we hit the town in St
Julian's Bay. Jack Charlton sang *Dublin in the Rare Auld Times* for
a group of the supporters in a pub just beside the hotel which we
took over for the night. The team, the press and the fans made
tracks for Styx, the best nightclub on the island of Malta. I was no
stranger to the club. I had been there on a United visit just years
earlier with Norman Whiteside – and we nearly missed our plane
home the next morning. We were fined then of course but this was
a night now with Ireland, not to worry about fines or clubs or
anything else. It was a night to celebrate with the Irish fans.

That's exactly what we did. Sporadically the huge crowd in the
club – it seemed like five thousand Irish fans had gathered there –
would burst into another chorus of "Ooh Aah Paul McGrath". I
was embarrassed but so proud. I was on my way to the World Cup
finals. A year after Alex Ferguson and Manchester United had
offered me an insurance pay-out to quit the game I was going to
Italy.

The draw did us no favours that December. We were thrown
in with England and Holland again, with the unknown quantity of
Egypt to worry about. We were also sent to the islands of Sardinia
and Sicily. I felt sorry for the fans. This was not what we expected
the World Cup finals to be. But at least we were there. And I had
something to be happy about again.

My first season at Villa couldn't have gone better. We lost the
league to Liverpool at the final hurdle but the prospect of a World
Cup finals helped ease me over that disappointment. Before I left
to join the Irish squad that summer Graham Taylor called me into
his office. He told me I had been a great buy for Villa, that I had
justified his faith in me. He told me I could be the greatest player

World Cup stage if I believed in myself, that there was an opportunity there waiting to be grabbed. He told me to be proud and committed for Jack Charlton. And to get Ireland on to that World map. Did I not like the sound of that? Of course I liked it.

I took note of what Graham had said. I also knew this was my chance to show the footballing world just what I could do. International football has always been a terrific challenge for me. It is so different to club football. Speed of thought and movement is everything. Central midfield was also a different challenge then. It was my forte under Jack at that stage of my Irish career and I knew going to Italy how important it was to the Irish team. My performances alongside Andy Townsend were going to be crucial to our hopes of progressing beyond the first stage.

I had a gut feeling about that World Cup. A feeling that it was going to be a great tournament for Ireland and for me personally. I prepared so seriously before the squad had even gathered for the trip to play Turkey in Izmir and then on to Malta. I gave up the drink. I watched what I ate. I left the Dublin nightclubs alone, staying instead with Frank Mullen out in Dalkey and getting myself right mentally and physically for the challenge to come.

I played against the Turks in Izmir in what can only be described as a greenhouse. The weather was incredible, the temperatures over the hundred. There was no air, no oxygen. I had never experienced anything like it. I just couldn't breathe. Jack had taken this game to give us an idea of the humidity in Italy. Surely it couldn't be that bad.

Then we were off to Malta for a training camp. We took a curious route. Instead of going direct, about an hour by plane, we flew via Istanbul and Rome. A one-hour journey became 12 hours before we checked in at our Maltese hotel.

Our last visit there had ended with a carnival. This was no party. Malta acclimatised to the Irish instead of the other way around – the weather was dreadful. The sun took a holiday, the rain arrived, all the way from Ireland just to make us feel at home.

We got a good laugh out of that rain. And out of the day we got on the team coach, a school bus, and somebody spilt a bottle of Ballygowan water at the back. The driver thought somebody had done something else to wet his floor – and kicked up murder. That gave us all a laugh.

Jack and Maurice worked us hard – it was like pre-season training all over again. I hate training at the best of times. This time

I made allowances. I wanted the ball all the time. I wanted to work, to build up a sweat, to get myself right for the World Cup opener against Bryan Robson and England.

Every day we worked hard. It was a shock to the system for players who were used to Jack winding us down rather than up before games in Dublin. We had all finished long and hard seasons with our clubs. This was different though – this was a World Cup finals.

I counted down, day by day. I remember sitting with Kevin Moran in our hotel room in Malta one night and remarking that there were only seven days left before the opener against England. The seven days flew. We moved to a brilliant hotel in Sardinia, the Is Molas. England had used it for their training camp before moving to a sister hotel in the Forte village. It had its own beach, top-class facilities – and an armed police cordon around it. This was the real World Cup. As soon as we landed on Italian soil we were the focus of attention. Even the team bus was a different class with leather seats and the height of luxury. This was what it was all about.

England were our first opponents in the Group of Death on those Italian islands. It added spice to the event even though everyone thought about the *déjà vu*, about familiarity breeding contempt for our World Cup opener. It was never going to be a classic World Cup game, more a traditional English league derby. The purists expected too much from the fixture. We had beaten them in Germany. They owed us one for that. We knew them inside out. They knew us outside in.

I was a little nervous before that game as the heavens opened in Cagliari. The tension in the air was as charged as the atmosphere while the rain and the lightning swept down on a stadium packed with Irish and English fans and a few thousand bemused Italians.

This game was our World Cup. Irish fans were looking no further than that opening match. They wanted another Stuttgart, another kick in the teeth for the nation that had given the game of association football to Ireland and the world. This was our World Cup final as far as Jack's Green Army were concerned. We knew victory against Egypt and Holland would mean nothing if we lost to England. That explained the nerves in the hotel the morning of the match when Jack named his side. I waited for my name and I heard it. That was all that mattered to me. Ten seconds after Jack had named the side I couldn't have told you who else was going to play.

Before the game Jack told me to play my normal midfield role for Ireland, to act as a spoiler in front of the back four and to cover for Mick or Kevin if they were drawn out of position. It was a role I was accustomed to by that stage. A role I was beginning to enjoy even. It also brought me into confrontation with Bryan Robson again – and with Paul Gascoigne.

That was to be Gazza's World Cup for England. But there was to be little evidence that first night in Cagliari. The weather ruined the pitch and the early goal scored by Gary Lineker threatened to ruin our night and our World Cup. I'm still convinced that the ball had crossed the touchline before Chris Waddle whipped it across for Lineker to score so early. Steve Staunton was adamant at half-time that it had crossed the line. But the goal stood and we were fighting an uphill battle. It was time to roll the sleeves up again. That's exactly what we did.

We got stuck in for the second half. And then came a wonderful equaliser from that sweet left foot of Kevin Sheedy's. He gave the ball away to Steve McMahon on the edge of the box, robbed it back off McMahon and let fly. Peter Shilton had hardly moved by the time it hit the back of the net. We had saved the point and the World Cup as far as our fans were concerned.

To draw with England was as good as a moral victory. That night we celebrated, not as loudly as we had done in Germany two years earlier, but there were celebrations nonetheless. Some of the wives, including Claire, stayed at the hotel and Jack wasn't happy. He was right of course. He had laid down the ground rules before we went to Italy and they stipulated that the hotel was off limits to the wives. He gave us a ticking off. There was even a threat of disciplinary action. But it was all forgotten about the next day as we made our way from Sardinia to Sicily through the crowds of Irish fans at Cagliari Airport, all celebrating their moral win and acclaiming Kevin Sheedy, the new recipient of "Who put the ball in the English net?"

Palermo was back to basics, modest rather than conservative. The hotel was primitive. The rooms were tiny. Some of the lads were expected to sleep in camp beds. Imagine the length of Niall Quinn in a camp bed. These were the side issues though; the main topic of conversation was the next match against Egypt. We watched them play like Brazilians against Holland the night of our arrival. They drew thanks to a penalty from an impressive midfielder called Abdel Ghani.

Holland looked disjointed but the Egyptians looked good in that game because they wanted to play football. When they came to play Ireland in Palermo, though, the Egyptians just put 11 mummies behind the ball and refused to make a game of it. We were frustrated. We could find no way past a side that didn't want to know about a game. It takes two to tango and two to make a match.

Their sweeper Ramzy had a great game. He was there when we got forward. Fortune saved them when he was beaten and Steve Staunton, Ray Houghton and Tony Cascarino got close to scoring. Apart from one surge forward stopped by a brilliant tackle from Kevin Moran they never looked remotely interested in crossing the halfway line.

It was probably inevitable then that the game finished scoreless. Jack slaughtered the Egyptians at the press conference for their negative attitude. He was right. We were slaughtered by elements of the media at home. That was unfair. The fans were as frustrated as we were but it was wrong to suggest we lacked commitment or ideas. Of course we wanted to win it. Of course we tried to win. Things don't always work out as you want.

The fans at least stood by us. They were everywhere that week, wishing us well before the last group game.

And so we entered the final match against Holland knowing that the time had come to produce a result and a valiant performance worthy of the World Cup final itself. Jack made one change against the Dutch – big Niall Quinn came in for my Villa team-mate Tony Cascarino. It was a godsend from Saint Jack!

The Dutch, suspect as they were at the time, got off to a great start after ten minutes when Ruud Gullit scored one of his great goals. We had given away possession and a free-kick just inside our own half. The Dutch reacted with lightning speed, Gullit played a one-two with Wim Kieft and the ball was in the net. I was heartbroken as I was about an inch away from stopping him.

Disaster was on the cards until Niall took the chance he had been waiting so long for. Five years earlier an Irish team in that position would have thrown the towel in. Jack's arrival had changed all that. We replied to Gullit's shock with the determination of a team fighting for survival. For the next 60 minutes we produced one of the best away performances ever seen from an Irish team. We hit Holland where it hurt, fired on by those green, white and orange clad fans on the terraces who left the Dutch fans trailing in their wake.

Then we got the goal. Packie Bonner hoofed it forward, the defender made a mistake in his effort to get the ball back to Hans Van Breuckelen and Niall steered the ball inside the 'keeper and the post. That was the goal of his career. I don't care what else he has done, he could not have matched that one for value and for timing. Not even when he scored against England at Wembley.

The goal was enough. We all but came to a gentlemen's agreement to give up the ghost of victory with the Dutch when we heard England were one up against Egypt. We effectively stopped playing. There was no danger of another goal from either side after that effort from the Mighty Quinn. The game died. When the referee blew the final whistle we were through and the Dutch and English were with us. Elation once again. The Group of Death had ended with all three teams through to the second phase. Now the World Cup could begin in earnest for the Irish. The Italian mainland was beckoning.

Lots were drawn to decide who went where. The Dutch got the Germans and went out in the second phase in Milan when Voeller and Rijkaard were sent off. Ireland drew Rumania, a side we had played only once before in a Dublin friendly before the European finals. We had won that one 2-0 but we knew the Rumanians were a different side in competitive football. They had a guy called Gheorge Hagi in their side – and a certain Daniel Timofte, now a household name in Ireland.

At last we were off the islands and on to the mainland. Welcome to the real World Cup. We knew as much when we flew to Genoa and checked into the splendour of the Grand Hotel Bristol. Now this was luxury. Rooms big enough to swing a leopard in compared to the cats' quarters on offer in Palermo. Food fit for a king. Just looking at the spread in the dining-room put weight on – and caused Eddie Corcoran and Mick Byrne to have heart attacks about our waistlines. A freshwater swimming pool to relax by. Oh – and there was the small matter of a World Cup quarter-final place waiting for the winners of the match against Rumania.

That quarter-final was likely to be against Italy in Rome. And we had promised our physio and the players' best friend Mick Byrne all along that we would fulfil his lifetime's ambition and get him to Rome to meet the Pope. Mick was on about it all the time in Genoa – we dared not let him down. We didn't.

The game in Genoa, on a pitch once graced by Liam Brady with Sampdoria, was nail-biting. Hagi was flashing shots in from all angles but Packie Bonner was equal to anything he could produce. At the other end Kevin Sheedy and Tony Cascarino were having a party all of their own – without the ball obliging with the goal we needed. Some 90 minutes failed to produce a winner or a goal and we drifted into half an hour of extra-time. Again no winner and no goal. The dreaded penalty shoot-out beckoned.

I'm terrible at penalties. I'd lost a fortune to Niall Quinn at the training camp in Malta when he gave us three penalties for a fiver. If he saved one you lost the fiver – I lost count of how much I owed him fairly quickly. So when David O'Leary was looking for volunteers I went missing.

Penalty shoot-outs had not entered our way of thinking going into that match. There was no plan of action. David just took it on himself to get them organised and what a job he did. He even offered to take the final kick, a hell of a responsibility for any player, particularly for one who had never been noted as a penalty-taker.

The Rumanians went first. They scored their first four past Packie. He was close a couple of times but not close enough. I don't remember the order but I remember Ray Houghton, Tony Cascarino, Andy Townsend and Kevin Sheedy. Four Irish penalties. Four goals.

The Rumanians sent Timofte up to take number five. I couldn't watch. I turned away and watched the Irish fans behind me. I focused on one face. I knew Timofte was about to shoot. The guy with the green jersey had my World Cup dream resting on his facial expression.

Timofte shot. A twist. A smile. A jump for joy. A face contorted with ecstasy. The guy went mad. He jumped around like a lunatic. Packie had saved it. One more kick of the ball and we were Rome and dry. Step up David O'Leary. He shot. He scored. We all got pissed on emotion. We were in the quarter-finals of the World Cup. Ireland! The Republic of Ireland were off to meet the Pope and that Sicilian hitman called Toto Schillacci.

It was too good to be true. I was waiting for a linesman to order the penalty to be re-taken, for the referee to wake me up from a dream. He didn't. It was true. We were in the last eight. We just swamped David O'Leary on that penalty spot. He was the hero. Packie was the hero. We were all heroes. Jack was a god. And Mick Byrne was off to meet the Pope.

We let our hair down in moderation in Rapello that night. Next morning we were off to Rome. The Irish had arrived. When we landed in the Eternal City I declared Eternal Love for Jack Charlton. I wanted to kiss the ground – just like the Pope.

Because we were playing the Italians in their own backyard, the Christians from Ireland about to face the lions in the blue shirts, we were the centre of attention. Tony Cascarino was besieged by Italian press, radio and television. Because of his Italian ancestry the "Ice-Cream Man" as Jack calls him became a celebrity before that game.

They're quite clever over there – they employ some very pretty women in the media. You can tell a male press man to get lost. It's not as easy to tell a pretty girl to go away when she asks for a quote or two. Tony became a media darling. And we wound him up something rotten. We told him to tell the cameras that they should have employed Irish builders to build the Colosseum, that McInerney's, the builders at home, would bring some Paddies over to finish it off if the money was good.

We had a laugh at our own expense. And we had a good laugh at the team hotel some 30 miles outside the city near the village of Frascati where the wine is produced. The rooms in the hotel were a joke. Kevin and myself were given a broom cupboard – the two of us couldn't turn in the room. Jack kicked up murder. The FAI officials were thrown out of the hotel and we were given a room each. That was better. Spirits were up. They were raised further when news came through that the Pope would see us in St Peter's. Mick Byrne's lifetime ambition was about to come through.

That was a great occasion. We met the Pope and he talked about football with Charlie O'Leary, with Mick Byrne and then with Packie Bonner, two goalkeepers together. How could we lose to the Italians in the battle of the Catholic nations with God on our side?

By now all of Ireland wanted to see this match. More fellows went sick off work, borrowed money for new cars off the banks and the Credit Unions just to be there. They chartered every plane left in Europe to enable the Irish fans to make their Italian Connection. There was a great story when they were on their way home. There was no such thing as boarding cards at the charter airport in Rome – they just put the first hundred on to the first plane, the second hundred on to the second plane and so on.

Those fans had trouble enough getting there. They also had problems getting tickets. We knew that all along. We knew how much they inspired us in Italy and wanted them with us in the Olympic Stadium. I still don't know how the FAI managed it but there must have been 25,000 Irish fans in the stadium that night. And even at that they were drowned out by the Italians.

I knew we had really arrived on the world stage when we trained at the Olympic Stadium less than 36 hours before kick-off. We were in the big time now. I had played at Wembley and loved it but there was a feeling of shock when I looked up into those empty stands in Rome and realised they were going to be full the following night, full of Italians looking for blood and Irish fans looking for a semi-final place. It was a daunting task ahead of us. But a task we were confident about. We knew the Italians were suspect to our type of pressure. We knew they feared the way we worked as a team.

They had big names in their team. Walter Zenga the goalkeeper who's afraid of the light but little else. Franco Baresi, my idol, the best sweeper in the world and an inspiration to me as a defender. I'd be happy to lace his drinks never mind his boots. Giannini, Donnadoni, Baggio, Vialli and Schillacci. Great names, great players.

Jack had us up and pumping before the game. Why should we fear them? We had a great track record on big occasions. We had survived Stuttgart and Hanover in the Euro finals. We had come through against England and Holland in Italy. What could the Italians do to us that the likes of England and Russia had failed to do?

We were determined and confident. When we stood in the tunnel in the Olympic Stadium our captain Mick McCarthy shouted at them with a message for us. "Look at them – look at the fear in their eyes!" he screamed to inspire us and frighten the Italians. He was right. They were as afraid of us as we were of them.

They had a look of fear – but they also had the ice-cool hero called Toto Schillacci in their ranks. He turned out to be the difference between the sides.

There was a lump in my throat when we turned away from the dignitaries to face the Irish flag for the national anthem. FIFA hadn't liked that in the earlier games and threatened to fine us for not obeying protocol. Sod protocol. We were respecting our flag and our anthem. We were proud to be Irish. And we gave the Irish a team to be proud of that night.

We settled into the game very quickly. We even had the audacity to go close to a goal when I crossed, Niall Quinn met it with a perfect header and the great Zenga somehow pulled it out of the night sky. You don't get too many chances against a side like Italy in their own backyard. If that had gone in we were made, just like Northern Ireland when Gerry Armstrong scored against hosts Spain and put them out of the 1982 World Cup finals.

My worst fears were realised in the 37th minute. We lost possession near halfway and Giannini came at us like an express train. He released Donnadoni whose screaming shot could only be parried by Packie on our line. Schillacci needed no second invitation. He reacted with the speed of Carl Lewis, got there ahead of me as I made a despairing lunge and buried it off the angle. I nearly stopped him just as I had nearly stopped Gullit scoring in Palermo. Nearly, though, wasn't enough. The Italians took the lead and the stadium went berserk.

Now the Latins were in their element. They dictated the pace. Before the goal Baresi was nervous, a sign that we had 'em under pressure. After the goal he strolled around at the back with the proverbial cigar in his mouth. We had a John Aldridge goal disallowed. He had another half-chance that went just wide. All the time the home crowd were singing their side to victory. Our fans were singing, drowned out incessantly by the sheer volume of the Italians in both numbers and noise.

We gave it our best shot and our best shot was almost good enough. Now we were out. Not in disgrace but out in a strange kind of glory. We had gone to the Republic's first World Cup as underdogs and ended it as beaten quarter-finalists, victims at the hands of that Sicilian assassin called Schillacci. We held our heads high as we left that Olympic arena in Rome. We had been mauled by the Lions of Italy and we were still standing.

That night the pressure valve of the previous six weeks blew in the team hotel. Guinness sent us out two barrels of their black beauty – we rolled out the barrel. Chris de Burgh sang *Lady in Red*. Jack Charlton sang *Dublin City Ramblers*. I sang Smokey Robinson and looked forward to a return home, back to the Ireland of a hundred thousand welcomes for this soccer team.

Nelson Mandela got to Dublin before us that day – and he couldn't believe the welcome he received. He honestly thought the million people lining the streets were there to welcome him and greet him after his release from prison. He thought they were all out on the streets to witness the presentation of the freedom of the city of Dublin to one of my heroes. Nobody had the heart to tell him otherwise but I think he found out fairly quickly that it was us they were waiting for. When the crowd sang "Ooh Aah Paul McGrath – That's Paul McGrath's Da' " in his direction they just might have let the cat out of the bag.

We arrived a few hours later after a raucous flight from Rome. We got that *Cead Mile Failte*, the hundred thousand welcomes. And more. Ten times more. A million people lined the streets of Dublin for our sort of homecoming. A homecoming in triumph. You'd swear we had won the World Cup, such was the reception.

Being Irish we had, of course, won the World Cup. We should have beaten the Italians. And they were beaten by a poor Argentina side. And *they* were beaten by an Andreas Brehme penalty in the final by West Germany. So idealistically we were the world champions.

We were champions alright that Sunday afternoon in Dublin. Champions to a man as the people of Ireland lined the route from Dublin Airport all the way into College Green. "Ooh Aah Paul McGrath" rang out all the way in.

Home were the heroes. I was crowned RTE Television's "Player of the World Cup", a great honour in itself. I picked up the Opel "International Player of the Year" award again for that World Cup. In College Green Jack publicly vowed to win the World Cup in America. So did I privately. I could smell the World Cup final the night we played the Italians in Rome. I could smell America already.

Miracles do happen – just remember Italy 1990.

CHAPTER THIRTEEN

Où est Paul McGrath?

I LOOKED in the mirror and I wanted to die. Here I was, distraught and hungover, deep in the bowels of the Dublin International Airport Hotel. My team, the Republic of Ireland, were playing Turkey some 12 miles away at Lansdowne Road in a European Championship qualifier.

This time I had gone overboard. I had disgraced myself. I had let my family down. I had betrayed Jack Charlton. I had put alcohol before the Irish team for the first time in my life and I knew I had done wrong. Drink was the root of my evils once again, only this time I had gone too far. I had missed my check-in time with the Irish team, I missed the training session on the Monday before the match with Turkey – I missed the game itself all because of a stupid alcoholic binge.

Life was a problem for me again that October, just three months after I had experienced the greatest sporting moments of all my living days at the World Cup finals. In that short space of time I had gone from a national hero to a national disgrace, all because of my knees and the mental anguish they cause me every time they hurt so bad that I can't play. It had all been so different the previous June when I tripped the light fantastic with the Irish team, danced with the 20,000 fans who followed us all over Italy and celebrated with the millions back at home who shared in every glorious moment.

Two years after Alex Ferguson told me I'd never play for him again I had marked some of the greatest players in the world at a

World Cup finals. Two years after United wanted me to quit I had played out of my skin on the biggest stage of all. Two years after I was rejected and betrayed by United I was one of 22 Irish heroes, wanted and loved by my own people like never before.

It was the sweetest summer that any of us had ever experienced. I thought I had made it now, that nothing could go wrong for Paul McGrath of Ireland and Aston Villa. I was never as far from the truth. The summer was short after the glories of the World Cup and I was soon back to work with Villa after the briefest of family holidays. I'd been over in Ireland while I was off and I had revelled in the glory of the World Cup.

Suddenly what we had achieved out in Italy came home to me. I came to realise just what a team of footballers had done for the Irish people and the Irish nation. We had unified the country, we had brought the people together like never before. For once Ireland was making the headlines all across the world for the right reasons. There was no carnage, no guns fired, no bombings, just hundreds of thousands of people out having a good time and celebrating the feats of their soccer team. They were still celebrating when I went home that summer and eventually those celebrations were to cause me the biggest problem I've faced since I became a professional footballer with Manchester United.

For the first time in my life everybody in Ireland wanted to know me, they wanted to share me, they wanted me to be a part of their family. I was wanted, I was loved by a nation and everywhere I went those people felt a need to show me their love and share their lives with me for a few minutes, a few hours or a few days.

The big problem though was the way they wanted to welcome me home and thank me and the rest of the lads for what we had achieved out in the World Cup. The most usual way of showing their appreciation was also the most lethal as far as I was concerned, not that I realised it at the time. Everywhere I went they wanted to buy me a drink. In the pubs, in the hotels, in the discotheques they'd come over with a pint of Guinness or a short and say, "Thanks Paul" or "Well done – this is for what you did in Italy."

I was so wrapped up in it that I didn't see what was happening. I played along with the fans because I was so happy to be wanted and loved. I drank the drink they put in front of me. I sang the songs with them. I shared the craic. I enjoyed being a part of their lives even if it was only momentary. They didn't know that the drink they were buying me was doing me damage. They didn't realise that the pints of plain – as we call Guinness at home – were going to threaten my international career in the space of three months. They didn't know and I didn't care.

I didn't care because I was having a good time, I was a hero and I was living up to it and exploiting it every single minute I was in Ireland. When I went back to Villa for pre-season training I was so high I could have flown to Birmingham on my own without the aid of a plane. I'd had a great World Cup, I was a hero back home and Villa were looking forward to the challenge of bettering our second spot in the league the previous season.

Everything was set up for me. I was as fit as a fiddle after the World Cup, I was ready to battle for the First Division title again, ready to show Jozef Venglos, our new boss, that I was a part of the future for Aston Villa. But life is never as easy as that, particularly when you're a professional footballer, and slowly things started to go wrong. We lost matches at the start of the season, our league form was a disaster, we had trouble understanding the new gaffer.

I went to Dublin for the friendly against Morocco that September and Jack decided to rest me. Then the knee started acting up again. All the highs were rapidly disappearing. The final straw came at Barnsley the week before the international against Turkey in Dublin. My troubles began that Tuesday night of the week before the game against Turkey. I had told the gaffer Josef Venglos that I wanted to miss the match because my knees were sore. For the first time since the World Cup finals I was feeling some discomfort in my right knee and it was beginning to worry me. I skipped training on the Monday and when I reported for action on the Tuesday I explained that my knees weren't up to it and that I wasn't fit to play.

The coaches didn't believe me, they made me do a fitness test on the pitch before the game and even though I protested that I wasn't ready for action they told me I was alright, that I would have to play against Barnsley for the sake of the team. I played in that match under protest and afterwards the knees felt awful. They were swollen the next morning and suddenly all my old fears about my future, about my career prospects, came flooding back. I was depressed after that match, worried that I wouldn't be fit for the international the following Wednesday in Dublin, a game that meant so much to us and the fans after the success of the World Cup finals. My fears prompted a reaction that was to change the course of my life – I went on a binge, a binge that was to bring me to grips with my problem. A binge that would prove to be a turning point in the life of Paul McGrath – footballer.

The binge that threatened my career was ultimately the best thing that ever happened to me – but it took me an awful long time to realise that. Villa had no game that weekend because there was a blank fixture list in England in the build-up to the European Championship games. That meant I was free on the Wednesday and I turned to the only comfort I knew in times of worry – alcohol. It started with a small-time session in Birmingham. By the time I reached Dublin on the Friday I was ready for more alcohol – a lot more in fact.

And here I was the following Wednesday afternoon staring blankly into a mirror, recovering from the binge of a lifetime. In no state mentally or physically to do what I do best. In no state to play football for my country.

It was the imperfect end to an imperfect week. I had a problem. I was in trouble. I was crying out for freedom.

It was no more than was to be expected after seven drunken nights. Seven days of rumour and counter-rumour. Espionage and intrigue. A James Bond movie perhaps? No, just another week in the life of Paul McGrath.

Cast your mind back to October of 1992. Where were you the day Paul McGrath went missing? I don't know – I still find it hard to remember. The day or the week or the realisation that I had indeed got a drink problem. I couldn't get enough of it that week.

Apparently it goes something like this.

The rumour factory in Dublin was working overtime as an outbreak of innuendo greeted the news that Paul McGrath had gone missing and had failed to report to the Irish team headquarters at the Dublin International Airport Hotel just three days before the European Championships opener against Turkey at Lansdowne Road.

Officially Irish boss Jack Charlton was saying little, telling the assembled press that I had been given the day off, that my mother wasn't well and that I had gone home to see her. He covered up for me, said I had only arrived in Dublin that morning and was whisked off straight away to Crumlin to see my mother. Jack, protective of me as ever, was calm and collected when he first broke the news of my non-appearance at a lunchtime press briefing before the assembled Irish team went off to train that Monday afternoon.

It wasn't the first time I had failed to arrive on time. Chances are the doors would open and I'd pop my head around rather sheepishly any minute now. Besides he had other problems to worry about before the first competitive game in the wake of Italia '90. He was more worried about the injuries to Ronnie Whelan, Chris Morris and Kevin Sheedy than he was about the current whereabouts of one Paul McGrath. The journalists were suspicious, however. Word had filtered over from England that I was back on the booze in a big way. There were whispers from Birmingham that I had been drinking in the city during the week after the Rumbelows Cup match against Barnsley. That I was drunk at the airport in Manchester on the way over to Ireland. Some hacks allowed their imaginations to run wild as they went to watch the team train at Dalymount Park, expecting to see me in the lobby when they came back. By six o'clock their suspicions were becoming bigger, the doubts increasing as I was still absent from the team hotel.

"There's no problem with Paul," said my guardian angel Jack. "His mother is sick, I've given him the day off and he'll report later tonight, train at Lansdowne tomorrow morning with the rest of the lads then play against Turkey on Wednesday."

Behind the scenes Jack was worried. He knew I had been in town since the previous Friday morning, he had heard stories about me drinking in various Dublin hotels. Reports were verified that I had been seen in Rumours and various clubs down Leeson Street. Charlton knew only too well how dangerous it was for me to drink. He knew the repercussions both mentally and physically and the dangers of three or four days of life back on the bottle. He was worried about his star player, worried for a player he treated like a son, a player he regarded as one of the best he had ever handled.

Irish physio Mick Byrne was told to make discreet enquiries around town, to check out the stories about this latest drinking binge, see if they could find me in one of the watering holes I frequent around my native Dublin.

The initial enquiries drew a blank. Yes, I had been seen drinking over the weekend but nobody knew where I was now. Then the phones in the hotel went down – nobody could ring around to find me nor could I ring in to explain where I was. Jack was more worried as evening approached.

After dinner the Irish team went off to the pictures, our normal Monday night habit in the week of a home international. Most went to see *The Field* well aware of the missing wanderer but expecting to see me back in the hotel on their return. When the players and most of the press departed the team hotel, the search for Paul McGrath began in earnest. Byrne and Trevor O'Rourke, the PR man for Irish team sponsors Opel, went off in O'Rourke's car to search the streets of Dublin. They checked out various pubs, rang various friends, then contacted the police and an APB was put out to see if anyone had seen or heard of the AWOL Irish player.

By now the majority of the journalists had left the team hotel – most prepared to accept the official story, some wondering if the old days were back again for Paul McGrath. One paper even sent a journalist around the pubs of Dublin looking for me but he drew a blank after several reported sightings earlier in the day.

Some journalists stayed on in hope – waiting for a glimpse of the man they wanted to return to the hotel before they would be forced to write a story about a player's drinking that nobody wanted to see published. Like Charlton the Irish press men loved Paul McGrath the player, they respected me as a footballer, they knew all about this drink problem but they wanted to forget about it in a professional capacity. Nobody wanted to write that Paul McGrath was back on the bottle, that I had let my country down by drinking instead of reporting for an international fixture. But the tabloids were lurking in the shadows, they smelled a rat and only the fact that the local press repeated stories that I had gone home to my mother's, that I had arrived in Dublin at the weekend, kept them at bay.

I had gone over early for the Irish launch of *The Manager*, the Terry Venables board game. That was on the Friday. I went over on the Thursday depressed and lonely. I was having problems at home, I was having problems with my knee, I was in trouble at Villa. When I met my biographer Cathal Dervan to discuss the book on the Friday after that launch I was desperate for someone to talk to. I explained how I had played a game on the Tuesday night against my better judgement in the Rumbelows Cup against Barnsley.

Jo Venglos, then the Villa boss, was no Graham Taylor. His English was limited, his understanding of a player with my problems limited even further. I did not want to play that night. I did a fitness test and still felt uncomfortable. They made me play against my wishes – that was the fuel to ignite the fires of doubt burning in my soul.

I opened up that Friday, my tongue loosened by the Guinness and the vodka that flowed freely in the bar of the Burlington Hotel. I spoke candidly about the pains that were coming back into the right knee for the first time in months, spoke openly about the inherent fear that this time the problem was real again and not a figment of the imagination.

We parted company. I went out with a friend from Manchester and a couple of Dublin mates. We did the usual circuit, some food, some drink, a disco, a club on Leeson Street. Next morning I headed off to Trim for some promotion work with the radio station Atlantic 252 at the local Trim Celtic football club. They sent a car to collect me at the Burlington. I was the worse for wear but we got there, slightly late, and I was surrounded by hundreds of kids.

I needed a drink. We had a few in the Judge and Jury in Trim then we headed for Cathal's hometown of Dunshaughlin. We had some grub at his house. We talked books and soccer. We went to his locals, Murray's and Lawless's. Naturally we had some Guinness. The barman in Lawless's, a favourite haunt of Niall Quinn's, didn't know me. The owner of Murray's got an autograph for his daughter but he had no camera for a photograph. I was happy to co-operate, I was feeling good and ready to talk. Really talk.

We left for Dublin and my mother's house around eight o'clock. By the time we had left Dunshaughlin and were heading for Clonee I had dropped the bombshell to the one journalist I trusted above all others. This was to be my last match for Ireland.

My battered knees could no longer stand up to the pace and the pressures of playing in the centre of midfield for the Irish team. I told Cathal he had a world exclusive on his hands, to wait until the day after the game and he could break the news that Paul McGrath's playing career for Ireland was over. I was so down I felt I couldn't do Jack Charlton or the team justice any more, that the twisting and turning in central midfield was too much for those damaged knees. Paul McGrath the footballer was at a crossroads, I had reached a crisis in life and I was reacting in the only manner I knew – I turned to drink. I knew I was drunk when I was telling him my international career was over, I knew I was talking through drink, getting things off my mind that were kept locked away during normal life.

Cathal knew then that Paul McGrath was a troubled man – to be fair he told me he'd talk to me about the story and my desire to quit at the team hotel on the Monday when I was sober. I never made the team hotel that Monday – I was still high on an alcoholic cloud, oblivious to Jack Charlton and to my country's needs. I didn't know anything about a football game by then and I didn't care.

I was brought home that Saturday night in time to go out around town with a few friends. I felt I needed to drink even more because I was to record a single the next day with former Horslips drummer Eamonn Carr and I was worried and nervous about that. I loathe microphones at the best of times, but the prospect of going into a recording studio with a bunch of musicians and trained singers really frightened me. I couldn't handle the idea of recording a song. I needed drink inside me to give me the confidence and the composure to face that microphone the next day. That's why I had a few in the Judge and Jury in Trim, that's why I had a few more in Lawless's and Murray's in Dunshaughlin, why I hit the town in Dublin on the Saturday night. I was nervous about the record and worried about my knees. I sought solace in the only way I know, through alcohol.

It was the same on the Sunday. I was out early for a few drinks at lunchtime before I hit the studio. I was a bundle of nerves but the drink did the trick, it relaxed me and I managed to do the few lines that were required of me. I even fancied the girl who was singing on the record – I made that known but I was wasting my time. She wasn't into me, full stop. For once the blarney had failed.

Not that I was too bothered. Now I was in the humour for drink, I wanted more. All ideas about international matches and playing for Ireland and my responsibility to the squad went out the window. I was having a good time, I was having a drink and a chat and a joke and a bit of crack with people I'd never met before. I kept saying I'll have one more than I'll head off. As usual one became two became three and before I knew where I was Sunday night had turned into Monday morning and I was still on the binge. I thought about reporting to the team hotel in the morning but decided I needed another few pints to calm me down enough to face Jack. This was the week I was going to tell him I couldn't play in midfield anymore. This was the week that I was going to stand up and say that my knees couldn't bear the strains of playing in midfield, that my career wouldn't last much longer if I was twisting and turning, checking and marking.

It was a different role to the one I played in at Villa and I had convinced myself in that drunken haze that I was going to quit the international team that week. I had told myself over and over again that I couldn't do the Irish team justice any more, that my knee problems meant I was going to let the team down, that I was a liability to the squad.

I was afraid of making a mistake in an Irish shirt, a fear that was fuelled by my problems against Barnsley and a week on the beer. That's why I kept delaying my return to the team hotel, that's why I shied away from meeting Jack and convinced myself that everything would be fine if I just had another drink. I knew I was doing wrong but I wouldn't admit it. I knew that Monday afternoon that I should be training with the team instead of drinking with people I hardly knew in a Dublin pub. I knew it would get out in the papers that I was back on the jar. I knew I should have phoned my wife Claire and explained where I was. But all the doubts and all the questions were drowned in a sea of alcohol and I was getting more relaxed about the whole thing as I got drunker.

By the time Mick Byrne found me late that night I was in no state to represent any country or any team. I was a mess, a crumpled mass of emotion now distraught at the reality of what I had done. He found me in that girl's brother's house out in Mulhuddart. How they tracked me down is incredible.

A girl I knew in Dublin had come with me to Trim Celtic on the Saturday. I brought her with me to Cathal's house in Dunshaughlin to do some work on this book. We left her talking to his wife Elizabeth. How he explained who she was I still don't know. I can't remember the girl's name even now – but when Cathal went home on the Monday night and it was explained to him that I was missing he said the last person I had been seen with was that girl. His wife Elizabeth knew her name and where she worked. He passed the information on to Mick Byrne, they rang the job, got her number, spoke to her mother and discovered that I was in her brother's house in Mulhuddart.

When Mick got there with Trevor it was like a scene from a Roddy Doyle book. There were kids outside the house chanting "Ooh Aah Paul McGrath". I was inside, oblivious to the world, drunk as a skunk and determined not to leave. They eventually got me into the car, but even on the way back to the Airport Hotel I was more interested in more drink than I was about the repercussions of missing two days with the team.

I was in a cold sweat though. Reality was beginning to set in and I knew just what that meant. It meant facing the music, facing up to my responsibilities, facing Jack Charlton, facing my team-mates, facing the fact that I had let him, my fellow players and my country down.

When Mick brought me back to the hotel Jack treated me like the prodigal son. He welcomed me back into the fold with open arms, he told me I was the most important person in all of this, to get a grip of myself, to get off to bed, that we'd talk about it in the morning. He was forgiving and I was remorseful, ashamed of what I had done.

They put me to bed. They left me alone in a dark and quiet room to reflect on what I had done and my remorse. I tried to sleep before the drink wore off. That made me worse but I felt better. Sober, I could realise what was going on around me; drunk, it was somebody else's problem. So I slept, slept off the immediate effects of the over-indulgence but not the long-term effects of a week-long session.

That Tuesday morning I woke up late, looked in the mirror and I wanted to die with embarrassment. I was a disgrace to myself, to my family, to Jack Charlton, to the Irish team. How could I face the boss? How could I look the players straight in the eye? I got a fright, the biggest fright I had ever had.

This was not Paul McGrath the footballer. This was Paul McGrath the mess. Paul McGrath the drinker. Paul McGrath the liability. Those were the thoughts that went through my mind when I walked around the pitch at Lansdowne on the Tuesday. They were the same thoughts that filled my mind when I went back to my room that afternoon and attempted to sleep off the drink. They were the same thoughts that flashed through my mind when I underwent a fitness test on the Wednesday morning just hours before the game with Mick, Jack and Villa physio Jim Walker, flown over especially by the club when they discovered the state of collapse I was in. My knee was sore enough but my head and my heart really hurt. My pride was in ruins, my dignity in tatters.

I couldn't face a match in that condition and I knew it. Jack wanted me to play, said so as we got on to the bus. But as we made our way to Lansdowne I got the shakes, I went through the withdrawal symptoms with the hot flushes and the cold spells and the shakes in the arms and I was afraid. For the first time in my life I realised how bad my drink problem was. I realised I was on the verge of serious problems and I vowed there and then to stop. This was to be the turning point. Or so I thought.

When the bus got to the ground I decided to put my foot down. I told Jack I couldn't play, I wouldn't play and he wasn't happy. He took the team in, I stayed on the bus, hiding from the reality of what I had done, ashamed to show my face in that dressing-room and see what effect I had had on the team.

Jack came out to the bus and brought me in but I remember little or nothing of what happened. He let his feelings be known in no uncertain terms and I just sat there and took it like a little boy without a word to say for himself, a guilty boy who knew he'd been caught. All I can recall is sitting in the dressing-room oblivious to what was happening then leaving the ground and going back to the hotel. That night I knew there was no turning back. I had a problem and I was going to face up to it.

If Jack Charlton was as good to me now as he had been before he would help me. I hoped and prayed that he would, that he would see me through my rehabilitation and help me rebuild my life and my career. I prayed that I would still be a footballer in a month's time and play for my country against England at Lansdowne Road. It was going to be a long and painful journey.

I did make that game for Ireland. I did play for my country again. But by then Villa had put me through the mill in an effort to sort my life out. Jim Walker escorted me back to Birmingham and booked me into a private clinic, the Woodbourne in Edgbaston. I was there to dry out, to come down off the drink craze that was ruining not just my career but my life.

They put me through the detoxification programme. They gave me tablets to stop me drinking, to make me sick if alcohol touched my lips. They examined me from all ends up, went through my past, spoke about the future. They decided I was not an alcoholic. I am a binge drinker. I can give it up if and when I want. By the same token, once I get a taste for it I can keep going for days even though my threshold is quite low.

Villa were in a different class. Doug Ellis picked up the bills, ensured everything was done to get me better. They hid me from the press, made excuses for me when I missed a couple of games, never let on I was drying out. The clinic put me on a six-week programme. After four weeks I felt well enough to leave and return to a normal life.

A year later I went back for a top-up session. That went as well as the first visit. Just to be sure, the club booked me into the Ashby De La Zouch health club in Derbyshire. It became my home for four months. I was on the way back.

I did indeed get back into Jack Charlton's side, sooner rather

Now that's what I call training: Dublin Airport training ground
(Noel Gavin/The Star)

PFA Awards 1993, with Bobby Charlton and Ryan Giggs
(Courtesy of the PFA)

Dalkey re-united, 1994 club dinner. Left to right: Frank Mullen,
Tom Cullen, Paul McGrath and Johnny Dunne

*Best of times: Football League Centenary Team, Wembley
(Courtesy of Chris Cole/All-Sport)*

*A galaxy of stars, old and new: Bryan Robson, Paul McGrath, Liam Brady
and Pele (Courtesy of Bob Thomas)*

A king amongst his own: training again with Ireland, summer 1993
(Jim Walpole/The Star)

Some people have to train you know, Alan: watching the Irish team go
through their paces with Alan Kernaghan, November 1993
(Jim Walpole/The Star)

*Mine's a Guinness: pulling pints at the Blackthorn Bar in Boston, June 1992 (Noel Gavin/*The Star*)*

Still Z-ray after all these years: with Z-ray singer Maria Walsh recording 'Ooh Aah Paul McGrath' (Noel Gavin/The Star)

The happiest man in the world: with Betty McGrath and her husband Noel Lowth on their wedding day, summer 1990 (Noel Gavin/The Star)

Happy families: Christopher, Mitchell, and Jordan say Cheese, Manchester 1994

than later. A month after my Turkish fright I played at Lansdowne Road in the 1-1 draw with England.

Graham Taylor was manager by then and played right into our hands when he dropped Paul Gascoigne and left him on the bench. We couldn't believe that when we heard it in the dressing-room. He was the one player we really feared in the English team. There was a rumour going round that Taylor didn't play him because the player felt threatened by the occasion and the atmosphere. I can't believe that. It was Taylor-made, if you'll excuse the pun, for a player of his class. I was scared to death he'd be running at me in midfield, I'd had enough of a job trying to keep Bryan Robson quiet at the World Cup finals.

That European Championship campaign is still one of the biggest disappointments of my international career. We should have gone to Sweden '92, not England. We gave them an early goal in Dublin through David Platt and did well to level late in the match through Tony Cascarino.

But at Wembley the following March we played them off the park when Lee Dixon scored early off Steve Staunton's foot. That was the kick-start we needed. We dominated from then to the end but got only one goal, a great finish from Niall Quinn to show George Graham up for letting him leave Arsenal two years earlier for Manchester City. That night was my favourite game in an Irish shirt and, modesty prevailing, my best performance for my country. I was recently given a video of the game thanks to Maurice Reidy in RTE television sport and I love every minute of it.

It was sad as well. We effectively ended Bryan Robson's England career and caused Graham Taylor, in language that was later caught on camera during the World Cup, to admit he had "shit himself" when Ray Houghton should have scored a late winner.

As usual we didn't make home rule count for the rest of the qualifiers. After Wembley expectancy was high. We drew 0-0 at home to Poland on a disgrace of a pitch at Lansdowne Road. We drew in Poznan against Poland when we were 3-1 up with 25 minutes to go. We won handsomely in Istanbul in the last game on a night when Gary Lineker scored his last competitive goal for England with 12 minutes remaining in Poznan to level against the Poles and put us out. Graham Taylor, my old Villa boss, was through by the skin of his teeth.

But I wasn't too unhappy. At least I was still playing for my country. After my Turkish escapade that was a delight in itself. And

161

a relief that Jack Charlton still had enough faith in my ability as a footballer to turn a blind eye to everything else. Almost.

CHAPTER FOURTEEN

Where's Albania?

DRINK – the curse of the working class. And the footballing class. At least it was in the summer of 1993 when the season ended in disappointment for Aston Villa. There was heartbreak in our efforts to stop Manchester United winning the league title.

My personal life was collapsing all around me. There had been revelations about my activities off the field where the women were concerned. There was a story in the newspapers about a child by another woman. That came three weeks before we surrendered the title to Manchester United. The timing was terrible. My long-suffering wife Claire had had enough.

On the field though I was still getting away with it. From a purely selfish professional point of view the season could not have gone much better, aside from the disappointment of not winning the league. I was named the first winner of the resumed Midlands Football Writers Player of the Year. At the dinner in Birmingham I even got a chance to meet the lovely Karren Brady from Birmingham City Football Club. Every club should have a managing director like that – even if she was under the impression that Ron Atkinson (who's white) and Dalian Atkinson (who's black) were father and son.

Before that Midlands award my fellow professionals bestowed the highest honour possible on me – they named me their senior Player of the Year. That was the ultimate accolade – when your peers reckon you're the best player in England it really means something. Gordon Taylor rang me with the news – and we had a good laugh about the day he represented me when Alex Ferguson wanted me to quit. He insisted that the PFA wanted me in London to collect the award and it was twice a delight when I was presented with the trophy by Bobby Charlton, a person I loved as a player and a man I have respected greatly since he quit the game and moved into the executive side of things with United.

That was the personal glory. The collective emotion at Villa was all of the sorrowful variety. We had a great team and a good season – but not a great season. We went out of the Coca Cola Cup in the fourth round to Ipswich. We went out of the FA Cup at the same stage to Wimbledon, on penalties. And we handed the league to Manchester United when we might well have beaten them with a little bit more belief in our own ability.

The Sunday afternoon on the first weekend in May that we lost at home to Oldham and surrendered the league to United was a bitter day indeed. I read later that Alex Ferguson had gone golfing that afternoon – and came home with the title in the bag. That Fergie title made the pill of defeat all the harder to swallow for me.

That night of the Oldham defeat we had a supporters' club presentation at the Holte End suites. Rumour has it that Ron came out with a great line. Allegedly he said the good news for the supporters was that he was going to line the first team up against a wall and get them shot. The bad news was that Ray Houghton was doing the shooting. Sorry about that one, Razor!

Losing the league was enough to drive a man to drink. It did. Mainly because I had other problems on my mind. My wife was in hospital and I was looking after the children on my own. I had found a new love called Caroline Lamb from Liverpool and I was as happy as I could be with her. I still am.

At the end of the season all I wanted to do was to get divorced, go home to Ireland, play in vital World Cup qualifying games, all away against Albania, Latvia and Lithuania, and go on holiday. In terms of the football two out of three wasn't bad. The first game, though, was a disaster.

Albania was a lucky omen for me, I thought. I had played against them in Dublin in the opening match of our World Cup campaign. I scored the second goal in a 2-0 win, a header in the 80th minute. My sister Okone had a baby that day, a lovely little daughter called Miawa. Okone and her husband were proud as punch. My mother was as proud as punch. So was her husband

Noel Lowth. I was delighted for her. That day I dedicated my goal to my little niece – and vowed to get Ireland to America on her behalf. It was the best present I could give the latest addition to the family.

By the time the return leg was played in Albania I was the one behaving like a little child again. And owing another apology to the Irish people and to Jack Charlton. I never played against Albania in Tirana on 26 May when Ireland won 2-1. I missed the pleasures of the land that time forgot. By then I was AWOL, on holiday in Israel, escaping from my footballing sins with Caroline and a friend of mine from Birmingham called Dave Abou, commonly known amongst the Villa footballing fraternity as Israeli Dave.

My problems began when Villa took the first team squad off to Mauritius with their wives for a friendly game and a thank you gesture for the season. I travelled on my own and I didn't play. I didn't want to risk my knee on the island of dreams with three big World Cup games coming up. Instead I had a drink at the game, quite a feat considering alcohol was banned. One local official looked after me though; he had taxi-men scurrying round the place looking for some beer, then organised some policemen, of all people, to shield me while I drank it. That's how bad I was after losing the league in the manner in which we did.

I left Mauritius before the rest of the players, five days early, complaining of my knee. I flew back on my own via Paris, anxious to get back to England to meet up with Caroline and then head off to the town of Crosshaven in Cork for a coaching session with my old friend Joey Malone. Joey had organised the coaching clinic for the local kids and I was the star attraction. I was to train with them and do a talk-in at a local pub on the Friday night. I fulfilled my obligations despite reports to the contrary and I enjoyed myself. I had a few pints and I relaxed. On the Friday night, 48 hours before Ireland were due to meet up for the Albania game, I spoke in front of the local soccer club in a question-and-answer session at one of the local hotels in Crosshaven.

I enjoyed Crosshaven. The locals claim if you stare hard enough you can see America across the Atlantic waves. By the time I left Cork I was in danger of not seeing America at all this summer.

I forgot about my fear of microphones at the talk-in that night. I was quite good, I thought. Joey, who conducted the session, said I was even funny. When that was over I did have a few drinks but only after I had carried out the talk-in.

I was due to leave Cork on the Saturday and go with Joey to the Irish PFA'S annual dinner, a show I like to visit as a former winner of their Player of the Year award. Drink was getting the better of me though. We retained the room in the Crosshaven hotel and went off to the dogs in Cork – myself, Caroline and Dave. Joey went off to his dinner after I promised to follow him by Sunday.

We went to the greyhound racing that Saturday night. I was enjoying myself but I was still aware of my responsibilities to Jack and to Ireland. I had every intention of flying up to join the Irish squad the next day at lunchtime.

What's that saying about the best-laid plans of mice and men? I was a mouse that weekend. On the Sunday lunchtime we were just about to check in for the Aer Lingus flight to Dublin from Cork Airport when I changed my mind again. We'd stay in Cork and I'd go up on the Monday instead. Jack would understand. He was my friend.

Instead of taking the flight I took a cab into Cork and asked the driver to take me to any decent hotel. He chose the Silver Springs in Tivoli on the Dublin Road, a very good choice. We checked in, went for a meal in one of Cork's many fine Chinese restaurants and had another good night.

Of course I never went to Dublin on the Monday. We never came out of the hotel room all day. By now the papers had wind of my disappearing act. I was national news once more. I didn't know as much until the Tuesday morning when Caroline and myself went for a walk up the road to get a paper at the local garage. I was getting funny looks off some of the guests in reception and I couldn't figure out why. It was the same in the garage. Then I saw the papers. The *Cork Examiner,* the *Star,* the *Irish Times,* the *Irish Independent,* the *Irish Press,* the *Sun,* the *Daily Mirror.* They all carried the same story. "Ooh Aah Paul McGrath goes missing" was the gist of the headlines. Oh, oh – I was in trouble.

I hid my head on the way back to the hotel. Caroline didn't know where to look. If she had known me longer she'd have put me on the first flight to Dublin and sorted me out with Jack. Instead I told her to ring the Dublin Airport Hotel and tell Jack that I had a sore knee and wouldn't be coming into work today.

Now I was in trouble again. Turkey revisited. The hotel agreed to keep our secret. The receptionists in the Silver Springs were brilliant about it. Anyone who asked was told I was not there. I made arrangements to go back to Birmingham on the Tuesday, then home to Manchester and on to a sunshine break in Israel to get away from it all with an Israeli friend.

I was in trouble and I was running again. Running scared. Claire was now in hospital and that was causing me worries. The children were at a friend's. I was in the news in Ireland. I needed to get away. Israel and the sun seemed a great idea. At Cork Airport I told reporters that my knee injury was serious, really sore, and that I had sent word to Jack. When we arrived in Birmingham there were more cameras and reporters. Dave Abou became my minder, according to the media. I told them to go away, that I was very angry and had nothing to say.

By the time I got to the resort of Eilat the whole of Ireland seemed to be looking for me. I was headline news on the front pages as well as the back pages. They were running sweeps in pubs on when I'd be seen again. One pub in Cork opposite Jury's Hotel, the Windmill I think, had a picture of me staring out of the door with a few of their regulars on the Saturday night and a caption that read: "When Ireland was looking for him we knew where he was." They were right of course.

That disappearing act had its funny moments, although Jack Charlton might not see the joke. When I left Cork on the Tuesday the good people at the Fitzpatrick's Silver Springs hotel arranged for me to get the flight at the last minute and arrive at the airport in one of their vans. I got there just as the flight was closing, checked in and was escorted to the tarmac. There were a couple of reporters hanging around – and one in particular became the centre of attention. His name was Marty Morrissey, a nice fellow from the county of Clare who works as a newsreader with RTE Radio Cork during the week and as a Gaelic games commentator with RTE television sport at the weekends.

Because he was the right man in the right place, poor old Marty got lumped with the job of following me around the airport with the RTE television news people that day for footage that was to be the mainstay of their main evening bulletin. The bold Marty, a friend of a friend of mine called Tony O'Donoghue, awaited my arrival and saw his 15 minutes of fame pop up right in front of him. He followed me through the airport and out on to the tarmac. He tried to ask questions. I ignored him, muttering that my knee was sore and that I had told Jack Charlton I would not be going to Albania.

He persisted in following me. I saw the steps to an aeroplane and I went straight up them. He followed. The hostess smiled and intervened. Wrong plane. This was an Aer Lingus jet going to Heathrow. I was due to go back to Birmingham on a Brymon European Airways flight. Back down the steps we went. Back up the right steps to the Birmingham flight we went. Me and half of the RTE crew. All captured on film of course. All highly amusing for the Aer Lingus hostess.

This all appeared on national television that night. And when Marty was seen in all his glory he got a ticking off from one of the most unusual sources of all.

Christy Moore is the finest singer in Ireland, a folk singer who has crossed over to contemporary rock and made his mark with Planxty, Moving Hearts and as a solo artist. He has always been a favourite of mine. When I was on the run, so to speak, in Cork that weekend I saw posters for his latest album and I even said to Caroline that I'd love to see him live.

The respect was mutual. I didn't know Christy was a big soccer fan – and a big fan of mine. He was disgusted at the way I was treated by the media that weekend and he wrote to Marty Morrissey to lambast him. Marty got the letter alright – and just in case he thought it was a hoax he was soon put to rights by Christy himself. They crossed paths a few weeks later at a Gaelic football match between Dublin and Kildare in Croke Park. Christy, there to shout for his native Kildare, called Marty over, confirmed the letter was his and told him to leave me alone and stick to Gaelic football. I was flabbergasted when I heard the story.

And so we flew across Europe, across the Mediterranean and on to the golden Isreali coast of sun and sea. I was not oblivious to the fact that I had let my country down again. I was in a nice hotel. The sun had his hat on. Caroline was at my side. What more could a man ask for?

Then reality slowly began to dawn. It crept up on me first when I realised the fuss I had caused at home. Next thing a photographer mysteriously arrived on the scene at the hotel and wanted a "nice" picture of myself and Caroline. I smelled a rat. The picture was worth good money back in England and Ireland.

I knew we were in trouble staying at the resort. We fled. Caroline and I headed across the desert in a madcap four-hour taxi journey. We arrived in Tel Aviv knowing nobody and spent hours looking for a travel agent to get a flight back to Manchester. Caroline spent hours with me as I went looking for a drink.

I couldn't find a ticket office or a bar. We went for a walk, the pressure getting to me by the minute, the guilt growing by the hour. We had an incredible experience when we saw this weird-looking character in the desert in front of us and thought he was about to shoot us. It was a statue. Hallucination once again.

We stayed one night in the city before we could arrange a flight home. From the hotel I rang Jack and asked for forgiveness once more. As ever he was forgiving and told me to get back to Dublin and back to work. I did both.

While I was taking the sun in Eilat the boys in green were looking after my World Cup interests in Albania. A 2-1 win in Tirana courtesy of goals from Super Steve Staunton and Tremendous Tony Cascarino did the business and kept Jack and me, I hoped, on the road to America.

When I met Jack I confessed that I was in danger of taking a wrong turn down the road to ruin. I apologised profusely. I asked for forgiveness once more. He was as good as ever. I was back in the camp on the strict understanding that it was not to happen again. Ever. Step out of line again and I'd be crucified. That was a fair swap for World Cup solace.

I apologised to the Irish nation and the Irish team for my bad behaviour. I returned to the Irish side for the World Cup qualifier in Latvia on 2 June and scored a goal for good measure. A fortnight later I was on the Irish side that won in Vilnius against Lithuania. Three away games, three good wins and we were on our way to America.

Villa were due to go to Japan in July for a tournament that had been arranged with me as one of the central attractions. Because of my PFA award the Japanese were particularly anxious to see me. Villa insisted I had to travel. I insisted I couldn't go. Our au pair had gone back to her home in Croatia. My wife was in hospital, very sick. I had three children at home who needed me. Even if it meant giving up football I was not going to walk out on my children.

I skipped that trip to Japan. I missed the flight from Heathrow. My family came first, football second. If I was presented with the same choice tomorrow morning I would take the same course of action. I have no doubt about that.

That decision to stay home alone when Villa went East cost me a lot of money. Ron fined me two weeks' wages. He warned me publicly and privately about doing it again. He understood my problem but had to take action for the sake of club discipline. I knew that and I accepted it. A fine of two weeks' wages stung my pocket but my children mattered more to me.

I was fined again in January 1994 when I missed the FA Cup third round tie at Exeter and hit the headlines all over again. This time things just got right on top of me in the days before the game. We were due to play Leeds the previous Monday and the match was postponed because of heavy rain. I went out that night with Caroline, Dean Saunders and his wife and a couple of the press lads including Rob Shepherd from *Today* and Cathal Dervan. We had a drink in Mulligan's at the Four Seasons Hotel and a few more at Yesterday's.

The next day was Doug Ellis's 70th birthday and the club threw a bash for him. That was good crack as well. By Friday and the trip to Exeter I was down though. My knee was sore and the pressures of my court cases against my wife Claire and my private problems were becoming too much. The press had been plaguing me all week to do a story – they had heard rumours that Caroline was pregnant. I just couldn't see myself playing against Exeter. I told the club so and I skipped the bus to the West Country. I went for a drink at the Barley's pub near the training ground and the landlord got Caroline to come down from Manchester and pick me up. Of course somebody in the pub rang the newspapers.

Next day I was the villain again. The newspapers had me facing the sack, in trouble with Doug and Ron and on the way out of Villa. Ron was hopping, he told me as much on the phone on the Friday night and again on the Monday when I went in for training. Result? Another fine. Another two weeks' wages down the drain. Only this time Ron came up with a wonderstroke for the rest of the lads. He used the money to take them away for a five-day break in Tenerife before the FA Cup fourth round game at Grimsby. Nice one, Ron. The lads went to the sun and I paid for it.

I didn't even get any benefit from the fine myself. I missed the flight again, but with permission. My young lad Jordan was in hospital that week for an operation on his ears and I stayed behind with him. With Ron's blessing of course. Like I said – my family comes first.

And I'm just grateful that Jack Charlton and Ron Atkinson are the heads of my football family. Very grateful. I have been the wayward son too often. They have always welcomed me back as the Prodigal Son. They understand me. They punish me. But they always welcome me back, through thick and thin.

I have tested Jack Charlton and Ron Atkinson to the absolute limits. I have pushed their patience to the limits and beyond. I have done enough to have been sacked by Villa and discarded by Ireland. Thankfully they've both welcomed me back.

They haven't let me get away with it. Any time I'm out of order with Ron especially he will fine me. He will never let me away with a thing because of the problems that would cause with the other lads, which is right. If I miss a day's training he fines me and he fines me a lot of money. I deserve that.

Jack, to be fair, has always spoken dead straight to me. He's always said "do it one more time and I'll slaughter you". I've got away with murder but I don't actually think I've escaped punishment. The publicity and the problems I have caused have been punishment in themselves.

I feel I've done some bad things and then I've tried to work my way back in. It's not because I actually do things deliberately. I do things on the spur of the moment, things that I always regret afterwards but things that I never see through or think through. I don't think about Ron or Jack, about fines or punishment. About letting Villa or Ireland down. I just get off on a tangent and away I go. Drink today, worry about it tomorrow.

I wish Jack had some facility where he could reprimand me because then I'd feel like I had been really punished, that I had served a sentence worthy of the crimes I've committed against that man and against Ireland.

Ron has a different facility. He will fine me and that hurts me financially but it has never actually stopped me doing it again. I think they both understand that when I do those things I'm not always thinking rationally, that a part of me knows it's wrong but is powerless to do anything about it.

I wouldn't have been surprised if Jack had told me to take a hike after Albania. Of course I was worried. When I come down from these binges I do worry about Jack. Half the time I think he should say don't bother coming with us again, I picked you and you weren't there. But to be honest about Jack and Ron they've been nothing but brilliant to me. They don't deserve what I do time and time again. At the same time I don't do it because I want to hurt them or Villa or Ireland. They both sympathise with me, they both judge the personal problems that I have for what they are then judge the punishment by what I do on the pitch.

I'm not saying I've got huge problems but my personal life has been a mess and there are times when it takes its toll – normally during the football season – and either Jack or Ron gets hurt. They understand at least – even it they don't always sympathise. They weigh up both sides and do what's best for them. If I couldn't give them something on the pitch they would have given up on me a long time ago. If I can play the games and do them justice and do them proud, that is all I want to do. I will have my ups and downs but I love playing football, I love performing to the peak of my ability for club and country. They know I haven't always been at my peak physically but they've made allowances and when push has come to shove I've stood up to be counted for both Ireland and Villa.

Both of them will know when it's time for me to quit. Jack knows now that it's time for me to go from midfield and maybe altogether after the World Cup. But I still think I can do a job for Ireland at the back and I'm going to try.

Jack has taken me under his wing more than any other Irish player. He has treated me far better than I ever deserved to be treated. There have been times when I have totally and utterly betrayed his trust, I've spat in the face of his respect and his affection for me and kicked him when he's been down.

There are things people will never know about the relationship between me and him. He's been not just a manager but a good friend to me. He's covered for me, he's dug holes for himself by making excuses for me. He has always defended me no matter what the weight of evidence against me. He should have told me to skip it in rather more colourful language after the last episode when I went missing for the Albania game. But he hasn't, he's always brought me back in, tried to cover for me. I've tried to repay him on the pitch. A lot of the time you can't. He's been like the old mongrel, no matter how many times you kick him he will always come back on my side. He really has been a great friend to me.

Maybe I can repay him. I'm going to try.

CHAPTER FIFTEEN

Bye Bye Billy – and Good Riddance

JACK CHARLTON came down the aisle of that Aer Lingus charter from Belfast with a double for Paul McGrath. A message and a warning that triumphant Wednesday night.

The champagne was flowing freely, the party had begun but the words from Jack's mouth were laced with realism. The truth, his truth, hit me like a bolt from the blue as Jack spelt out what the rest of a season of hope and expectancy meant to my future as an Irish international footballer and a prospective World Cup star.

I was on a high. We had just shut Billy Bingham up, shoved his rantings and ravings down his throat by booking our place in America. We had done ourselves, Jack and Ireland proud. We had drawn with Northern Ireland at Windsor Park, Alan McLoughlin had scored the goal of his life and I was in the mood to party. The boss was determined, though, to bring me down to earth with a bang.

"Six months, Paul – that's all I want. Six months away from the booze and the problems, six months to the World Cup, to the games of your life for Ireland. That's all I want," said the big man with the heart of gold and the great expectations of a nation now resting on his shoulders after lift-off for our American dream.

He was sincere and honest with me that night when it would have been easier to bask in the reflective glory of the 1-1 result. Drink was talking all over Dublin and beyond. Guys were promising their best friends they'd be on that plane to New York, telling their wives it was, just like Italy, the trip of a lifetime, a once in a lifetime chance not to be spurned. Sod the money – they were all going by hook or by crook. I assumed I was going too until Jack put it all into perspective.

I could understand his worries that night. It had been a great World Cup for Ireland but I had hardly covered myself in glory throughout the campaign. I had missed one game through injury in Copenhagen, one through suspension at home to Lithuania and one through stupidity when I had gone AWOL for the visit to Albania. Some of the lads reckoned I didn't fancy life in the most backward corner of Europe where mini-bars were small units in the hotel lounge.

But I had played my part and felt I was worthy to be there when the rewards were going to be reaped in America. I also knew that I had let Jack down along the way; his concerns were voiced out of worry and a realistic view of my age and my problems.

I promised him that night that I would do my best. Even with that Exeter disappearing act I was still determined not to let him down when our flight of dreams took off from Dublin Airport on 6 June.

And I have bad news for Alan Kernaghan, Phil Babb, Brian Carey, David O'Leary, Kevin Moran, Andy Linighan or anyone else who fancies taking my jersey for that opening match against Italy in the summer. Forget it. It's mine and I'm keeping it.

I had no intentions of retiring quietly before the World Cup began. I would consider such a prospect after America, I would probably move over and let the new kids on the block get their chance for the 1998 World Cup. I'll be as old as Kevin Moran by then. But there's no way I would be abdicating my throne before the last throw of the dice in the stadiums of New York, Orlando and beyond. This World Cup was not my farewell. It might be my last shot at the greatest stage of them all in terms of the World Cup. Not my last contribution to the history of Irish soccer.

I understood Jack's concerns. He has watched me a lot this season. He knows I'm struggling in terms of fitness and pace, struggling with injury and that perennial problem of mine – self-doubt. But this was a struggle and a battle I would win.

The fitness problem is simple. Villa are playing too many games. All the talk about the advent of the Premier League reducing the demands on the top players has been absolute rubbish. All it has done is maximise the demands on our time and on our bodies. Sky Television may have been good for the game in terms of exposure – it has been a nightmare for the players. We are now treated like circus clowns, expected to perform on the traditional Saturday, Sunday afternoons, Monday nights, Tuesday nights and Wednesday nights. The only days sacrosanct, it seems, are Thursday and Friday – how long before they become part and parcel of the football calendar?

What the ageing bureaucrats down at Lancaster Gate have forgotten in all of this is the effects of live televised soccer. The fans who traditionally watched their team on a Saturday afternoon and maybe on a Wednesday night are now asked to travel on Sundays, to take time off work on Monday to make the big match. The players are being asked to play more games instead of less – it is no wonder technique and skills are lagging behind the rest of Europe.

English football still rates amongst the best in the world despite the country's failings at international level. The Premiership is one of the best leagues in the world – in spite of the administrators. I know it's an easy excuse. But the demands on my time are stopping me playing to a standard I want to reach and a level I know I can achieve. That was one of the reasons Jack was worried about me, probably the main reason.

The problem with fitness I've had is down purely and simply to the demands of English football, the advent of Sky television, the refusal of the FA to cut down on the number of games in the Premiership. The increased fixtures for Villa, with the Coca Cola League Cup, FA Cup and Europe as well as the Premier League, all had their effect on my knees. I simply haven't had the chance to do the exercises that I should be doing for my knees because we have been playing games all the time. If I do the necessary remedial work in the gym the knees ache the next day and I can't play. That's no good when you're playing on a Sunday, then a Wednesday, then a Saturday, then a Tuesday, then a Saturday and then a Tuesday again. All season I'd either been playing matches or travelling or doing training on the pitch with the lads the day before a game when I had to join in. I had no time to do the work in the gym that my dodgy knees demanded.

I used to do a lot of gym work to try and keep myself going. That was the plan when I first joined Villa. I don't even get time to think about it now. I need to start doing more training but the schedule of games is so intense that I just don't get the chance. The matches are supposed to keep you fit but obviously your fitness levels drop. I don't go out to run about, I maximise my energy at the back. I feel it's a lot harder now.

For someone at 34 who doesn't train, all this play and no work in the gym is making me a very dull boy in terms of performance. People think that I am naturally fit but I've been dead lucky that I haven't had to train as hard as the other lads, that I had the chance in the past to do most of my work in the gym and that I can still run back with the young lads and make those saving tackles. But it's getting harder by the game.

That's just nature. When I first went to Villa I spent a lot of time in the gym and on the bike. I did a lot of sit-ups. The other lads used to think I was taking the mickey when they were out on the training pitch and I was in the gym. Invariably I'd have a cup of tea in my hand and be in having a chat with the ladies in the canteen when they'd come off the pitch. That used to get up their noses but I swear I was working hard. Graham Taylor gave me the freedom to work at my own pace.

Now when I do sit-ups I get a pain in some other part of my body because I'm getting older, so I've had to knock them on the head. Then I do my bike work but I've cut it down an awful lot. I might do 15 minutes a day – nothing like Sean Kelly or Stephen Roche. I use it to get a sweat up, to get out of breath at least once a day. I don't feel I'm doing an honest training session if I don't. Now, though, with so many games a lot of the time I can do nothing better than sit in the bath and soak.

On the day of games, for example, I opt out. If the lads are going for a light work-out I just sit around or go for a walk around the pitch. I don't do a lot with Ireland before games. I'm sure people watching the team train at the AUL complex or at Lansdowne think I'm taking the water. They must think I'm having a laugh at everyone. But I know I'm not fit and, thank God, Jack and Ron and everyone else who works with me knows that. I'd love to be able to go out with the Irish team and take a full part in the five-a-sides but I know that if I do that then the next day or the day after I'll start aching, the knees will start acting up and it's debatable whether I'll play or not.

I've walked every blade of grass at Lansdowne with every member of the Irish squad. There's always somebody with a knock to keep me company. The lads look after me like that but I've never had a regular companion.

Looking back on the World Cup campaign, I think we fully

deserved to qualify. I know that Peter Schmeichel and Denmark are not happy with the way they went out in our group. I know how gutted Dean Saunders was after Wales failed to get the results they needed. The same applies to England and France who were so close and yet so far. But the great fallacy about qualification for the World Cup is the claim that one or two games cost a side their place in America. My old boss Graham Taylor had a right go at the FIFA observer and the linesman in the Holland match when they failed to send Ronald Koeman off for a professional foul on David Platt. That definitely deserved a red card and perhaps it would have changed the whole complexion of the game. But you do not lose a World Cup place in one match. You qualify or not on the basis of what you achieve over a series of group games. We qualified because over the 12 games in our group we were one of the two best sides. We got the results that mattered – they got us to America.

We went to Spain and Denmark and came away with draws. We could easily have won in Seville when Roy Keane had his best game yet for Ireland and had even Maradona drooling. Some day soon Keane is going to end up as the Franz Beckenbauer of the Irish team. I can honestly see him taking over from me at the heart of the Irish defence in years to come and playing his way out of trouble like Mark Lawrenson used to do – and I'd love it. He was unbelievable that night in Seville. It was obvious then why a club like Manchester United would break the domestic English transfer record to get him from Forest.

Then, in Copenhagen, Packie Bonner kept us in it with a tremendous save. I know he's been getting stick recently but people should remember that save and what Packie has achieved over the years in an Irish shirt before they talk about discarding him.

The big difference between us and Denmark came in our performances away from Lansdowne in the other games. We went to places where they only drew and we won comfortably. That end-of-season tour last year paved the way. I missed the win in Albania – I was on the beer in Israel when the lads were looking after my World Cup interests. But the wins in Latvia and Lithuania were sweetness itself – and the light at the end of our World Cup tunnel.

This last season we got a fright. I was suspended when we struggled at home to Lithuania and the danger signs were flashing all across Lansdowne Road in September. But we won. Another two points in the bag and the nation went crazy.

People were saying after the Lithuanian game that we were home and dry. I don't think people quite realised that we were lucky enough that day. They might have had a couple of goals, we should have had a lot more. But there were warning signs. We weren't as dominant or as confident as we like to be. There was something missing that afternoon, something that was still missing in those last two games.

That night I kept saying to everyone that we had two really hard games coming up but the whole of Dublin was partying and saying not to worry. Then we got the shock of our lives against Spain at Lansdowne. They came out firing on all cylinders and we were three down before we even had time to reach for the rosary beads. Jack's hand was forced that day when John Aldridge pulled out 24 hours before the game with an injury that had plagued him and kept the newspapers and the Spanish guessing. Jack put out the story that Aldo had a chance of playing and that Tony Cascarino would partner Niall Quinn if he didn't make it. That was done to keep the Spanish guessing. But the day before the game I knew I was playing in midfield again and that Niall was doing his Christy Moore impersonation, a solo show on his own upfront.

I worried about my role. My legs ain't what they used to be. I'm finding strikers are getting quicker and quicker when I'm playing at centre-back and they're running at me. That's easier to counteract because you can see them coming at you. In midfield, pace is so much more vital. I knew I was struggling on that front. My worst fears were realised. They hit us like a bull charging through the streets of Bilbao itself. The five-man midfield was a disaster. Kevin Moran got injured and went off after the third goal. I was back in defence, John Sheridan was in the middle and pulled one back, but it was too late. We had gambled and failed. Ron Atkinson, in Rotterdam with ITV, spoke the truth at half-time when he said my days as a midfielder were over. He was so right.

The lessons of Lithuania had not been digested by the team. We had let Jack down in his hour of need. The light at the end of that World Cup tunnel was dimming rapidly.

And so our World Cup fate rested on a game in Belfast. A game that was the final fixture in a group balanced on a tightrope. When the fixtures had been set three years earlier everyone expected Windsor Park to be Coronation Street for another Republic World Cup send-off. It was intended as a stroll for Jack's Army before the plans began for America' 94.

How wrong we were. Belfast was the game we needed to win to be sure. A draw would only be enough if Denmark or Spain won in their game in Seville.

World Cup survival was incentive enough. But the best reason to be positive and determined about Belfast came about rather unexpectedly. And it was sad. What can only be described as footballing vitriol poured forth from the mouth of Billy Bingham in the build-up to the real All-Ireland football final.

And suddenly we were given the perfect excuse to qualify for America and ram his words back down that bitter throat of his. It became more than a World Cup mission – it became a mission to shut up Bingham, a man I had respected so much before that November. I wanted to tell Billy Bingham that I am Irish. I am not, as he has suggested, a mercenary. I went to Dublin when I was six weeks old. I class myself as Irish through and through. The funny thing is that all the lads who play for the team do as well. They are more Irish than the Irish themselves, just like Strongbow. The lads playing for us would die for Ireland – they think it's a disgrace that a man of the stature of Billy Bingham should drag up something like that.

It was a difficult enough time for everyone without us being upset, frightened or hyped out of it. I don't think anyone needed that. I had heard him the previous Saturday talking to Cliff Morgan on Radio Five and he was just as inflammatory. He was talking about us not being born in Ireland – if he wants to make that accusation to my face I know exactly what I'll do. He won't like it.

It wasn't a very gentlemanly thing do on the eve of such an important game for us and a farewell for him. I've been fined by the FA in England for bringing the game into disrepute for less than that. I used to think a lot of Billy Bingham. I had great respect for what he had achieved as a manager with our brothers across the border in Nothern Ireland. What he forgets is that people in the South cheered as loudly as the supporters in the North when Gerry Armstrong scored that great goal against Spain at the 1982 World Cup finals in Valencia. I remember watching that game on television at home in Dublin and being delighted for Billy and his boys. I wouldn't be so happy for him now – in fact I'm glad he's gone out of international soccer and retired. Thankfully he won't be in charge when we play them in the European Championship.

That's a sad thing to say about any fellow professional. I always thought he was a nice man. I was shocked that someone I had a lot of respect for should come out and say that. He will have lost a lot of respect through a silly remark. That was his last game and I would have liked nothing more at the end of that game than to have clapped him off. Instead I wanted to use my hands for something else that night when I realised that we had qualified. I thought he was above that kind of cheap remark.

I have always got on with people from the North. I've been up there a lot and I love the place and the people. When I got close to Norman Whiteside at United I always wanted Northern Ireland to win but I had supported them before that. It was an Irish team playing, as far as I was concerned.

I would like to think that what Bingham said was said in the heat of the moment but I have my doubts. He made similiar remarks in January when the draw was made for the European Championship qualifiers in Manchester. Obviously he hasn't learned his lessons and he means what he said.

It worked against him in November 1993. It annoyed us and it fired the lads up as well. Some of the lads were incensed by it. It didn't do us any favours on the night, on a night that was so nerve-wracking. I have never played in a game like that – it was just so nervous, there was so much pressure on us. It was unlike any other game I had been involved with for Ireland and that includes the World Cup quarter-final against Italy back in 1990. Normally once the lads gell together again we relax in each others' company. That's been one of the beauties of the Irish system – it's always been like a great big happy family.

But that weekend was different. Jack had us over on the Friday – and I actually managed to turn up which caused a great laugh in the squad. They even offered to open a book on when I'd go missing over the few days up at the top-class Nuremore hotel in Carrickmacross before we travelled to Belfast. I didn't oblige of course – this was a time to stand up and be counted.

That was reflected within the camp. It was total pressure. You could tell from the moment we met that we had to get something out of this game. There was no relaxation – we were there to do a job and we just had to get to those World Cup finals. Even on the Sunday night when we made our usual November jaunt to the Opel International Awards the atmosphere wasn't its usual self. Jack allowed us to have a couple of pints and celebrate with Steve Staunton, who won the senior award, but that was it. We were back on the bus and back to Monaghan for the real work of the weekend.

It was a weekend with very strange travel arrangements,

thanks to the security problems. It was incredible, driving a hundred miles from Dublin to Monaghan on the Saturday, up to Dublin and back on the Sunday, then down to Dublin again on the Tuesday for a flight to Belfast – we were nearer Belfast than Dublin when we left Monaghan that Tuesday.

It was an unusual fixture all round. The political climate in Northern Ireland at the time was so volatile. There were a lot of problems and there was a lot of debate about the game going ahead at Windsor Park. I was always confident it would. I never believed for a minute that FIFA would move it away from Belfast. That would have been a mistake, even though it was all quite different for us going up there.

There were a load of factors in that game that will never happen again. If I never get nervous for another game I think that's the one that I used up all my nervous energy in. It wasn't because of all the hype about North playing South or the stories about the game being moved out of Belfast because of the delicate politicial climate there at the time. I had played there before. I had been up to the North before on a number of occasions, sometimes with Norman, and I knew there would be no problems from that point of view. But I was nervous about the game itself and the result and the World Cup. There were so many people depending on us getting something out of the game. So many people with World Cup trips booked, holidays planned, arrangements made for the summer of their life in America. People were saying it was worth a hundred million pounds to the economy, that there were jobs dependent on it at home, that the country would make so much money.

Then there was the family pressure as well. I'd been telling my sons and Caroline that I was going to bring them to the World Cup next summer, that they were going to see me play for Ireland, possibly for the last time in a World Cup game, in America.

There was just pressure right across the board. On the night in the dressing-room we were wondering if England would make it or Wales. I remember thinking if Wales got through and we don't there would be ferocious stick in the dressing-room off Dean Saunders when we got back.

The security thing never bothered me. Yes, it was funny to go to training and see armed soldiers and police and whatever all around the place. I half expected that but to see so many policemen surrounding 22 players and the staff was a bit daunting. And then we had to do the job that the Republic of Ireland wanted. It was a bit tense that way.

It wasn't even similar to the last time we had played up there on the way to Italia '90. That seemed a lot more relaxed but it was the first game in the group. Whoever picked this one as the last game needed their head examined.

In terms of pure football it was never going to be a classic and it lived up to that billing. I thought it was a terrible game. The first 20 minutes I just couldn't believe the way they were coming at us. I know people will call me a hypocrite but they came at us like they were the ones who could qualify. I was a bit naive, I thought one or two of them would not lie down and die as such but would at least give us a chance without rushing around as if their lives depended on it, lifting our lads into the air with tackles.

I just couldn't believe that. When I thought about it afterwards I said fair play to them, it was an international, they played with pride when they put on that Northern Ireland shirt. But they could have saved it for some other fixture. After all, one of our politicians even offered them the Six Counties forever if they'd let us through!

Eventually it settled down for me after about 20 minutes when I realised that I was having a nightmare and needed to do something about it. I just took a few seconds for some thought and turned to Alan Kernaghan and said to just calm it down. They still hadn't scored despite their headless chicken impersonations. I just took a deep breath and relaxed.

I never took a blind bit of notice of the crowd. They were calling me nigger and all sorts. Afterwards I thought that was funny – I'm about as close to a Black Protestant as you'll ever find in Ireland. Apparently I was getting all sorts of abuse. I never heard them – if I did it would only have wound me up to do even better.

We settled into it eventually. At half-time it was still scoreless and Jack just said to take it easy, to keep our shape and our composure, that we would wear them down. Out in the stadium Billy Bingham was doing his cheerleading bit, getting the crowd to shout even louder for his Northern Ireland in his last game.

Then came the nightmare. We were all over them when they scored – Jimmy Quinn just belted one into the top of the net. It was all your worst fears come true. There were 17 minutes left and we were in trouble. But I never thought that was it. I felt the aggression rise in me. I said to myself just don't let these bastards beat us – if there was a prize there for us to go to the World Cup there was no way these lads that we know, that we play week in and week out, were going to deny us. They were trying to take it away from us – nothing would have thrilled them more than to walk off that pitch thinking we were not going to make it to America.

At that stage when they scored I just thought, let's keep fighting, gee everyone up and keep going. Something might break. Then substitute Alan McLoughlin came up with that cracker minutes after he entered the arena.

From where I was standing it seemed so simple. He just went whoof, bang and it was in the back of the net. He was so cool about it. I thought, that's going in there, and he was hardly moving, we were hardly reacting. It was like a Sunday league game when he scored and we were all trotting back. That one goal and the draw was enough.

I was thrilled for Alan. He is part of the family; he's one of those lads who's hardly had ten games but he's there every month when the call comes. I remember him as a slight young lad at United when Ron let him go on a free transfer, so it was lovely to see him come on and get that bit of glory. It's that Three Musketeers thing – one for all and all for one. The day we forget that will be a bad day for Irish football.

And there was a great story about Alan back in Dublin. In the video, *The Road to America*, the cameras that followed us around the qualifiers were in the Submarine Bar out in Terenure on the night of that game. At half-time, when things were looking dodgy, the reporter asked a girl what should be done. She said to put on Alan McLoughlin and that he'd get a goal. Fair play to her she knew more about the tactics for that one than the rest of us.

The only thing that worried me after the goal was getting through. I didn't know even at the final whistle that Spain were still a goal up with ten men against Denmark in Seville. I turned around and thought, Jesus, we were out. Then there were lads flying at me from all angles. I got an instant heart attack when we were told that the game in Seville wasn't over yet. That had to be the longest four minutes of my life.

I just walked straight off the pitch and into the dressing-room. I couldn't bear the thought of going through that agony in public. I was effing and blinding on the way, cursing the fact that Jimmy Quinn had scored such a brilliant goal, that we had managed only one reply through the great Alan McLoughlin, cursing the North for not lying down and letting us qualify easily.

I was just waiting for the ridiculous to happen and news of a Danish goal. When I got into the dressing-room Eddie Corcoran was the first man I saw and I just kept shouting at him, "It's not over yet. It's not over yet." Then he got on to Donnie Butler on the radio and learned it was official – Spain had beaten Denmark and we were through on goals difference or goals scored or something like that. I didn't care. We had qualified for the World Cup and all hell broke loose. I wanted to kiss Alan McLoughlin there and then – but there was a queue.

Everyone was singing and shouting and screaming, it was a bloody great evening. The champagne was out, the party had begun even as we made our way on to the bus to Aldergrove Airport under armed escort for the flight back to Dublin.

The funniest thing on the way out was the bloke giving Niall Quinn stick on the steps of the coach as we got ready to go away. He was telling Niall to "fuck off back to Dublin, you Fenian bastard". Niall, cool as a cucumber, just turned to him and said, "I'll send you a postcard from America, pal." I nearly wet myself with laughter.

It was incredible when we got back to Dublin at half past one in the morning and the airport was packed. It was like coming back from Italy all over again. There were kids there and I was thinking they should be in bed but they just wanted to see their heroes. Caroline was with me and we had such a good night with the lads and their wives. We went into town and let it sink in. Even going back the next day we were still lapping it up. When we got back to the club everyone was congratulating the four of us from the Irish squad.

It was an incredible night in Rumours. There was just so much relief that we had qualified, it meant so much to so many people. It was bad enough playing in it but to have watched a game like that must have been so hard.

It surpassed qualifying the last time. That will always live in my memory, that game in Malta and the incredible party in Valetta. But this meant more, just the manner in which it finished up. The other one will always stick in my mind for the time that we had over in Italy but we didn't know what to expect. This time we'd have been there before, we would know what was needed to succeed beyond all our dreams in America and we'd be ready to bust a gut to do it. It would be the last World Cup chance for quite a few of us. As I said about Villa not winning the title, you appreciate something that much more when you've been there already.

People were saying after the Belfast game that Spain had done us a great favour and booked our ticket to America but that was wrong; you qualify for a World Cup over ten or 12 or 14 matches, not over one game. That's the mistake Graham Taylor made when he blamed Koeman for England's World Cup exit in Rotterdam. England didn't lose the World Cup away to Holland, they lost it in previous matches at home to Norway and Holland when they were ahead and drew both times. The same applied with us. We got 18 points from 12 games, we had actually done it over the 12 games. We went away where Denmark got draws and won. At the end of the day we got ourselves through.

People also talk a lot of rubbish about Dad's Army and the age of our squad going to America. It will be nice in ten or 20 years when my kids are grown up and I can talk to them about qualifying for the World Cup with Ireland when I was 34 – ahead of European Champions Denmark. Even Terry Yorath came out with some rubbish that Ireland weren't in a tough group. Who is he trying to kid?

I felt for Wales and I felt for Graham Taylor. We were in the dressing-room before the match in Belfast when we heard England were a goal down away to San Marino. The lads were shocked – and I wondered if the poor man's life could sink any lower. I really do feel for him because he is a nice man.

It's been an incredible six years for Ireland. Since Jack has taken over he's lifted us to a new level of belief. We've lost a lot of great players over the years. Liam Brady for me was one of the best in the world, the best player to ever play for Ireland. Mark Lawrenson was in a class of his own. Frank Stapleton was a great target man, a great captain for Ireland.

We've missed Mick McCarthy badly at times in this campaign. If he had been there against Spain we wouldn't have dared to let in three goals as quickly as we did. He'd have killed us on the pitch. I spoke to him in Dublin recently and I told him that he had as much right as anyone to come to America with the lads.

I wouldn't be surprised if he's the next Irish boss. He gave us incredible belief and confidence, he was the best lad to have at your back. He ran the show, screaming and shouting, fighting and kicking everything that moved. He once cleared a ball into the top of the stand at Maine Road and explained afterwards that he did it because he'd never seen anyone score from row Z. That was typical Mick, organising the players in front of him and giving it

100 per cent commitment. He deserves as much credit as anyone for getting us there. He played in some of the early games. It must be hard for him to see things moving on without him.

It gets tricky when people start talking about using veterans like myself and Kevin, David O'Leary and even John Aldridge. You have to look at it realistically. If we missed out on America we would feel aggrieved. A lot of us will have to face up to the reality of life beyond international football fairly shortly. I've gone along for the last four years not doing any training but believing that I can still play football. This past season I have dropped a level in terms of performance, I've had a lot of personal problems as well and sometimes I'm amazed that I'm still able to play at all with everything that's going on around me. I wonder how I turn up on a Saturday to play games because I'm thinking I've got to do this on Monday or that on Tuesday. Go into court, sign this or sign that.

There's going to come a time when somebody is going to have to replace us. Kevin is going to have to go as well as myself and David O'Leary. There are lads like Alan Kernaghan who have come in and he'll get a right few games now. I think he's still settling in.

There's no way, though, that I'm going to say to Jack, okay, let some kid come in. No – I'm going to be fighting all the way to get fully fit and keep myself as fit as I can. If at the end of the day Jack leaves me out of his 22 I'd feel aggrieved – I want to make it impossible for him to leave me out.

I think Jack has developed and run his squad in a very good way. He's brought players in when he's needed them. The likes of Denis Irwin, Terry Phelan and Roy Keane have all established themselves since the last World Cup finals and there's no way anyone could say that they've weakened the side. The same applies to Alan Kelly, who's now an established member of the squad as Packie Bonner's understudy. And Alan McLoughlin had to wait patiently in the squad system before he made his presence felt in Belfast.

Jack has done it carefully, he doesn't have the resources that Graham Taylor had at his disposal or that Terry Venables has now – even if he did I don't think he would have used 59 players in three and a half years. He's used the friendlies well, he's looked at players in a non-competitive situation then, when the chance arose, he's used them as he needs them. He's kept the ones who can do a job for him and dumped the ones who won't. Then there are young lads like Gary Kelly, Brian Carey and Phil Babb whom he brought to Belfast last November. I'm sure they'll get a chance along with the likes of Scott Fitzgerald at Wimbledon. I think Jack has stood by the players because it's worked for him. We've worked hard for Jack because we wanted to.

I believe England never got the support from the media that they should have in the World Cup qualifiers. There were a lot of players who shouldn't have been used but that's what you put a manager there for. I think even Graham might hold his hands up and say he didn't do everything the way he should have done.

I was surprised he wasn't a big hit as an international manager. The amount of quality players in England is phenomenal – they just don't seem to gell on the park like we do. But it's off the park where we get our inspiration. Jack treats us like adults, let's us have a drink together on the Sunday night when we meet up and that helps develop the one for all and all for one mentality. The team that drinks together stays together – I know from talking to the English lads that there is so much pressure and so much seriousness in their camp.

When we report to Dublin on a Sunday it's like going back to your family. We've got a much more settled atmosphere off the field and that carries on to the pitch. It carries on in our relationship with the media as well. I've been drunk with Irish journalists at home and abroad. I've been out with them and that in itself builds up trust. You know the good guys and the bad guys – but if a journalist becomes a friend they're much less likely to have a go when times are tough. We have a mutual respect.

It's a shame England didn't make it to the USA. The World Cup misses something with England not there. I remember watching them in '70 when Bobby Moore was my hero. After that Holland game I felt there would be something missing at this World Cup finals with England not there.

Bryan Robson would make a great England manager. I'm delighted for him that he has been appointed to work with Terry Venables, Don Howe and Dave Sexton at England level. That was an inspired choice by Terry and a good sign that England are preparing now for the future.

Bryan has all the attributes for international management. He's the most competitive player I've ever known. If he can transfer that battling spirit into management you couldn't bet against him becoming a success with United or with England. If he puts his mind to doing it, he'll get there. I'd back him every time – he's an amazing fellow. He knows football through and through. He's been there, he's done it, he has the tee-shirt and the caps. I always thought he would get into club management first but he will be a success with England.

I was gutted for Wales and for Dean Saunders. It's sad to see the World Cup denied the talents and quality of a player like Ryan Giggs. He's got years ahead of him to get there but the likes of Dean and Mark Hughes won't have so many more chances for the World Cup.

At 22 years of age, though, Roy Keane of Ireland has it all ahead of him. If you look at any World Cup it is a shop window. My old Villa team-mate David Platt has become a millionaire out of the last World Cup. Because he scored a great goal for England against Belgium he became a superstar overnight. Since then he's moved three times from Villa to Bari to Juventus and now to Sampdoria. That goal made him.

Roy can follow in his footsteps. He's got a great energy about him, he can run all day, he can play, he can pass. As long as he stays away from the pitfalls of Manchester life that I fell into he's got a great chance. He's got to realise that there's plenty of time after football and now is the time to concentrate on his career. He's already made one right decision by going to United but the sky is literally his limit.

I can see him playing in my position for Ireland in years to come. His passing is not utilised enough by United or probably by Ireland. He tends to run on to things for club and country but his brain is so good and his vision so clear. He could become a great libero moving out from the back, opening up defences and sweeping forward every so often himself. He could do that at a doddle. I played against him when he was there for Forest last season and he was unbelievable. None of our lads upfront got a kick. He has too much energy and too much to give in midfield to play further back for Ireland just yet but one day he will do it with his eyes closed. He's got so much vision and he's good in the air.

I was so impressed with him in the World Cup qualifiers, especially in the Spanish game when we were under the cosh going to Seville, but he played as if it was his backyard in Cork. He was so calm, he ran the show against some very seasoned internationals and even the great Maradona was taken by his skills. He could be the next big export from the English game to Italy – and if he does it I'll be both delighted for him and jealous. I would have loved the chance to play abroad in my career – if he gets it he should grab it.

It must be frightening for him – at his age I was only coming over from Ireland. I'm just delighted he's one of us. He can do my running for me! I still think he's learning. He's much more confident about himself since his move to United. He can handle the big stage now. He's getting stronger now, he does things that are beyond a young fellow.

CHAPTER SIXTEEN

Amigos

FOOTBALL has been good to me – despite all my moans and groans.

It has given me the chance to see the world, to meet new friends, to get a glimpse at a lifestyle that was otherwise beyond me growing up in a Dublin orphanage. It has opened some doors, slammed others in my face, exposed the world to me and me to the world. All those things have come at a price but there are friendships I have developed before football and through football that I would never swap for love nor money.

Klasf Lee was my running partner in The Bird's Nest. We had a lot in common in the home. We were both black and we both knew how to stand up for ourselves. We don't meet that often now but, like any true friendship, when we do it's as if we were never away.

John Young was my first real friend outside the orphanage. We grew up together, going to the same school, playing for the same football team. Frank Mullen, Tommy Cullen and Johnny Dunne at Dalkey were always there when I needed someone. They still are

Billy Behan did more for me that most people could imagine. He stood by me when I was sick. He ensured Manchester United stood by me in my hour of need, long before I had ever signed my life to their cause.

Joey Malone has been a good friend since our days together at St Pat's. The same can be said of Paul Birch, once of Aston Villa, now of Wolves. He's always been there when I've needed a shoulder to cry on or to fall on. Many's the time I've phoned him for advice, often in the middle of the night. He always listens with sympathy and understanding.

At United it was Kevin Moran, Norman Whiteside and Bryan Robson who kept me sane, who kept me on the straight and narrow and off it a few times as well. We were a regular foursome in the drinking holes of Hale and Altrijncham, regulars in the sin bin with Ron Atkinson and Alex Ferguson. But we were always one for all and all for one.

One of the biggest mistakes that Alex Ferguson made was getting rid of Kevin Moran so early. He lost not just a great player and servant to the club but a spiritual leader as well, a father figure in the dressing-room. I know that Kevin still visits United regularly and is often to be seen in the players' bar and the dressing-room leading to the inner sanctum. That doesn't surprise me in the slightest. The United staff, the players and the fans all hold him in such esteem. That was proven last season when he got one of the biggest rounds of applause of the night when he went back there with Blackburn on the evening United received the first Premier League trophy.

For me Kevin has always been more than just a work colleague. He was the big brother I never had since I caught my last glimpse of Denis and Mrs Donnelly out in Whitehall all those years before. He was a sporting hero of mine long before I crossed the Irish Sea. His achievements with the Dublin Gaelic football team are legendary in Ireland. He was one of the greats from the first day he arrived for training under the legendary Dublin coach Kevin Heffernan on the back of his Honda 50 motorbike. He was always in the wars even then. I can still remember that great All-Ireland clash with Kerry in 1976 when Kevin ended up with bandages swarming around his head and playing like a Colossus. How often was he to do that on the playing fields of England?

When I signed for United in 1982 Kevin was already a legend at the club. His bravery won him the hearts of the fans, his commitment won him the heart of Ron Atkinson. As a player he has always been as honest as the day is long. And he is the best central defensive partner I have ever had for club or country. With United and with Ireland I always knew where I stood with Kevin. When I started playing with him he taught me more about the art of defending than any coach in England.

Kevin understands that a good central defensive partnership is based on communication and trust. He always talked me through games, let me know where the striker was, when to stay in, when to stay out. If Kevin said to leave a ball I left it because I had 100 per cent confidence in his assessment of the situation. I play better with a player like that alongside me who will talk me through the game. Latterly in my career I have been the talker – and some of the time that hasn't worked with Villa or with Ireland.

He has always been more than just a friend to me. When Kevin was around he always made sure I got home in one piece. Had he not left United for Spain when he did I would probably not have tried to drive home the night I wrote the car off after a session with Norman and ended up lucky to be alive.

I should also have taken advantage of his business expertise over the years. He'd have known what I should have done with my deals and my money. And I always envied him his move to the continent when he signed for Sporting Gijon after his free transfer from United. But even Kevin's move to Spain and Sporting Gijon landed me in trouble.

His going-away party was at the Four Seasons Hotel in Hale, near both our homes. It's a great hotel, run by an Irishman called Seamus Kilroe, and boasts the best Guinness outside Ireland in its trendy bar, appropriately called Mulligan's. It was natural that Kevin would have his going away bash there – and of course all the Irish lads at United gathered to see their best friend off in style the night before he was about to fly out with Eleanor and the kids. We had a right session. I was drinking away with Kevin and his missus and with Norman and his wife Julie. Towards the end of the night Norman was off talking to someone else and he'd left a pint behind. I said to Julie that I might as well drink it since he wasn't going to bother. But of course walls in Manchester have eyes as well as ears.

The next day in the *Daily Mirror* I was reported as being so drunk that I went around the bar picking up half-empty glasses and knocking the drink back. They even quoted an eye-witness. Since that was a private party I couldn't believe the story and the way it was done. But mud sticks in these situations.

I was fuming and so were the club and Kevin. It was absolute rubbish. If I had been desperate for a drink I could have bought one – I had plenty of money in my pocket. I simply drank that pint because Norman wasn't going to – nothing more and nothing less.

I chased the PFA to get an apology for me. Even Alex Ferguson was so incensed by the story and the damage it did needlessly to my reputation, without any grain of truth, that he kicked up a storm with the newspaper. Kevin, too, before he got on that plane to Spain, spoke in my defence. That was typical of the way he has looked after me all through the years.

Before Fergie arrived there was always a nice little Irish posse at United and that is important for any lad from home going to any club in England. You need some of your own to help you settle in. United then was a home from home, with Kevin, Ashley Grimes, Frank Stapleton, Liam O'Brien and youngsters like Pat Kelch, Derek Brazil, Martin Russell and later Joe Hanrahan, the brainy one who refused to be browbeaten by Fergie and went home rather than put up with the rantings and the ravings and the arguments from Fergie. Joe was too clever to listen to all that and had a university degree and a career with Shamrock Rovers to fall back on. If I had that luxury I'd have skipped it home as well.

Both sides of the Irish border were represented in the dressing-room, without partition or any problems. There were quite a few lads from the North when I went there, like Norman, Phil Hughes and Kenny Scott. Now it seems you have to be Irish and from Cork to sign for the club. Witness Roy Keane, Denis Irwin and Brian Carey, the last three major signings from the Republic, with Brian now moved on to Leicester.

In my early days Ashley Grimes was the joker in the pack, the man who teamed up with Lou Macari to cut the tops of your socks while you were out training or stick wintergreen down your jockstrap before a match. That pair were always at it. They thought they were Laurel and Hardy.

Years later I was close to signing for Lou when he was in charge at Swindon and I was going through my bad times with Ferguson. That would have been interesting. West Brom's Kieran O'Regan, another Cork man, has told me about the strange training habits Lou used when they worked together at Swindon. Since I don't train anymore I don't know how I'd have coped with his army camp sessions and his long cross-country runs.

Frank Stapleton was quieter and more reserved. But he was a great footballer, a tremendous worker on and off the ball. I really appreciated that the night in Hanover during the European Championship finals in '88 when I was in the stands and really studied what he was about. I know Frank too had his problems with Alex Ferguson and gets almost as much criticism as I do in the book *Six Years At United*. That was unfair – and bore scant regard to the service Frank had given the club in previous years. He has been a great friend to me over the years and so has wife Chris. They are the sort of people you can always rely on.

Fergie makes a lot in his book of the relationship between Norman Whiteside and myself. We were much more than bosom buddies – we were blood brothers, often brothers in arms when things got really scary.

I met Norman as soon as I went to United on trial and was put in digs with him, Barry Kehoe and Phil Hughes, with a lovely woman called Bet Fenham out in Chorlton. I hit it off with Norman straight away. He was six years younger than me and on his way with Northern Ireland to the 1982 World Cup finals and a tournament that was to put his star firmly into the ascendant.

My first footballing move of any note at United was to set Norman up for a goal in a reserve team match at Newcastle. Even then he was such a handful for defenders, a teenager in age but a man in stature and physique. He was so confident on and off the ball. He took the world by surprise with his performances in that Spanish World Cup finals but I wasn't shocked in the slightest. It was no more than I expected, having watched him at first hand for three months. He played like a 24-year-old. He had that arrogance about him, the swagger that suggested he had done it all before. His goal that night was top class. In one of his earliest games in the United first team, he chipped the 'keeper at Ipswich with a finish that would have done a Brazilian proud.

The pressure on Norman at 16 was so intense but he handled it all. He was in the Northern Ireland team at the World Cup, he came back from there as the great white hope for Manchester United. It was bound to take its toll eventually and he ended up in as much trouble with Ferguson as I did. We became the Terrible Twins of Old Trafford.

We were lumped together by the media as soon as I had crashed my car and been close to doing myself in back in 1987. That was the first time I was really in the headlines for all the wrong reasons – and attracting front-page interest from the tabloids. I can remember the day of the crash but not much about the crash itself. Norman had some builders over at his house putting on an extension and they were close to finishing the job. As a thank you gesture he had invited them down to the Four Seasons

194

Hotel in Hale for a meal and a few drinks. I went along with Norman's father-in-law and we had a great session altogether. The drink was flowing, the crack was good and the whole day was an unqualified success.

Of course drink and driving don't mix. But I was in no condition to realise that. I insisted on driving home, a distance of about a mile and a half from the hotel to my house. I refused the offer of a lift from Norman's wife Julie when she came to collect her husband and her father. I refused their advice to take a taxi and leave the car at the hotel. I refused to listen to common-sense. I got into that car because I was convinced I was alright to drive. Mistake number one. Mistake number two came about half a mile from home when I lost control of the car completely. I was aware of what was happening but it all went by so quickly it was as if I had no control over it. The car took off on its own, mounted the footpath, went into a garden, through another one and came to a stop in the grounds of a third house. Luckily I had been conscious enough getting into the car to put my belt on. That didn't prevent me from getting whacked on the head by the steering wheel. Not that I felt much pain. I had my own anaesthetic on board.

When I came round somebody was opening the door and attempting to drag me from the wreckage. I looked up and laughed – I was trying to make a big joke of the whole thing, not realising what had happened. As soon as they moved my head blood came gushing out everywhere. The next thing I knew I was in hospital – and a blood test was taken for drink driving. I was three times over the legal limit.

To be fair to Alex Ferguson he never had a go at me about the crash. He has said since that he was amazed I was still alive – and that's why he left me alone. He also knows that the accident awoke me to a lot of things. It made me realise how bad drinking and driving is – I was banned for two years but lucky just to survive that smash.

It also made me realise what life was really like as a bad boy in the media. They dragged Norman into it as well because I had been seen with him all that day. That started all the bad publicity. After the crash we couldn't turn for somebody ringing the club and telling Fergie that we were on the beer in this pub or that pub. People resented seeing Manchester United players out having a good time. Norman and I developed a reputation as the heavy drinkers of Old Trafford. If we had a day off, of course we'd have a few beers. If we finished work and fancied a pint, of course we'd have one. But so would any group of workers.

We got slaughtered. Every second week Fergie was hauling me over the coals, passing on second-hand information that I had been in this pub or that pub. Norman was having his problems as well with the boss – and we were always lumped together. When we both asked for transfers I was ahead of Norman by about six months. Yet it came out that we had planned it together. That wasn't the case at all. A few people tried to buy us as a pair but United weren't keen on that idea at all. Eventually I escaped to Villa and the same summer Norman went to Everton. Sadly, he's had to quit since through injury. Now he makes his money as a physio and an after-dinner speaker. I hope I make it into a few of the stories after this book!

The one thing about Norman was his loyalty to his friends. We were from opposite sides of the tracks back home in Ireland. That was never an issue between us. Norman is very misunderstood in Ireland, probably because of his background in the Shankill, in the heart of loyalist Belfast. That has built up an image about him in the Republic that is completely unfair. I have spent the best of times with him in Belfast and a crazy night in Derry. We have holidayed together in Donegal – he loves it up there, as does Paddy Crerand. And we have had some great nights in Dublin.

He was always Irish as far as we were all concerned – and that prompted one of the funniest nights of our relationship. The Wolfe Tones, the best rebel-rousing ballad group in the world, were on tour in England and playing at the Carousel in Manchester. The lads in the band have always had a great rapport with the Irish soccer team since the days of the footballing Ray Tracey and his banjo, when Liam Tuohy was the manager of the national side. In fact one of the rituals with the Irish side now is a Wolfe Tones tape on the bus on the way into every match we play. We belt out the ballads with the tape – that really gets the blood worked up before kick-off. After that you'd die for Ireland on the pitch.

That night in Manchester we were all going to see them. Kevin was there, Frank, Ashley, Liam O'Brien and a few of the younger Irish lads. Norman came along – and I'm not sure he realised the rather political content of some of their songs. Of course he got a hard time from a few of the punters – a couple of them even thought about roughing him up in the loo. But Norman's a big bloke and he can handle himself. He took it all in good humour and we had a good laugh with the band about it afterwards.

We had another great laugh in Glasgow when we went up together for the 1989 Scottish Cup final between Celtic and Rangers. Celtic won, Mick McCarthy lifted the Cup and we had a wild night celebrating. At least I was celebrating with my winnings from Norman. He wasn't too impressed with the result – or the fact that he had to hand over the stake money to me afterwards.

Glasgow, of course, is almost as bad as Manchester for football gossip. We'd barely got off the shuttle from Manchester when the word was out that United were selling their two wayward sons north of the Border. According to the reports I was signing for Celtic and Norman was going to Rangers. It never happened of course. We got a good laugh out of that one.

Norman was with me for one of the highlights of my career when we met Sir Stanley Matthews out in Canada the summer after we had won the FA Cup in 1985. Norman and I were invited out to play for an international team against the Canadians as part of their centenary celebrations. While we were there we met a local judge who was a personal friend of Sir Stanley. He took us out for a day touring the area and visiting the Niagara Falls. We had a great day, then on the way back he said we'll take you up to see Sir Stanley Matthews. I was saying no, don't trouble the man, but he landed us in on top of Sir Stanley and it was a great thrill to meet a living legend. We just crashed into his home and he was delighted to see us. He knew all about what was happening back in England and he spoke to us about the Cup final and how we'd won it. He was still playing in Canada at that stage and he told us all about the local team and how they were doing. He even gave me a bit of encouragement about my knees. It was fabulous to see him, especially so soon after we had won the Cup, a competition that meant so much to him as a player.

Then at the start of the 1987-88 season we were picked together for the Football League team to play the Rest of the World in their centenary match at Wembley. I was amazed when I got the call-up for that game – I couldn't believe it. I was actually back home in Dublin on holiday when news came through that Bobby Robson had called me into his squad for the game.

I was having a few pints in the Harp on O'Connell Bridge when this fellow called Donnie Flynn, a United fanatic originally from Cork but at that time home on holiday from a welding course in Manchester, walked up to me and said congratulations, you've been picked for the English league team to play the Rest of the

World at Wembley. I thought he was taking the piss out of me. I thought, get out of that, you're having me on. Then when I discovered that I had been picked I thought I'd just be with the squad but I wouldn't actually play in the game itself.

Manager Bobby Robson had always been good to me. When I first joined United and started to make waves in the first team he was aware of the fact that I had been born in Ealing. That made me eligible for England – and he wasn't slow to get the message down the grapevine. After one England trip Bryan Robson came back to Old Trafford with a message for me from his gaffer. There was talk at the time of Eoin Hand finally getting his act together and picking me for Ireland – Bobby sent the message to wait and he'd get me into the England set-up. Ray Wilkins, the best player I've seen at United, encouraged me to wait as well.

I was flattered by the approach but rejected it out of hand. England had been badly stung by the loss of Mark Lawrenson to the Republic when Johnny Giles was manager. They were always moaning about losing Lawro and years later they would make the same remarks about my Villa Park buddy and Irish captain Andy Townsend. I think that was one of the reasons that Robson made his interest in me known so early. But it was one-way traffic. I may have been born in London but that was purely through circumstances as far as I was concerned. It is no more than a line on my passport. I had spent only six weeks in the capital, I did not feel that any part of me was English. I was still struggling for recognition with Ireland under Eoin Hand but I never considered turning my back on my country. I would have missed international football altogether rather than play for any country other than the Republic of Ireland.

By the same token, if any of my boys show any sign of footballing skills, and Christopher the eldest lad is a lot better than I was at his age, then they'll play for Ireland, if I have anything to do with it. Of course they'll have a choice – so long as they make the right one!

That was my answer to Robson but to be fair he never held it against me. He was always full of praise for me as a player – publicly and privately. Back in 1985 he had locked horns with Ireland in a friendly at Wembley. England won 2-1, Gary Lineker scored his first international goal and I was involved from the Irish midfield until Eoin decided to give me the hook, for little reason, at half-time. Before the match was the best part for me though. In the English papers the previous Sunday Robson discussed the game at length. He spoke of the qualities of Lawrenson and Liam Brady, obviously the stars of our Irish side back then. When he was asked to pick the best player in the Irish squad, though, he sprung a surprise – he opted for me. According to Robson I was the best prospect in England right then. I was close to becoming a regular then at centre-back in the United side and he could see nothing but a great future for me with club and country. He spoke of my pace and my ability to get out of trouble – and he spoke of my potential as a midfield player at international level. That was ironic because years later I would play in the centre of midfield against England on a number of occasions, including that famous win in Stuttgart in Euro '88, a date inscribed on Irish hearts everywhere. Bobby Robson saw something in me that was not obvious, and Jack Charlton had the same foresight years later.

Robson maintained his loyalty to me when he picked that Football League side for the game at Wembley. It was a magnificent feeling to go back to the Twin Towers as part of that representative side and to play alongside such great players as Maradona, Ossie Ardiles, Chris Waddle, Peter Beardsley, Bryan Robson and our own Liam Brady. I enjoyed every minute – and Robbo the manager made me his man of the match. To say I was on the same team and the same field as those greats will always be one of the highlights of my playing career.

Bobby Robson came across as a nice man. He pushed us quite hard in training even though it was only a representative match. He took it seriously, he wanted to win it and he came across as a good manager. He was tactically astute.

The next time I came across him was in the European Championships out in Stuttgart – and the circumstances were slightly different that day. He ended up playing us twice as England boss – he lost one in the Europeans in Stuttgart and he drew the game in Italy at the start of the World Cup. There was a lot of rubbish written by those so-called experts about that game in Italy and indeed the match in Stuttgart. We were knocked for playing long ball, for being the Wimbledons of world football. That was rubbish. We were battlers and we had our pride. We played to a system that maximised our skills and our potential. If England had found a system that suited them over the last four years they might have been in America with us.

Robson never made such excuses. He knew what he was in for, he never kidded himself that it would be all pretty football with

John Barnes belting down the wings. He knew the way we'd be, he accepted it for what it was and gave credit where credit was due. He probably felt he deserved something out of the first game but he would certainly have been happy with the result the second time.

I have a lot of respect for Bobby Robson. I only spent a couple of days with him. I've seen him since but I've never had a long conversation or anything. For me he was grossly mistreated as England manager. He should have been honoured for what he achieved with his country on the pitch, not lambasted for what he did off it. Like me he enjoyed the good things in life. Like me he got caught. There are people in the corridors of power in this game who have behaved in exactly the same way. There are people who set themselves up as judge and jury against the likes of Bobby Robson and myself yet they commit the same cardinal sins all the time. There are double standards rampant in football.

We were at a World Cup training camp in Izmir at the end of May 1990 when news broke that Bobby Robson was to resign as England manager after Italia '90. There was dismay in the Irish camp. A lot of the lads knew him and liked him and Jack regarded him as a friend and a good manager. Jack let his feelings be known to the media. He wasn't happy with the way his friend had been treated. He said it just typified why he would never take the England job, why the Irish job was human compared to the England situation.

If Bobby Robson had been manager of the Irish team he would have been treated so differently. It's amazing that anyone should be allowed to take that sort of criticism and that sort of stick from the so-called experts in the newspapers. I felt for him because I have been that soldier so many times in the past and no doubt I will be again. It was disgraceful – murderers wouldn't get the sort of abuse that he was getting. He took it with a lot of dignity, he never kicked back or lashed out. He would have been justified in my mind if he had done. If it had happened to Jack he would have given the reporter a mouthful then sorted it out. Bobby took it well but he should never have had to take it. Thankfully the Irish people never treat their sports people like that.

I felt a similar sympathy for Robson's successor Graham Taylor when he decided to call it a day as England boss after failing to make the World Cup finals. Graham played a huge part in my life. He rescued me from an Old Trafford hell and gave me reason to live again at Villa Park.

One of the great regrets of my career is never getting the chance to work with Terry Venables, the man who has just taken over from Graham as England coach. Jimmy Armfield never asked my opinion on who should take charge of England but he got it right anyway. We have been close to working together – twice I almost became a Tottenham player. Both times I was encouraged by my good friend in Dublin, Krish Naidoo, to sign for his beloved Spurs. I actually launched the Irish edition of Terry's board game *The Manager*. I just wonder, will he now rename it *The Coach* since that's his England title?

Terry is a real player's man. I know from talking to him and watching him in action that his is one of the most astute brains in the business. He commands respect on the training pitch and that breeds respect in the dressing-room. I have no doubt that he will be a success with the England squad. And I sincerely hope he is. I think the domestic game in England needs a successful England side. It's a shame that the Republic qualifed for America on our own without England, Scotland, Wales or Northern Ireland for company.

England have a major advantage for the next European Championship finals in 1996 – as hosts they're already qualified. That will take a huge amount of pressure off Terry, pressure that Graham Taylor was always living under.

I know myself from the disappointment we suffered by not making the 1992 European finals what non-qualification means. Terry doesn't have to worry about that. He has two years to grow into the job – if the FA give him the time he will need to work with the players. He certainly has some great talent at his disposal. I have a lot of time for the likes of Paul Ince, David Platt, Gazza, Ian Wright, Alan Shearer and Tony Adams. They are the backbone of his side. The talent coming through the ranks is quite strong too. Terry already knows all about Nicky Barmby and Darren Anderton at Spurs. They are exciting prospects. So too is our own Steve Froggatt at Aston Villa and that goal machine called Andy Cole at Newcastle. I can't catch him, he's so quick off the mark. Greame le Saux at Blackburn, who thought he had an Irish grandmother, is another to come into contention for Tel.

English football must want success for its national side though. It's great for Ireland because the English game educates our best players. Of course we suffer by playing too often at club level – if they get that right they will benefit their own national side more than anyone else's. England have a great opportunity with Terry Venables in charge for 1996. They must not blow it.

CHAPTER SEVENTEEN

Knees up Mother Brown

THEY'VE BEEN talked about in bars, debated in pubs, prodded by specialists, opened up by experts, fondled lovingly by nurses in the course of their duty – and beyond – and manipulated by physios for club and country. They've been opened up, ripped up, dragged up and written off. But they're still there and they're still getting me through 90 minutes of action for Aston Villa and Ireland. I refer, of course, to the Paul McGrath knees, that well-known institution in Irish soccer's talking circles. People back home are always asking about the knees, asking about the latest state of play with the joints that have threatened my career, asking me will I get through the next game for Jack or Big Ron.

Jim McGregor, Jim Walker and Mick Byrne have spent more time cursing my ligaments and cartilages, working the muscles in my knees more than they have done with any other part of any other footballer's body. In reality my knees were past it years ago. In any other walk of life, if that's the right phrase to use in these circumstances, my knees would have been declared redundant. If I was a horse I'd have been declared lame and put out to grass long ago.

But professional football is seldom about commonsense when it comes to injuries. There are players scattered across the world who are now feeling the pains of past injuries, living the realities of the games they shouldn't have played, the chance they shouldn't have taken. Years from now I could well be a cripple, unable to turn or walk properly, confined to a wheelchair even, and paying the legacy of my years playing on the dodgiest knees ever to come out of Ireland. Eight operations later I am, as Elton John might suggest, still standing. But only just. The knees, as they say in Dublin, are on their last legs. They're cracking at the seams and wilting at the joints.

Jim Walker, the Villa physio whom I've abused as much as my knees with my antics on and off the field, wants me to go in and have another scope about once a year, let the doctors have a look around the joints, clean away the grit and the dirt and get me ready for another season of English football. I don't know about another op – I've had so many now that every time they open up the knee I fear it's the end, the operation that's going to produce a terminal result for my playing career.

My old Irish mate Jim Beglin has had so many problems with his knees that he's been forced to quit the game at a tragically young age and give in to the injury. But Jim has a great saying and attitude about the problems. He reckons that in ten years' time they'll have developed a total cure for knee injuries, that knee replacements will be as common as hip replacements are now. I live and wait in hope – because I sure could do with a new pair of knees.

Although I've had eight operations, at this stage it's the right knee that's causing me all the problems. It's leading by two ops – and rising. I've had an operation on an Achilles tendon problem as well but the knees have caused me most pain and anxiety since I came to England and Manchester United. Incredibly though, before then I'd never had the slightest problem with injuries of any sort, good, bad or indifferent.

I did pick up the odd muscular problem when I first started full-time training with United, I'd had a couple of strains at St Pat's and I even got kicked up the arse a few times by Dave Henderson when I missed the ball or the centre-forward at Richmond Park. But I was strictly a virgin as far as injuries went when I first joined Manchester United. I sailed through my medical with no problems and I was far from prepared for what was about to come in the future.

The knee first went in a reserve match at the end of my first season with United – and it couldn't have happened at a worse time. I had just established myself in the Central League team and the gaffer Ron Atkinson was beginning to take a bit of notice of me. My name was featuring regularly along with Norman

Whiteside's in the reserve team match reports that appeared in the United programme and in the Manchester *Evening News* soccer Pink on a Saturday night.

I'd had my name in the papers at home while I was with St Pat's and I'd got a fair bit of publicity when I signed for United both at home in Dublin and in the press in England. But this was different. I got a real kick out of seeing the name Paul McGrath in the reserve team line-up, seeing the Manchester United team, any Manchester United team, with my name in it.

I was hardly three months in England but I was coming to grips with the pace of full-time training, adapting to life in a foreign city miles away from home and beginning to enjoy myself. My game was improving and even if I didn't quite give myself the credit I probably deserved there were plenty at the club prepared to tell Big Ron how well I was developing.

That development got me into the first team squad for an end-of-season tour to Canada, but disaster struck one night in Sheffield. A reserve team game against United at Bramall Lane is hardly the stuff that dreams are made of. But that night I had a point to prove to Ron Atkinson. I wanted to justify his faith in me for that tour to Canada. Until a big old striker decided to show this young upstart from Dublin a thing or two – and came crashing across my right knee with the sort of tackle that deserved judicial punishment.

That was the beginning of the end as far as my right knee was concerned. Instead of Canada I found myself back in Ireland for a spot of r 'n' r – rest and recuperation rather than rock and roll.

I was sent home to get myself ready for Operation Paul McGrath on my return to England that summer – the first in a long series of operations. Now I know the operating theatre routine inside out. I've been there so often I could tell Martin Walsh, the specialist who looks after the Irish team's medical needs, how to do his job. And as every knee-injury-prone footballer knows, once the knee goes it never really gets better. One thing leads to another – before you know where you are the stronger knee is weakened by the burden of the other one. That's how it is has developed with me over the years. I had so many operations on the right one that eventually the pressure began to tell on the left knee and it started to develop problems. It went during the Euros and the match against England and it's been at me ever since in dribs and drabs.

The United surgeon Jonathon Noble was always brilliant about things. I went to see him so often that it was embarrassing.

He warned me after a few ops that I could be in trouble. He was always cheerful and optimistic but he did warn me after the last few that I might not be able to play because it had been opened so many times and there was very little left to repair. He warned me that I'll have problems later in life – the fellow who examined me for Spurs in 1988 said I had two years left at most. He said it might be a case where I'll suffer later on, but I don't think about that now. It might trouble me when I'm 40 and I'm hobbling around the place and asking myself why I didn't look after myself a bit better when I was playing. But there's always the chance that by the time I'm 50 science will have come up with a way to rebuild the knee joints.

It's a case of just looking after your family and doing what's right for them. It's a case of looking after your livelihood and for footballers that means playing on, even in a situation where you pick up an injury. You have to get the cash from somewhere and even though I could have quit football altogether I had to think in long-term financial terms. I had nothing to fall back on.

If I had been an ordinary midfielder playing in a Dublin league or something like that I know I wouldn't be playing now. If I had just been playing the game for a bit of a laugh and the crack of good friends instead of for my living it would be a different story. I wouldn't have taken the risks that I've taken with my knees. I wouldn't have played on the nights when I've known I was making a mistake, known I was taking a huge chance by playing when the joints weren't up to it.

I shouldn't have carried on that day against England in Stuttgart. I shouldn't have played any further part in the European Championships after that game. I should have gone straight back to Manchester and straight into the operating theatre. But I couldn't bring myself to renege on Jack's team and let Ireland, my country, down.

There were times when I was living with Paul Birch after I first went to Villa when he'd ask me to tell him what the weather was like by the feelings in my knee. If it was damp or cold I had a pain. Nine times out of ten the knees were more accurate than the meteorological service.

But I hate crying off games and missing matches. A lot of games I've played I knew beforehand that I probably shouldn't but then they've gone okay and I've got through it. After games I've often said to myself, "Jesus you're an idiot", because I shouldn't have played in them.

I've often been told that it's all in my mind and there's nothing wrong with me. There was a stage at Manchester United when the club honestly believed that – but I never faked an injury in my life.

The worst time for suspicion and doubt at United was when I came back from the European Championships and told them there was something drastically wrong with my left knee, arguably my good one at that time. I knew it was so bloody obvious that there was something wrong. I could bend my knee and lift it and there'd be a bad click. I could actually see the knee moving as it clicked but for ages they didn't seem to believe that there was a problem.

There have been times when I've played for United and Villa and known it was wrong medically. But I always felt I was doing what was right morally at the time, no matter what the danger to my knees in the future. Once I play in a game I feel as confident as I've ever felt about how my knees will last up to the demands of professional football. When you start a game with an injury worry you have to let the adrenaline act as an anaesthetic, let it smother the pain and get you through the 90 minutes. You just can't give in to the pain or you're useless to yourself and your team.

I know that attitude comes with a prospective cost at the end of my career. If I see 36 and I'm still playing I'll be lucky, but I don't look that far ahead. I just look to the next game and the next season. I can't afford to look any further. After all those operations and months in plaster I, more than anyone else, know that you can't afford to take things for granted with injuries.

The knees have caused me pain, moments of doubt, hours of frustration in the gym building the muscles back up and keeping them up. I've spent a lot of time doing exercises on my own – and a lot of time not bothering to do what the specialists have told me I have to do to keep my job as a professional sportsman.

There were times when my knees have driven me to drink. Times when I got confident and cocky about it, when I thought that the knees were fine only for the old pains and the old problems to come back as regular as clockwork. That's when you have to go in and start all over again with the exercises and building the muscles up to where they were just a few days or sometimes weeks earlier.

My knees now determine my football life. They decide when I train with the other lads out on the pitch or when I do it on my own in the gym. There are some players at Villa who are convinced my knees are just an excuse for an old man to stay out of training. That's not the case at all. They're as bad now as they've ever been but I get on with it. I work them at their pace and they get me through. We have a deal. I look after them and they look after me. I don't wear bandages on them, although I have done a few times. I had my right knee strapped a few times last season when there were times it felt so bad that I needed a bit of reassurance that it was held together.

People think I'm crazy when I talk about my knees but I do have an incredible relationship with both my knees and all their joints and all their cartilages. I know some mornings when I wake up for games that I don't think I can play – normally I do.

CHAPTER EIGHTEEN

Next Stop Please

THE FUTURE is a far off, distant shore where most footballers are concerned. When you come into this beautiful game you dream only of the glory, not the reality of life at the end of the tunnel. There is no full-time whistle on your career as long as you're playing. You're only as good as your next match – and that final fixture is always an eternity away.

Then the years start to catch up on you. And more worryingly, the centre-forwards start to catch up and then pass you. You notice the opposition getting younger, the pace of the game getting faster. You fool yourself that it's the changing face of football. It is of course the passing of time.

It happens to us all. When I look back at the playing staff at United when I joined, so many of them are no longer playing at the highest level. Some are not playing at all, some are managing and others have drifted off down whatever path life had waiting for them away from the football pitch.

I know I face that decision very shortly. At most I have two seasons left in me, hopefully with Aston Villa if Ron Atkinson will keep faith with the worst knees in the English game.

At international level my time is almost up. The new kids are pushing for their place on the Irish block with the European Championship qualifiers just around the corner and a new generation of the Green Army waiting to show Jack their mettle on the way to his native land in 1996.

I don't think I'm cut out to get involved in management. I have seen too many of my friends in football go down that road and be scarred for life. Others have been great successes. Steve Coppell did well with Crystal Palace. Lou Macari has done the business at Swindon, Stoke and now at Celtic. And he's taken Ashley Grimes along with him. Mick McCarthy has done a great job at Millwall. Liam Brady is getting things sorted out at Brighton. Frank Stapleton has been a godsend in the boss's seat at Bradford. They're just a few of the players I've played with who are now in the management game. But they are all completely different animals to me. They have no problems dealing with people, dealing with the different mentalities that make up any dressing-room. I would be useless in a situation like that. And I could hardly be a strict disciplinarian. My track record on that score is hardly without blemish or good enough to tick players off for going over the top every so often.

I honestly don't know where I'm going to end up when my contract finally runs out at Villa. I always fancied a few years on the continent but that has gone beyond me now. I could try Japan like Gary Lineker and Gerry Peyton, but after my non-show with Villa last summer they'll hardly welcome me there now.

Nothing would please me more than to move back to Dublin with Caroline and bring the kids up in Ireland as Irishmen. I'd love that and they'd love it. And it might allow me to return to the League of Ireland for the twilight of my career. I could always go back to St Patrick's Athletic with Brian Kerr or maybe go to Monaghan United with Billy Bagster and Joey Malone. Imagine me playing alongside Joey again – all we'd need is Dave Henderson behind us in goals again when he recovers from his broken leg picked up with Bohemians in the FAI Cup.

Off the field is the problem. A year from now I'm going to pick up my pension as a footballer but I will still need some sort of a job to keep me occupied over the autumn of my life.

I know one area I won't be delving into – the recording business. And you can count out the media as well. A club as big as Manchester United attracts more press than any other club in England. The press box at Old Trafford is scattered with ex-players all making a living as analysers of the latest generation of Manchester United superstars. Take a trip into the watching box any Saturday and you'll see a roll call from United's past. You'll usually find former managers Tommy Docherty and Wilf

McGuinness working for radio. Denis Law, Paddy Crerand and George Best do it as well. My old Irish colleague Jim Beglin is at it now on television. But it's not for me.

I hate microphones of any sort. I hate cameras whether they belong to photographers or television. I just bottle up when radio and television people try to talk to me. I've always been like that. I know people in that business like RTE soccer commentator Gabrial Egan who say I'm only a fool to myself but I just get so nervous when I'm confronted with microphones. It was the same when I became a pop star and went into the world famous Windmill Lane recording studios to record my groovy single *Ooh Aah Paul McGrath*, a funky number one in the Irish charts I might add.

My good friend Krish Naidoo – who owns Rumours and the Rossnaree Hotel in Drogheda – did the deal on that one for me. Krish has been good to me businesswise and personally over the years ever since we met in Swaziland about a decade ago. He was there with the Spurs party and I was on tour with United. He actually ended up playing in a match against me, which had to be seen to be believed. And he's been at me ever since to move to Spurs. I've tried a few times but I reckon I'm destined not to move to White Hart Lane at this stage of my career.

I only had four lines – spoken really – on the song, a rap record. But even that was four lines too many. It was the weekend before the Turkey match in Dublin when I did my disappearing act.

Maybe that's an area I could go into – I could become a professional magician when my career is over. I've made myself disappear a few times before big matches. A few strikers have disappeared on me in my time as well. And I've been known to make pint glasses full of lager or Guinness disappear rather quickly too.

The first time I went AWOL was that Turkey game. And that recording session had a lot to do with it. I was frightened to death of the idea of singing on a record. Even though I was surrounded by professionals who are well used to such things it just phased me completely. I had to get tanked up in The Dockers, U2's Larry Mullen's and Joe O'Herlihy's favourite Dublin pub, before I'd even think of going into Windmill Lane with Eamonn Carr, a hero of mine when he was in Horslips, and a brilliant singer called Maria Walsh. It wasn't the best thing that will ever be recorded in Ireland but the girl was brilliant.

I was amazed when it got to number one in the Irish charts. It was so funny to be at home in my mother's one Sunday and hear Larry Gogan introducing my record as the number one on his 2FM Chart Show. I nearly fell around my mother's kitchen at the thought of me being a pop star but I suppose the success of the song was a carry-on from the World Cup and how well our own record *Put 'Em Under Pressure* – orchestrated by Larry Mullen from U2 – had done. I was the first player to get in there with a record afterwards – and I did far better in the charts than Mick McCarthy did when he teamed up with Linda Martin, the Eurovision singer. But I can promise all those budding number ones just one thing – I won't be challenging them this time around for that Top of the Pops slot. Once bitten, twice shy, as they say.

I have never been a great one for looking after my finances. I have signed deals that have been nothing short of a disgrace. I have lost out on a lot of money because of my hatred for cameras and crowds. A lot of the lads with Ireland, United or Villa have maximised their earning power and good luck to them. They know football is a short career, that only the cream of the crop get the chance to make the top money. They have put themselves out for promotion work, for advertising, for television appearances. I have never been able to do that. I've been offered spots on *A Question of Sport* or even *Match of the Day* and I've turned them down.

It has cost me a lot in terms of prestige and presentation. I know I have never been my own best salesman – and some of the characters I've let look after my affairs have done me few favours. Looking back over the years I have been ripped off so many times by agents and business deals. It's only lately that I have copped on to myself and realised what I was doing wrong. Krish Naidoo has turned down so many offers of work for me in my time because of both my reputation and my hatred for crowds. I have lost out big time ever since the World Cup in Italy when I should have been on the gravy train, on a rollercoaster ride to riches.

The 1990 World Cup changed life for every Irish player. It made us heroes – and saleable commodities. The thing I love about what's happened is that the game of soccer is now known all across the country. Ironically, though, its high public profile became a problem for me. There was nothing I liked more in the wake of the World Cup than going into any village down the country and having a few pints and a chat with the locals. I could relate to them in those situations and I could relax. There was no pressure on anyone when they were talking to me like they were talking to their friend. We'd have a few pints and talk about the games that had gone and the games coming up. They'd talk and I'd listen to their views and their stories. I was at one with the ordinary people of Ireland, my own people.

That has always been one of the attractions of going home to Ireland for me. I have always been able to relax in my own land, to let my guard down. It was so therapeutic, such a relief after all the pressures I had gone through living in a goldfish bowl in Manchester. I wasn't on trial all the time. The fans could ask questions but it wasn't like I was performing and getting paid for it. I was one of the lads having a laugh and they could ask me whatever they liked.

In England that situation is still possible but people get a lot more personal about their teams. If the club is doing badly at the time, like United were near the end of my career at Old Trafford, then you act like a magnet in public for all the awkward punters who demand to know what's going wrong. And they blame you personally. There's nothing worse for a footballer if you're having a bad time to have to listen to something like that.

I look at the money some players are making these days and I want to cry. Players have come into the game as teenagers and been close to five figures a week before they're even 21. That is frightening.

I still feel I was cheated financially at Manchester United. It still hurts. It wasn't until I went down to talk to Villa that I realised just how badly off I was. Doug Ellis and Graham Taylor were able to double my money when I moved to Villa Park without me even demanding this wage or that wage. The money they offered me was the norm for Villa. For any big club. But not for me at United.

That made me realise how wrong my dealings with United had been, how bad it was at Old Trafford. I was shocked.

There were United players in my time at the club on big money. Myself and Norman were in the team with Robbo at one stage and earning less together than he got on his own. I'd never begrudge Robbo all the money in the world because he has been the greatest player ever at United. But I had been Player of the Year two years in a row with the Supporters Club and I was on peanuts. Now I pick up the paper and Alex Ferguson is giving Cantona and Ince and Keane more than £5,000 pounds a week – £10,000 a week in some cases – and that all seems a bit hypocritical to me.

I was still on buttons when I left. They used to say to me that I should be proud to wear the red jersey when I was on a pittance. I was proud alright – but pride never paid a mortgage. I wanted the same as everyone else was earning. I was amazed by the fact that they thought I should be happy just to play for the club. They had me on a seven-year contract and they thought I should be pleased about that. They got me for next to nothing, they paid me next to nothing and they eventually sold me for next to nothing.

Back in 1988 Norman Whiteside was on more than I was but we decided that this wasn't on any more, that we weren't going to be exploited any more. People think that Norman went in first looking for a move but it was me. I demanded better wages or a transfer. Fergie didn't go public on me. I asked if I could go to the papers but he wouldn't let me. After Norman requested a move it got out that I had looked for a move as well. People thought we were in cahoots.

No one would put up with that situation at United any more. You can't expect the likes of Cantona or Giggs to be happy just to wear a red shirt. Players of the talent of Arsenal's Ian Wright deserve all they get. They're entertainers as much as anyone else.

CHAPTER NINETEEN

Mon Amour

BREAKING UP is hard to do. Not – as they might say in *Wayne's World*.

One of the saddest things about life in the spotlight is the effect it has on your private and personal life. My marriage to Claire has been dragged through the newspapers and through the mire. We've been on every page from the front to the back of the papers over the last 12 years since I came to England. We've been in court, out of court, in love, out of love, and now we are no more.

There's only one woman in my life now. The mystery blonde. Caroline Lamb, a fine-looking girl from Liverpool, 27 years old and the best thing that ever happened to me.

I met Caroline on a night out with a mate up in Liverpool. We went for a drink in Kirkland's, a rather trendy watering hole on Merseyside. The first thing I noticed about her as she sat up at the bar were her good looks. She's a stunning blonde – a mystery blonde in Ireland last summer and a mystery to me that night in Liverpool. But not for long as Cupid slung his bow in my direction. And Caroline's.

We got chatting. Caroline was home from London to see her parents. She had character, personality and a warmth to match her looks. And I got her number. Football cut no ice with her – she wouldn't have known me even if I had played for Liverpool or Everton. She certainly wasn't interested in Aston Villa. Caroline was sports-minded but not my sort of sport. As a teenager she was a fantastic prospect as a sprinter. That promise developed to the stage where she sprinted for England. She's certainly faster than I am over 100 yards – not that that's too hard a feat anyway.

We got talking about life in general. We chatted and we got on. We realised there was an attraction there. It seemed right to just have a drink and talk. And talk. And talk. Football entered the conversation but it was not central to the conversation. I liked that – somebody who was interested in me as an individual, not because I played football for a living.

At the time I was still living with Claire but our marriage was long over. We shared the same roof and that was that. We had split up many times before only to patch things up and try again for the sake of the children. This time it was over for real. There was no way back. I needed a fresh start in my personal life. Caroline gave me that new meaning in my life that I had craved.

We swapped phone numbers and we began to talk over the telephone line. Our relationship developed. I began to visit Liverpool. We got beyond the curiosity stage and into a meaningful relationship. I was happy. So happy. Happier than I've been for a long time. With Caroline I am relaxed and natural. She understands me, understands how I need to be looked after. She goes out with me all the time. We've been over to Ireland a few times, over for the Texaco Awards dinner when our photograph appeared on the front page of the *Irish Times* no less. We've had a ball with Niall Quinn's sister-in-law, Valerie Roe, at Lillie Bordello's, the trendiest nightclub in Dublin these days. We even helped Valerie clean up one night while we waited for a taxi back to the hotel.

All the while Caroline has been the constant rock of sense on my arm. She keeps me on the straight and narrow. She knows when my eyes go and it's time to go home.

She's been brilliant with the kids. That's the incredible part of our relationship so far. Whatever our deep feelings for each other, I was always worried as to how Caroline would react to three children. When we discussed living together at the house in Manchester she reckoned it wouldn't be a problem. I thought after two or three days she'd have had enough and be on her way. I couldn't have been more wrong. She's taken to the children like a duck takes to water. She's just been brilliant to them. They love her and she loves them. We're one big happy family now and that means so much. To all of us. And to me especially. I've always had a soft spot for women. Romance has never been a problem. Love, though, was another story altogether before I met Caroline.

Before I left Dublin for Manchester I had gone out with a lovely girl called Jeanette Corcoran for about two years. She was a secretary in the Civil Service, the first love of my life. We did all the usual things couples do when they're courting in Dublin. We went to the pictures, went out for a drink, even though I was still off it at the time, went to nightclubs, to restaurants. We were close but my move to Manchester put an end to any hope of that relationship becoming permanent. Absence makes the heart grow fonder but it also put an impossible barrier into our relationship.

Then Claire entered the scene. We met in Majorca on one of my first club trips away from home with United, a sunshine break for four days on the Spanish island. People think those trips are for training in good weather. Wrong. They're a bit of r'n'r for the lads, a chance to let your hair down away from the glare of the media.

The night before we were due to go home we let our hair down alright. And that was how I met Claire. She was 19, a trainee nurse back in Manchester. She was in Spain on holiday with a friend, ironically called Caroline. They were in the next hotel to us and they were out one night at a club when our goalkeeper Gary Bailey started chatting up Claire's friend.

Claire was left sitting on her own like the lemon. When the pair of them went off to the ladies Gary came over and asked the lads for a bit of help. I was still very shy at that stage, not long over from Ireland. But since I was the worse for wear I was the one nominated for this Spanish version of *Blind Date*. I was dragged over to make up the foursome – and that's how I fell for Claire.

We started talking and I discovered that she was from Manchester. That was interesting. There was a problem though. She was a Man City fan who had stood on The Kippax in her time even though all her family were United fanatics. I decided to forget that little *faux pas* and ask for her phone number. I got it eventually and we left for home the next morning.

By the time she got back from Majorca there were messages all over the board at her nurse's home that this Paul McGrath had called to see her and to ring me back. She called and we started dating. Within a year we were married.

The happiest times for us were the births of our three sons. Christopher and Mitchell arrived while I was at United, Jordan was born the Saturday night of my Aston Villa league debut.

Christopher is very much like I was as a child. He's a good athlete and a good footballer. I've watched him play at school and he's got bags more talent than I had at the same age. If he decides he wants to follow me into the professional game I'll give him every encouragement. I'd even let him play for Manchester United if they were interested. But I would draw the line at playing for England. He was out in Italy with Claire for the 1990 World Cup and he had a ball. When they were staying in Ceffalu on Sicily the Irish fans there made him a real hero. They were playing football with him and chanting "Ooh Aah Mini McGrath". He loved every minute of it.

Mitchell is the character of the family. He's the middle boy and he loves to be the centre of attention. He's quite an actor, far more outgoing that I ever was at his age. And he likes to play a bit of football as well.

Jordan is the baby of the family. Just four years old and spoilt rotten. He has his daddy wrapped around his little finger. Anything he wants he gets.

I live for my three boys. I would die for my three boys. They mean the world to me. Throughout all my problems they have been the steadying influence on my life.

Marriage, though, was never easy. Claire had to live with me through my worst times at Manchester United and that put a strain on our relationship. We were constantly in the papers. I know she didn't like the idea of living in a goldfish bowl. Any time I went missing or drinking the newspapers were round at the house, tormenting Claire, even quizzing the kids about their daddy.

My relationship with Claire is over and done with now and very bitter. We've just had a huge custody battle for the three boys and she had made some damning allegations against me in one of the Sunday newspapers. It all stems from the time it emerged publicly that I allegedly fathered a child 11 months earlier by a woman from Manchester. She had run to the newspapers with the story – and received an incredible amount of money from one Sunday paper for blowing the lid on our affair. I do know her and I did have a fling with her – but I have asked to have DNA tests to ascertain that the baby, a little girl, is mine. That's because I don't know this woman well enough to be sure – no matter what she claimed in the paper. If the child is mine I will support it. I will not turn my back on the baby. But I need to be certain in my own mind.

This woman said in the article that we had met at a Manchester wine bar. It was actually the Townhouse in Hale the night before the Irish team flew off to a World Cup match from Manchester Airport. She claims we had a passionate and long affair – I was in her house and her company about seven times at most over the space of four years, once for a couple of days when I was on a binge. If that's a long and passionate affair I must be living on another planet.

She did bring me to a party one night – and I got extremely drunk and fell asleep on the couch. When I was asleep she had a photograph taken of me conked out and her beside me with a glass of wine in her hand. Of course that photograph ended up in the papers – and I got a terrible ribbing about it from the lads at Villa.

Claire took that newspaper revelation very badly. We said publicly that she was standing by me but by then our marriage was as good as over. I was seeing different people in Birmingham. Even in Manchester we were living in the same house but not living together as a couple.

Claire has already sold her side of the story to the papers. She revealed how she took a sleeping tablet overdose and ended up in a private nursing home for 11 weeks. Then she met her new boyfriend, Matthew Shutt.

She claims her problems were due to my drinking, my behaviour and my alleged child. She claimed I used to drink a bottle of vodka on my way to training in Birmingham – how could I drive with a bottle of vodka down me? Why would I drive if I had already served a two-year drink driving ban after a crash in Manchester? And how could anyone who knows how low my threshold for drink is expect me to get away with a bottle of vodka before training? Surely Villa would have known if I had that much drink inside me and they'd have quite rightly sacked me if it was true.

Claire claimed I was told by psychiatrists at a Birmingham clinic that I am an alcoholic. That's rubbish – the psychiatrists have analysed my drinking and come to the conclusion that I am a binge drinker. That is on my medical notes and Claire knows it. She's seen the medical notes but still she claimed I am an alcoholic.

She reckons I moved my new girlfriend Caroline Lamb into the family home while she was in hospital. That's rubbish as well – as is her claim that she went to see me in Birmingham three years ago and found Caroline in my house. I didn't even know Caroline when I had a house rented in Birmingham. That was at least 18 months before we met.

Claire also said I left her bruised during a visit to her new house, a house I am paying the rent on, last autumn. I did visit the house because she had done so many things to annoy me. And I did push her out of the way – but that was it. She went to her solicitor and virtually accused me of assault and I ended up barred from the vicinity. I have never hit a woman in my life.

Our whole relationship has turned nasty and that is a huge disappointment for me. I would prefer if we had parted on amicable terms and got on with our lives and our loves. Claire has found a new boyfriend in Matthew Shutt and I have found a new girlfriend in Caroline Lamb.

I am so happy with Caroline, the happiest I have been for a long time. Happiness has long been a rarity in my life. Now that I have found it with Caroline I intend to hang on to it. Forever, this time.

The other women in my life were my late sister Okone and my mother Betty. Okone married John O'Reilly and had a beautiful little daughter of her own called Mawia, born on the day Ireland played Albania at Lansdowne Road in a World Cup qualifier. She was a lucky charm for me that day – I scored and dedicated my goal to her.

Then there is my mother. This story started with her so it is fitting that it should end with her. The July we came back from the World Cup in Italy my mother and Noel Lowth became man and wife. I gave her away that day – the happiest man in Ireland. And the happiest woman.

Just as families should be. Happy and together. Through thick and thin.

Tragedy has never walked far behind my footsteps. It caught up with me again in March 1994 when my only sister Okone died suddenly in Dublin. She was only 32 at the time of her death, two years my junior, but death had been a cloud hanging over her head from the day she was born in Dublin. My sister was born with a blood disorder that was always life-threatening. It caught up with her that March and tragically she died only four days after falling seriously ill.

I was at the bedside in her final hours. We were as close in her last moments as we had been in life itself. I cried my eyes out in the St James's Hospital in Dublin, wondering how my only sister could be taken from this life at such an early age. There were tears too for her husband John O'Reilly and her little two-year-old daughter

Maiwa. In years to come we will look at Maiwa's pretty face and think of my sister. In years to come I will dedicate my achievements on the football field to the sister who was taken away from me long before she had the chance to fulfil all her own potential and dreams in life itself.

Life has always been hard. Her death one of the hardest blows of all to come to terms with. But life must go on. For me, for my mother, for my family. Life has to go on. And it will. The cry for freedom is still roaring in this heart of mine.